SPIRIT-FILLED
CHRISTOLOGY

MERGING THEOLOGY AND POWER

SPIRIT-FILLED
CHRISTOLOGY

MERGING THEOLOGY AND POWER[1]

"I have come as light into the world, that everyone who believes in Me may not remain in darkness." (John 12:46)

-Jesus

DAVID W. DORRIES, PH.D.

Aventine Press

Unless otherwise indicated, Bible quotations are taken from the New American Standard Bible, World Publishing.

© Copyright 2006 by David W. Dorries

First edition

Without limiting the rights under copyright reserved above, no part of this publication may be reproduced, stored in or introduced into a retrieval system, or transmitted, in any form or by any means (electronic, mechanical, photocopying, recording, or otherwise), without the prior written permission of both the copyright owner and the publisher of this book.
Aventine Press
1023 4th Avenue, Suite 204
San Diego, CA 92101

ISBN: 1-59330-390-4
Printed in the United States of America
ALL RIGHTS RESERVED

TABLE OF CONTENTS

DEDICATION	1
ACKNOWLEDGEMENTS	3
PREFACE	5
INTRODUCTION	7
Chapter 1 JESUS CHRIST: EMERGING LEADER	17
Chapter 2 MESSIAH	23
Chapter 3 DEATH AND RESURRECTION	31
Chapter 4 ASCENSION AND IMPARTATION	37
Chapter 5 CONTINUING PRESENCE	43
Chapter 6 DIFFERING INTERPRETATIONS OF JESUS	51
Chapter 7 SON OF GOD: Recovery Of The Old Testament Messiah	57
Chapter 8 SON OF GOD: The New Testament Witness	65
Chapter 9 SON OF GOD: Christian History And The Threat Of Arianism	73
Chapter 10 SON OF GOD: Christian History And The Threats Of Nestorianism And Liberalism	83
Chapter 11 SON OF MAN: Old Testament Background	93
Chapter 12 SON OF MAN: New Testament Witness	103

Chapter 13 SON OF MAN:
The Gnostic Challenge
To Jesus' True Humanity							111

Chapter 14 SON OF MAN:
The Apollinarian Challenge To The True
Humanity Of Jesus							123

Chapter 15 SON OF MAN:
The Eutychean Challenge To The True
Humanity Of Jesus							131

Chapter 16 JESUS: FIRST GIFT, THEN EXAMPLE
Christology and the Grace of God					143

Chapter 17 JESUS: FIRST GIFT, THEN EXAMPLE
Jesus As Gift: The Challenge of Pelagianism				151

Chapter 18 JESUS: FIRST GIFT, THEN EXAMPLE
Jesus As Gift: The Challenge of Semi-Pelagianism			161

Chapter 19 JESUS: FIRST GIFT, THEN EXAMPLE
Semi-Pelagianism and Conversion					169

Chapter 20 JESUS: FIRST GIFT, THEN EXAMPLE
Semi-Pelagianism and Sanctification					177

Chapter 21 JESUS: FIRST GIFT, THEN EXAMPLE
Semi-Pelagianism to the Present Day					187

Chapter 22 JESUS: FIRST GIFT, THEN EXAMPLE
Jesus as Example: Spirit Dependency					201

Chapter 23 JESUS: FIRST GIFT, THEN EXAMPLE
Jesus as Example: Spirit Baptism					213

Chapter 24 JESUS: FIRST GIFT, THEN EXAMPLE
Jesus as Example: Receiver of the Spirit				221

Chapter 25 JESUS: FIRST GIFT, THEN EXAMPLE
Jesus as Example: Empowerment — 233

Chapter 26 JESUS: FIRST GIFT, THEN EXAMPLE
Jesus as Example: Speaking in Tongues — 247

Chapter 27 CHRISTOLOGICAL RECOVERY
The Theory of the "Push Button" Divinity of Jesus — 271

APPENDIX 1
60 AFFIRMATIONS OF SPIRIT-FILLED CHRISTOLOGY — 287

APPENDIX 2
ORAL ROBERTS' LETTER — 309

APPENDIX 3
HOW TO RECEIVE JESUS AS YOUR PERSONAL SAVIOR — 313

APPENDIX 4
HOW TO RECEIVE THE BAPTISM IN THE HOLY SPIRIT — 315

NOTES — 319

DEDICATION

To Mariela,
my dream come true.
You are a tangible expression of Jesus to me.
Your faithful, tender love brings out the best in me.

ACKNOWLEDGEMENTS

That this book is now published is a tribute, above all, to the grace of God. I am thankful for His orchestration of all the events of my life to make this moment possible. To contribute to the family of Christians worldwide a treatise on the subject of the person and work of Jesus Christ represents an unspeakable honor for me. If Jesus' Lordship in church and world is extended on any level as a result of this book, I will be gratified.

Mariela, my wife, deserves my deepest thanks. She has been a loving support to me throughout the two years that this book has been in process. She has believed in me and in the importance of this book, and has bolstered my resolve to finish when the task seemed too overwhelming. My sons, Paul, Davis, and John have given me lots of love and encouragement, as well. Also, I wish to express my appreciation for the prayers and support over the years of my parents, Bill and Virginia Dorries, and my sister and brother-in-law, Martha and Clark Whitten.

I offer my sincere thanks to President Richard Roberts, Chief Academic Officer Ralph Fagin, and the Board of Regents of Oral Roberts University for the sabbatical time in the spring of 2004. Those months of focused writing at the beginning of the project were highly productive. Deepest thanks to my two Deans, Dr. William Jernigan in the Learning Resources Center, and Dr. Thomson Mathew in the School of Theology and Missions, who have gone above and beyond the call of duty to facilitate this writing project. I am sincerely grateful to my friend and colleague, Dr. Daniel Thimell, not only for his helpful feedback on many occasions during the writing of this book, but for his enduring friendship for more than twenty years.

I wish to honor the memory of my beloved mentors at the University of Aberdeen, Professors George S. S. Yule and James B. Torrance. Their efforts to ground me in the Trinitarian doctrinal essentials of the Gospel were apostolic in formative impact upon my life and ministry.

Though long since departed, I honor the memory of Edward Irving. To differentiate my Christology from that of Irving's is no simple task. I am thankful that he courageously taught the Jesus of holiness and power through the Spirit, and the Church's inheritance of the same. I am indebted to Irving's vision, and would like to think that this book in some way would extend his neglected legacy.

PREFACE

While addressing a group recently, I commented upon my area of academic specialization. I jokingly said that **my specialty is Jesus Christ!** Although my technical area is Church History, it is no joke that the discipline of the person and work of Jesus Christ (Christology) has dominated the content and motivation of my teaching.

This book represents the distillation of more than twenty-two years of researching, teaching and writing on the topic of Christology. The groundwork of *Spirit-filled Christology* was laid during my years of Ph.D. studies at the University of Aberdeen in Scotland. Professors George S. S. Yule and James B. Torrance were ideal mentors for guiding me through the writings and theologies of the Church Fathers and Protestant Reformers.

Choosing my thesis topic, the Christology of nineteenth century British pastor Edward Irving, proved to be providential. Irving endorsed the continuous expression of supernatural gifts, signs and wonders of the Spirit from a Christological foundation. Irving's writings assisted me in the merger of the implications of Incarnational Christology and the church's need for empowerment in mission. Augustine's critique of Pelagianism and Luther's corrective of semi-Pelagianism opened up for me the grace dimension. The believer's appropriation of the benefits of Jesus and the appropriation of His extended ministry always remain in the context of God's gift and initiative.

Nothing could have been more of a God-thing than being offered a position on the graduate faculty of Oral Roberts University straight out of doctoral studies. During the early stages of the Charismatic renewal, Oral Roberts envisioned a fully-accredited seminary as part of his university, anticipating the training of leaders to fuel this expanding international movement. He saw the significance of merging sound theology with the experiential dimension of the Holy Spirit's power. How revealing to view this statement by Oral Roberts on the occasion of the seminary's founding. "I believe that the charismatic movement has the power *without the theology* and that the church at large has a very critical theology *without the power*. I want the new ORU graduate School of Theology to put the two together, and I want to see the church become the church and therefore become the instrument of the Holy Spirit it is intended to be."[2]

Devoting my life to the task of training almost two decades of ministerial students within ORU's stimulating and diverse environment continues to be a high privilege and joy for me. As students latch on to the substance of *Spirit-filled Christology*, they leave our university with a theological/practical model capable of revitalizing the church with a fresh anointing of the Holy Spirit. My prayer is that this book will extend far beyond the classrooms of Oral Roberts University, making its way to the uttermost parts of the earth where church leaders who will never travel beyond their hometowns will be exposed to the same insights that our students enjoy in Tulsa, Oklahoma!

INTRODUCTION

Explosive Growth

Unbalanced Experientialism

Dangerous Trends

Exceptional Alternative

Third World Challenges

Christology the Key

Fresh Approach Needed

Movement From Reflection to Action

Biblically-based and Historically Informed

Spirit-filled Christology: **Pattern of Development**

Satan's Strategies

Training and Renewing the Intellect

Spirit-filled Christology: **Foundational Reinterpretation**

INTRODUCTION

Explosive Growth

Christianity is experiencing unparalleled expansion worldwide over the past century.[3] Especially noteworthy is the explosive growth of Independents (Christians unaffiliated with denominational organizations), representing more than 386 million adherents as of the year 2000. Among Independents, Neo-charismatics[4] represent more than 295 million members of that constituency. The growth of Independents is largely responsible for a major shift in Christian demographics. In 1900, the United States and Europe formed the demographic center of world Christianity. In 2000, the epicenter has shifted to Latin America, Africa and Asia.

Unbalanced Experientialism

Of course, there is much to celebrate regarding the rapid growth and diversification of Christianity. Yet a closer examination of these trends leaves us with cause for concern. An experiential orientation towards the Christian faith has been a general characteristic of the twentieth century Pentecostal/Charismatic movement. This continues to be the case among the Neo-charismatics as this Third Wave of Pentecostalism is making its mark among Third World nations. Emphasis upon experiences and practical ministry is good when balanced with sound Christian doctrine informing the teaching and preaching of the Gospel. Yet the current expansion of the church must guard itself against an experientialism that tends to be reactionary against the rational and doctrinal dimensions.

Dangerous Trends

The Independent sector of Christianity, being free from denominational control, operates without the protective covering of accountability for its beliefs and practices. This is particularly noticeable in its approach to leadership training. Independent churches prefer in-house, informal forms of training over traditional academic formats. Formal education in the traditional sense is no longer considered to be necessary or desirable. Content oriented theological disciplines often are viewed to be outmoded and irrelevant to the concerns of everyday life, and are being replaced by technique-oriented, hands-on ministry training, where trainees learn by doing. The spirit of the age that is making inroads within today's church is proudly anti-intellectual, anti-doctrinal, anti-theological and anti-educational.

Exceptional Alternative

Through the history of Pentecostalism, exceptional individuals have bucked the trend of anti-intellectualism. More than any figure in Christianity, Oral Roberts reconfigured the Pentecostal/Charismatic movement positively to attain a place of acceptance within American public life. Possibly his most far reaching endeavor was to establish a full-fledged, accredited academic institution, Oral Roberts University, to support the expanding Pentecostal/Charismatic movement. The university includes graduate-level theological education, offering the mushrooming Neo-charismatic international constituency with the highest level of academic theological training.[5]

Third World Challenges

Yet with the rapid growth and diversification of Neo-charismatics, existing institutions are hard-pressed to address adequately the changing dynamics and desperate needs of the twenty-first century church. For instance, new congregations are springing up overnight in Developing Nations, with no trained leadership to tend the flock. A case was reported in China where teenage girls were placed in charge of a huge congregation, simply because they were the only members of the group able to read and write.[6] Hundreds of leaders are in place over congregations, having no formal training and with little possibility of ever obtaining such. The challenge facing the few institutions capable of providing balanced theological training, most being geographically situated in the west, is to become more innovative and adaptable in relation to the developing context. Creativity, affordability, and mobility are obvious characteristics to be adopted if traditional theological programs are to become part of the solution for the new Independents. Streamlined, non-degree training, transmitted by means of satellite campuses and electronic links, hold promise for tomorrow's seminaries.

Christology the Key

Along with new delivery systems, equally important for addressing the urgent needs of the changing church context is the theological content of the training. No need is more critical than the reevaluation and reconstruction of the Christological factor in theological education. Christology is the foundation for all of the theological disciplines. The Apostle Paul illustrates this reality by comparing a building with the Christian church (Eph. 2:19-22). Setting the corner stone is the most vital part of the process. The strength of the foundation, which supports the entire building, is dependent upon the corner stone being set properly. Jesus Christ is the church's corner stone. Everything stands or falls with Him. When Jesus Christ is rightly known and experienced, the church that bears His name will be healthy and vital.

Fresh Approach Needed

This leads to my purpose in writing this book. The modern church, including the expanding Independent sector, needs a fresh approach to Christology. Therefore, I am proposing *Spirit-filled Christology* as a model for consideration. This approach satisfies two major needs. First, this Christology is faithful to the Biblical witness, and is consistent with the orthodoxy of the church's creeds and councils, Fathers and Reformers. This approach provides a sense of rootedness and continuity with traditional orthodoxy, in contrast to the relativistic individualism of our age. Second, *Spirit-filled Christology* necessitates the experiential dynamic of the Holy Spirit. This approach cannot be affirmed merely on a theological level. Theological agreement compels responsible action. One cannot authentically confess adherence to *Spirit-filled Christology* without responding to its behavioral consequences. Our spiritually hungry age needs a theological foundation offering authentic wholeness, health and vitality. Christ's incarnate life exemplifies maximum authenticity in these areas, and *Spirit-filled Christology* extends to every believer the maximum life possible in human experience.

Movement From Reflection to Action

In the face of a leadership crisis in world Christianity, no greater priority exists than that the implementation of an extensive educational effort to provide Christian leaders with the challenge of reevaluating our Christological beliefs to ensure that we are building upon an unshakable foundation. I believe that if this model is understood on a widespread level, it carries with it the potential for centering the diversity of present expansion upon Gospel essentials, producing healthy and vital Christian living. This is revolutionary truth, embodying the impetus for major revival and long-term reformation within Christendom. *Spirit-filled*

Christology moves from reflection to action, compelling believers to respond to the Spirit's initiative after the manner of Jesus in His public ministry and the church of the Book of Acts.

Biblically-based and Historically Informed

I have sought to address several challenges in the preparation of this book. *Spirit-filled Christology* is presented with substantive academic content, yet is articulated with an attempt to avoid excessive academic jargon and minutia. Also, a sound Christology must pass two tests. 1) **It must be unwaveringly biblical in its composition.** Christology that is not thoroughly biblical lacks revelatory authority, and is a human-made construction susceptible to destruction. 2) **A sound Christology also must be historically informed.** Christology, as a component of theology, has experienced historical development over a span of nearly twenty centuries of church history. Various theories regarding the person of Jesus Christ and the nature of His work gained recognition during periods of the church's history. As the church responded to those theories, a body of knowledge developed that greatly enhanced awareness of the subtleties of the Christological discipline. It is both naïve and foolish to advocate a Christological model for the consideration of today's church without reference to the wisdom that is to be accessed from the rich history of Christological development.

Spirit-filled Christology: Pattern of Development

Introduction – the dramatic changes in contemporary Christianity requires a fresh approach to Christology

Chapters 1-5: **biographical portrayal of Jesus Christ** from the Gospel narratives of Scripture

Chapter 6: differing interpretations of Jesus during the church's historical development

Chapters 7 and 8: Jesus' identity as **Son of God**, as developed in both Old and New Testaments

Chapters 9 and 10: challenges to Jesus' deity from the ancient church

Chapters 11 and 12: the Scriptural revelation of Jesus' identity as **Son of Man**

Chapters 13-15: historical challenges to Jesus' true humanity from ancient Christianity

Chapter 15: completes discussions concerning Jesus' unique natures as God and man, and the interrelationship between those natures

Chapter 16: Martin Luther's statement, **Jesus is first gift, then example,** begins a comprehensive study concerning the nature of God's grace revealed in Jesus Christ

Chapters 17-21: Jesus is gift - historical challenges

Chapters 22-25: Jesus' unique way of serving as example for the believer and the church (including the issues of **Jesus as Giver and Receiver of the Holy Spirit**, as well as the character of Spirit Baptism)

Chapter 26: **Speaking in Tongues**; its history throughout Christendom and its role in Spirit Baptism

Chapter 27: an analysis of contemporary Christological error, and the critique provided by *Spirit-filled Christology.*

Satan's Strategies

We wrestle against an evil foe, the master of deceit, whose resume spans centuries of conflict against the church. Satan has no more new tricks. He exhausted his arsenal of heresies against the early church, and was defeated on every hand. Since the Council of Orange, he has pursued his only advantage, which is to reintroduce his old tricks in new disguises. He knows that Christology no longer is a priority in today's church, and he is working on the premise that new competitors will be unaware of the ancient controversies, and of the successful strategies employed against him by former champions of the faith.

Training and Renewing the Intellect

Rather than lament this trend, I suggest that all believers, particularly those placed in positions of local authority, become informed students of Christology. Primary requirements are a passion for the preservation of Christological truth, and a measure of discipline in order to master the basic Biblical, historical and theological material. The true knowledge of Christ must be preserved in every generation. The believer whose intellect is renewed by the Holy Scriptures and trained by the study of historic developments concerning Jesus is more available to the Holy Spirit for the task of proclaiming and demonstrating the Gospel in today's world.

Spirit-filled Christology: Foundational Reinterpretation

Today's church needs a new Definition of Faith,[7] a foundational reinterpretation of Jesus Christ and His purpose, offering the opportunity to harmonize Christianity's diversity and resist divisive relativism. *Spirit-filled Christology* offers a fresh and dynamic interpretation of Jesus' person and purpose. Its authority is founded upon the Scriptures, and its insight and application is enhanced by perspectives of Christological development from Christian history. Enter upon this journey with the expectation of discovery!

Chapter 1

JESUS CHRIST: EMERGING LEADER

Jesus Was a Real Historical Figure
Jesus Embraced the Jewish Faith
John the Baptist
Jesus' Disciples
Making Individuals Whole

Chapter 1

JESUS CHRIST: EMERGING LEADER

Jesus Was a Real Historical Figure[8]

Jesus was born in Bethlehem, Judea, in 4 or 5 B.C. After living briefly in Egypt, His parents, Mary and Joseph,[9] settled in Nazareth of Galilee, where Jesus spent His early life. Jesus had brothers and sisters.[10] He followed in the footsteps of His father, taking up the profession of carpentry.

Jesus Embraced the Jewish Faith

Jesus' life up to the age of thirty must have appeared to be rather uneventful. Yet His Jewish heritage was shaping His identity in a profound way. When He reached thirty, He left behind the carpentry trade and launched out on a bold public ministry that ultimately would revolutionize world history.

Yet Jesus' emergence as a religious leader did not come through the formal channels of power within the Jewish establishment. Circumventing the power structure of the religious world, Jesus chose to link Himself initially with a controversial popular movement outside the establishment led by a prophetic figure named John the Baptist. Jesus and John were not strangers to one another, in that their mothers were kinfolk (Luke 7:28).

John the Baptist

Jesus chose the occasion of one of John's meetings to make His first appearance in public. Emerging from the waters of John's baptism, Jesus embarked upon the beginnings of His own traveling ministry among the Jewish people. John's movement would no longer be the same. He understood His brief encounter with Jesus to be the climax of His own ministry. He interpreted the prophetic awakening that He had kindled to be merely preparatory to the mission now being forged by Jesus. John explained, "As for me, I baptize you with water for repentance, but He who is coming after me is mightier than I, and I am not fit to remove His sandals; He will baptize you with the Holy Spirit and fire." (Matthew 3:11) Summarizing his own role in relation to Jesus, John declared, "You yourselves are my witnesses that I said, 'I am not the Christ,' but, 'I have been sent ahead of Him.' …He must increase, but I must decrease." (John 3:28, 30) As Jesus began His work, John ended his, releasing his followers to become followers of Jesus. John's life came to an abrupt conclusion when he challenged the immoral lifestyle of Herod, king of Judea. First imprisoned, John soon after was beheaded by the ruthless Herod.

Jesus' Disciples

So Jesus ventured out in ministry on His own, aligning Himself with the God of the Jews, but with no official backing of the Jewish religious establishment. Yet Jesus did not work alone. He handpicked twelve men with no previous religious training to form His inner circle of disciples.[11] They immediately left their jobs and homes in order to follow Jesus. The twelve lived with Jesus, traveling and ministering with Him. A female contingency also worked closely with Jesus and the disciples, some being relatives of the group. During the third and final year of Jesus' public ministry,

He appointed a larger circle of seventy disciples to engage in special mission tasks. This did not appear to be a permanent calling.

Part of Jesus' mission was to train His twelve disciples to assume the leadership of His ministry after His departure. He was continuously teaching them, and He often allowed them to minister to people in His name. Jesus' ministry rapidly gained visibility and recognition, and the majority of His time was spent preaching and meeting the needs of throngs of people. People flocked to Him everywhere He traveled, and Jesus often found Himself in such demand that He had difficulty finding time even to eat. Personal prayer with His heavenly Father was a vital part of His life, and it was not unusual for Him to sacrifice sleep in order to pray at night.

Making Individuals Whole

Jesus ministered to individual people. Even when crowds were flocking around Him, He was sensitive to the needs of individuals.[12] He cared for the immediate needs of people, as well as being concerned about their eternal condition. His ministry was to the whole person, encompassing the spiritual, emotional, mental and physical aspects of human life. Jesus equated His coming with the entrance of God's kingdom on earth, and He called people to enter into the blessings and benefits of the kingdom. As Jesus put it, "The time is fulfilled, and the kingdom of God is at hand; repent, and believe in the gospel." (Mark 1:15) Jesus preached and taught about the specifics of God's kingdom. To participate meant forgiveness of sins, spiritual rebirth with the promise of eternal life, deliverance from demonic oppression, healing and health for the body, and a life founded on God's truth and unconditional love.

Gospel means "good news," and Jesus' appearance in Judea certainly meant good news for the people who were willing to receive His message and ministry. The best news was that Jesus was offering people a relationship with Father God, a quality of relationship inseparably linked with His own life and destiny. Certainly, one who is able to mediate significantly the nature of relationship between God and humankind is no ordinary person, even if He is a prophet, teacher and miracle-worker. Jesus put Himself in an uncommon position attempted only rarely by previous Hebrew leaders. He identified Himself as the Messiah of the Jewish people. Jesus' life and ministry cannot be interpreted accurately apart from this self-assumed role.

Chapter 2

MESSIAH

According to Promise

Lamb of God

Jesus Anticipated His Death

False Expectations

Not a Political Kingdom

Chapter 2
MESSIAH

According to Promise

The promise of a coming Messiah had been interwoven into the fabric of the Jewish legacy since the time of Father Abraham. Messiah meant the "Anointed One" from God, "the Christ," the Savior of the people. The Hebrew prophet Isaiah foretold of the coming of the "Anointed One," and described the kind of deliverance that He would bring to the people. "The Spirit of the Lord God is upon me, because the Lord has anointed me to bring good news to the afflicted; He has sent me to bind up the brokenhearted, to proclaim liberty to captives, and freedom to prisoners." (Isaiah 61:1) A day would come when Jesus stood in the synagogue in His hometown of Nazareth, located the scriptural passage previously noted from Isaiah, and read it to the people. After closing the book, Jesus boldly stated, "Today this Scripture has been fulfilled in your hearing." (Luke 4:21) Another plain reference to Jesus self-understanding is noted in John's Gospel. As Jesus was dialoging with a Samaritan woman, she stated, "I know that Messiah is coming (He who is called Christ); when that One comes, He will declare all things to us." Jesus responded by saying, "I who speak to you am He." (John 4:25-26)

Lamb of God

Closely connected with the Messianic promise is the anticipation of a coming "Lamb of God," one whose sacrificial death would atone for the sins of the people. The notion of the death of a lamb would make no sense apart from an awareness of the sacrificial system of atonement in Jewish worship. The Hebrew God established this ritual of atonement during the leadership of Moses. God spoke directly to Moses, saying, "Command the sons of Israel and say to them, 'You shall be careful to present My offering. ...and you shall say to them, This is the offering by fire which you shall offer to the Lord; two male lambs one year old without defect as a continual burnt offering every day.'" (Numbers 28:2-3) The animal's blood would be offered to God at the altar by the priest to make atonement for the sins of the people.

Yet this system was not intended to be perpetual. It was given for a time, serving as a ritualistic portrayal of the need for a victim more adequate than animals to be presented whose undeserved yet freely offered death would be accepted by God as a final atonement for the sins of the world. The Hebrew prophet Isaiah envisioned a coming Lamb whose death would eliminate the need forever for animal sacrifices. "But He was pierced through for our transgressions, He was crushed for our iniquities; the chastening for our well-being fell upon Him, and by His scourging we are healed. ...But the Lord was pleased to crush Him, putting Him to grief; if He would render Himself as a guilt offering, ...He poured out Himself to death, and was numbered with the transgressors; yet He Himself bore the sin of many, and interceded for the transgressors." (Isaiah 53:5, 10, 12)

Jesus Anticipated His Death

Jesus appeared in Israel for the express purpose of serving as the sacrificial Lamb. He lived out His life in full realization and complete willingness that He was destined to lay down His life as an atoning sacrifice for the sins of the world. John the Baptist was aware of Jesus' destiny as the sacrificial Lamb of God. "The next day he saw Jesus coming to him, and said, 'Behold, the Lamb of

God who takes away the sin of the world!'" (John 1:29) The Book of Revelation honors Jesus as the victorious Lamb who conquered by laying down His life as an offering. "Worthy art Thou to take the book, and to break its seals; for Thou wast slain, and didst purchase for God with Thy blood men from every tribe and tongue and people and nation." (Revelation 5:9)

To prepare them for His departure, Jesus related numerous times to His disciples that it would be necessary to the fulfillment of His mission that He be put to death. Even as He predicted His coming crucifixion and resurrection, His disciples were not able to comprehend how such a fate could befall their Messiah. "From that time Jesus Christ began to show His disciples that He must go to Jerusalem, and suffer many things from the elders and chief priests and scribes, and be killed, and be raised up on the third day. And Peter took Him aside and began to rebuke Him, saying, 'God forbid it, Lord! This shall never happen to You.' But He turned and said to Peter, 'Get behind Me, Satan! You are a stumbling block to Me; for you are not setting your mind on God's interests, but man's.'" (Matthew 16:21-23) On another occasion, the disciples failed to see in a woman's humble gesture of pouring a vial of costly perfume upon Jesus' body a prelude of His approaching death. They saw her act as wasteful, but Jesus recognized the significance of her deed. "But some were indignantly remarking to one another, 'For what purpose has this perfume been wasted?' ...And they were scolding her. But Jesus said, 'Let her alone; why do you bother her? She has done a good deed to Me. ...she has anointed My body beforehand for the burial.'" (Mark 14:4-6, 8)

False Expectations

Jesus was being directed by a radically different interpretation of the role of Messiah than was typical of the prevailing view within Jewish culture. Even His own disciples, who had confidence in His Messiahship, had trouble seeing that suffering and death was a vital component. It became apparent that the Jewish religious leadership had succumbed to popular expectations of the Messiah's identity, even if it meant setting aside scriptural considerations that were informing Jesus' self-understanding.

This helps us better understand the ironic yet tragic development of Jesus' persecution by the religious authorities. They were maddened and threatened by Jesus' behavior because He did not come close to fitting their expectations of a Messiah. Yet in the very act of rejecting and disposing of Jesus, they were inadvertently assisting in the fulfillment of His Messianic purpose. By conspiring successfully to eliminate Him, they merely played a hand in the prophetic accomplishment of His Messianic mission to die as the atoning Lamb for the people's sins.

Not a Political Kingdom

"He came to His own, and those who were His own did not receive Him." (John 1:11) Religious leaders and the Hebrew culture at large failed to recognize Jesus as Messiah largely because they were not in touch with their own scriptural foundations. Had they been committed to the truth of scripture, they would not have misidentified Jesus. Jesus confronted a cultural mentality that too narrowly attached its view of a coming Messiah with patriotism and political ambition. The people longed for a coming deliverer with military/political power capable of liberating Israel from Roman subservience and shaping her into an independent nation.[13]

Jesus certainly was aware of the tension between the nature of His own kingdom being ushered in and the common Jewish expectations. He guarded against being cast in the role of a military/political leader. The tension was acutely real after He miraculously fed a crowd of more than five thousand people. Dazzled by the miracle, the people were ready to seize Jesus and take the nation by storm. "Jesus therefore perceiving that they were intending to come and take Him by force, to make Him king, withdrew again to the mountain by Himself alone." (John 6:15)

Jesus' Messianic mission embraced more lofty goals than that of social reorganization. King Jesus promised deliverance from the bondage of sin. Participating in His kingdom meant abundant life in this world, and eternal life in the hereafter. He came as the Jewish Messiah, but the bounty of His deliverance transcended the destiny of the Jewish people. The Messiah is also God's sacrificial Lamb, whose death must precede the initiation of His glorious promises. Since the curse of sin is universal, the Lamb's atonement likewise is universal. The Apostle Paul affirms that Jesus "gave Himself as a ransom for all." (I Timothy 2:6) The Apostle John testifies that Jesus "is the propitiation for our sins; and not for ours only, but also for those of the whole world." (I John 2:2)

Chapter 3

DEATH AND RESURRECTION

The Cross
It Is Finished!
Resurrection
Post-Resurrection Appearances

Chapter 3

DEATH AND RESURRECTION

The Cross

This struggle between conflicting Messianic expectations resulted in Jesus' death at the age of thirty-three, in 28 or 29 A.D. His public ministry burst upon the Palestinian arena like a meteor, only to be extinguished in three years. Blinded by jealousy and righteous indignation, Jewish religious leaders strategized to take Jesus' life. With the cooperation of one of Jesus' own inner circle of disciples (Judas Iscariot), religious leaders arrested Jesus and turned Him over to Roman authorities for execution. Pontius Pilate, Roman procurator of Judea, sentenced Jesus to death by crucifixion. Pilate found himself in an uncomfortable predicament, for he could find no wrongdoing in Jesus. Yet Jesus did not deny in front of Pilate that He was King of the Jews, and Pilate feared reprisals from his Roman superiors if he released a potential political rival of Caesar. The bloodthirsty crowd demanded Jesus' crucifixion, and Pilate acquiesced.

Nailed to a cross, Jesus was subjected to the cruelest death possible in Roman society. Crucifixion was the slow, agonizing death reserved for common criminals. Yet even the mode of death visited upon Jesus was another fulfillment of scriptural prophecy. In Hebrew Law, the punishment for sin worthy of death was to be hung on a tree. That one is considered to be under God's curse. "…he who is hanged is accursed of God." (Deuteronomy 21:22-23) Although innocent of sin, Jesus willingly took the punishment guilty humanity deserved. By taking the place of the sinner, He became subject to God's curse, thereby breaking the power of the curse and freeing the sinner from the consequences of sin. The Apostle Paul summarized Jesus' accomplishment by taking upon Himself our curse. "Christ redeemed us from the curse of the Law, having become a curse for us – for it is written, 'Cursed is every one who hangs on a tree' – in order that in Christ Jesus the blessing of Abraham might come to the Gentiles, so that we might receive the promise of the Spirit through faith." (Galatians 3:13-14)

For six hours, Jesus hung on that cross, suspended between heaven and earth. He was lifted up to death on the cross for the sake of the human race. As the soldiers raised Jesus' cross on that fateful day, with Jesus on it, they were helping to fulfill another of His predictions. "'And I, if I be lifted up from the earth, will draw all men to Myself.' But He was saying this to indicate the kind of death by which He was to die." (John 12:32-33) On the cross, Jesus suffered the spiritual, emotional, mental and physical consequences sufficient to pay the full price for the wrath of God against all human sins. As the unblemished lamb in Hebrew ritual was sacrificed in innocence for the people's sins, so the Lamb of God was offered for all sins, though He Himself was without sin. "He (God the Father) made Him (Jesus) who knew no sin to be sin on our behalf, that we might become the righteousness of God in Him (Jesus)." (II Corinthians 5:21)

It Is Finished!

In the final ebbing away of Jesus' life, He breathed His last words, "'It is finished!' And He bowed His head, and gave up His spirit." (John 19:30) Those words were the sweetest words ever heard by mortal man. "It is finished!" Since Adam's fall into sin in the Garden of Eden, a state of alienation between Holy God and the humanity created in His own image had been in effect. As the result of the successful accomplishment of the mission of Jesus the Messiah, alienation between God and humanity was now overcome. When Jesus spoke those words, "It is finished!" and gave up His spirit, a cataclysmic change in the human condition was established. Alienation was replaced by reconciliation. Now, from God's side, forgiveness and restoration are the norm. God considers that the full debt has been paid for human sins, and His arms are open wide for all who will come to Him in the name of Jesus!

Resurrection

The death of Jesus meant that His atoning work for sins was finished, but the entirety of His Messianic mission was far from over. Jesus had said that His death would be followed by resurrection on the third day. As proclaimed by the Apostle Peter in his Pentecostal sermon, "…this Man, delivered up by the predetermined plan and foreknowledge of God, you nailed to a cross by the hands of godless men and put Him to death. And God raised Him up again, putting an end to the agony of death, since it was impossible for Him to be held in its power." Peter continued by quoting a Messianic prophecy from King David. "Because Thou wilt not abandon My soul to Hades, nor allow Thy Holy One to undergo decay." Peter added more concerning David. "…he looked ahead and spoke of the resurrection of the Christ, that He was neither abandoned to Hades, nor did His flesh suffer decay. This Jesus God raised up again, to which we are all witnesses." (Acts 2:23-24, 27, 31-32)

Post-Resurrection Appearances

After His resurrected, Jesus did not depart immediately from the earth. For forty days He made appearances to His followers to confirm that He had risen from the grave. It took some effort to convince many of His followers that He was really alive. Once recognition was established, a critical event transpired. Jesus breathed on His disciples to receive the Holy Spirit. The Apostle John records this moment of the Spirit's impartation. "…Jesus came and stood in their midst, and said to them, 'Peace be with you.' And when He had said this, He showed them both His hands and His side. The disciples therefore rejoiced when they saw the Lord. Jesus therefore said to them again, 'Peace be with you; as the Father has sent Me, I also send you.' And when He had said this, He breathed on them, and said to them, 'Receive the Holy Spirit.'" (John 20:19-22) In this monumental act of imparting the Holy Spirit, Jesus was demonstrating now as the resurrected Lord that there is new life available for all who believe in Him. I believe that this signified that the new birth was now in action. The time had come in God's timetable for the new birth to be activated among His disciples, those who had confidence in Him and His redemptive work. "...if you confess with your mouth Jesus as Lord, and believe in your heart that God raised Him from the dead, you shall be saved; ..." (Romans 10:9)

Now that Jesus had confirmed with His disciples that their continuing identity would be in Him through the Spirit that He had given them, He set forth His commission for their earthly ministry. Jesus commanded them to preach, to baptize, and to teach in His name what He had taught. (Matthew 28:19-20) He commanded them to go to the uttermost parts of the earth. (Acts 1:8) After all, the good news of His salvation is good news to all people.

Chapter 4

ASCENSION AND IMPARTATION

Departure
The Day of Pentecost
Spirit Baptism
Not Birthday, but Empowerment Day

Chapter 4

ASCENSION AND IMPARTATION

Departure

The conclusion of His appearances on earth came as He ascended to the Father's right hand in heaven. Gathering His disciples together, He was taken up and a cloud received Him out of their sight. Awed and perplexed, the disciples were comforted by the words of an angel. "This Jesus, who has been taken up from you into heaven, will come in just the same way as you have watched Him go into heaven." (Acts 1:11) With these words a promise is made concerning the second coming of the Lord, which we yet await. He ascended to His Father to assume His rightful place of authority. Jesus now reigns over all as King of Kings and Lord of Lords (Revelation 19:16). His name is higher than all names (Philippians 2:9-10).

The Day of Pentecost

Before ascending, Jesus had warned His disciples not to venture into ministry hastily. When preparing them for His departure, He unequivocally commanded them to gather together for no other purpose than to wait and pray "for what the Father had promised, …but you shall be baptized with the Holy Spirit not many days from now." (Acts 1:4-5) This baptism of the Spirit He told them to expect would be a key factor in the accomplishment of their purpose. "…but you shall receive power when the Holy Spirit has come upon you; and you shall be My witnesses both in Jerusalem, and in all Judea and Samaria, and even to the remotest part of the earth." (Acts 1:8)

Spirit Baptism

In the Father's timing, Jesus fulfilled the Father's promise. As the ascended, resurrected Lord, Jesus became the Baptizer of the Holy Spirit. "Therefore, having been exalted to the right hand of God and having received from the Father the promise of the Holy Spirit, He has poured forth this which you both see and hear." (Acts 2:33) They were now the church, but were lacking the Spirit's empowerment. The hundred and twenty disciples had been waiting and praying in the upper room of a Jerusalem residence when the Day of Pentecost arrived. "And suddenly there came from heaven a noise like a violent, rushing wind, and it filled the whole house where they were sitting. ...And they were filled with the Holy Spirit and began to speak with other tongues as the Spirit was giving them utterance." (Acts 2:2,4) On that day, both men and women received the baptism of the Holy Spirit. All one hundred and twenty were baptized in the Spirit, not just the eleven apostles. Even Mary, Jesus' mother, was a recipient. All who would go forth, ministering in Jesus' name, required the supernatural enablement imparted through Spirit baptism.

That very day, these believers went out into the streets of Jerusalem, declaring the wonderful works of God. At first, they proclaimed the Gospel by means of speaking in other tongues. Even though their words were unintelligible to themselves, their tongues proved miraculously to be in the languages of those present, enabling those diverse people groups to hear and understand the Gospel. Then Peter preached a sermon, leading to the conversion and baptism of three thousand people. Now empowered, the church had taken action, with startling results. Armed with the Spirit's baptism, the church was now taking a bold public stance to proclaim the Gospel of Jesus Christ in the marketplace. The hundred and twenty disciples were the charter members of the church. But following the Day of Pentecost, the church quickly expanded, and would continue to grow.

Not Birthday, but Empowerment Day

At this point, an important observation needs to be made. The Day of Pentecost was not the birthday of the church. Rather, the Day of Pentecost was the beginning of the church's empowerment. Spirit baptism equipped the church supernaturally, so that she could go forth preaching, confirming the Word that they preached with signs following. The church had already been birthed when Jesus breathed on the disciples after His resurrection and said, "Receive ye the Holy Spirit." (John 20:22) They received the Holy Spirit through their confidence in His resurrection. They were born again believers, forgiven and cleansed by His blood. The new covenant was initiated already prior to the Day of Pentecost. All that remained was their need for empowerment, for their commission was an impossible one without supernatural enablement. John the Baptist had foretold Jesus' role as the Spirit Baptizer: "…He who is coming after me is mightier than I, … He Himself will baptize you with the Holy Spirit and fire." (Matthew 3:13) That prophecy was literally fulfilled on the Day of Pentecost.[14]

In summation, salvation was accomplished through Jesus' Messianic fulfillment of the old covenant. Jesus fulfilled the old covenant and established a new one, sealed by the shedding of His own blood. Then, as the resurrected, ascended Lord, He empowered the members of His church with Spirit baptism, equipping them for their mission to take the Gospel to the uttermost parts of the earth.

Chapter 5

CONTINUING PRESENCE

The Holy Spirit Specializes in Jesus

Jesus' Multi-presence

The Church's Early Growth

Christians Leave Jerusalem

Key Christian Centers

Paul's Conversion

Roman Persecution

Three Centuries of Persecution

Constantine and the Church's Triumph

Chapter 5

CONTINUING PRESENCE

The church is now functioning without Jesus' physical presence. Yet no misunderstanding should arise at this point that Jesus has been set aside and the church is able to operate effectively without Him. Nothing could be further from the truth. Jesus continues to be the focus and the center of this new covenant fellowship. In fact, Jesus is and always will be the rightful Head of this body. This body of believers is dependant upon Him as the source, the life, and the sustenance of this new community.

The Holy Spirit Specializes in Jesus

The New Testament presents the church as Jesus' living body on earth. Jesus resurrected from death to life, and ascended to the Father's throne in heaven. Jesus not only is at the right hand of the Father, but because He sent the Holy Spirit, He simultaneously is able to be on the earth, extending Himself in the midst of His followers. We find in the Gospel of John that the Holy Spirit's central purpose is to glorify Jesus and to reveal His life and His teachings to the disciples. (John 16:13-15) The Holy Spirit does not take us beyond Jesus. He takes us deeper into Jesus, into His living presence.

When Jesus gave the commission found in Mark, chapter 16, we find an interesting conclusion in verse 20. "And they went out and preached everywhere, while the Lord worked with them, and confirmed the word by the signs that followed." (Mark 16:20) Note what is clearly indicated. The Lord is still working. He is still extending His ministry. He has accomplished redemption, but He is not finished with the world. There remains a purpose to be achieved in history.

Jesus' Multi-presence

He is the Head of the church. He is continuing His ministry through the empowerment and presence of the Holy Spirit. Although seated at the Father's right hand, Jesus exercises multi-presence. He can be in multiple places simultaneously, through the agency of the Holy Spirit. He is in heaven, while also being in the church and the world. He is in each individual believer personally because the Holy Spirit has that capability. Direct access to the living Jesus, and continuous communication with Him, is normative for the church because the Holy Spirit has been given to us.

The Church's Early Growth

For nearly 2000 years, the church of Jesus has existed on planet earth. Rapid growth in terms of numbers of converts was apparent from the beginning, when the initial 120 believers were baptized in the Holy Spirit on the Day of Pentecost. As that day concluded, 3,000 new converts were added to the church. Further expansion followed on the heels of that event. In a very short while, 5,000 men were numbered among the converts of Jesus (Acts 4:4) The city of Jerusalem was the early center of Christianity (as the Christian movement came to be called). Jesus' brother, James, was the Jerusalem church's first bishop (leader), serving for thirty-two years.[15]

Christians Leave Jerusalem

Around the year 66, a massive migration of Christians occurred due to a vision received by certain members of the church, warning Christians to leave Jerusalem and settle in the Transjordanian city of Pella. Thus, Christians were no longer present when the city suffered one of the darkest days in its history in the year 70. In an effort to suppress Jewish political rebellion, Roman troops stormed Jerusalem, destroying the Jewish temple and leaving behind a horrible bloodbath of destruction.

Key Christian Centers

Other cities rose to prominence as major centers of Christianity. Antioch was an early strategic city for Christian expansion into Gentile territory. Alexandria, Egypt became a city of major Christian influence for centuries. Istanbul, renamed Constantinople during the reign of Constantine, became the eastern capital of the Empire and a major base for Christianity. Yet no city surpassed Rome in Christian influence. Rome being the capital of the Empire, and the Roman bishop being the first to face persecution, led to exalted status.

Paul's Conversion

The most prominent early convert was Jewish religious leader Saul (renamed Paul), who previously had persecuted the Christians. While on a mission to hunt down Christians in Damascus, Paul experienced a dramatic, literal encounter with the risen Jesus, radically altering his identity. After a season of reorientation, Paul spearheaded the expansion of the church beyond her Jewish roots, taking the Gospel message deep into the Gentile (non-Jewish) populations of the Roman Empire. His letters to various Gentile churches that he had founded soon became books included within the New Testament scripture.

Paul, along with Jesus' original twelve disciples (excluding the betrayer Judas), and a few others, served in the role of the church's early apostles. Apostles were leaders sent by God to spread Jesus' Gospel and establish new churches. Early decades of expansion lacked the resistance that would come later as Roman authorities began to recognize that the Christian church was not simply another Jewish sect.

Roman Persecution

Everything changed during the reign of Emperor Nero, as Christians became targeted for special persecution. Already viewed with suspicion and misunderstanding by the common populace, in that Christians refused to participate in the normal social and political activities of Roman life because of the rampant presence of immoral and idolatrous practices, Christians were easily victimized. In June of 64, a ravaging fire in the city of Rome destroyed ten of the fourteen sections of the city. The people believed that their emperor Nero was responsible for setting the blaze, for his intentions of rebuilding the city were known. Nero devised a way that he could relieve suspicion against himself. Since the sections of the city untouched by the fired included the homes of Christians, Nero turned attention away from himself by scapegoating them. Nero began massacring Christians by the thousands. His cruelty knew no bounds. He even lighted his gardens at night by using Christians as human torches. Intense persecution continued for four years, including the martyrdoms of apostles Peter and Paul in the year 67. Relief came in 68 when Nero was deposed by a rebellion that gained the support of the Roman senate. Nero committed suicide.

Three Centuries of Persecution

Although Nero was removed from power, his policies legitimating the persecution of Christian were not withdrawn. Some emperors simply ignored such policies, but the majority of emperors following Nero continued to persecute the church. Christians had become open game for the Romans. This practice continued off and on until the early 300's. Christians knew that when they were baptized in the name of Jesus, the likelihood of either suffering or dieing for their faith was a reality. However, attempts to exterminate Christians only served to spread the Gospel far and wide, leading to more converts and churches. Church leader Tertullian later would say, "The oftener we are mown down by you, the more in number we grow; the blood of Christians is seed."[16]

Constantine and the Church's Triumph

A turning point came in 313 A.D., as Constantine became emperor of Rome. In his quest for control of the empire, Constantine attributed a major military victory (Battle of Milvian Bridge) to the power of Jesus, after a dream or vision influenced him to go into battle with the insignia of Jesus on the shields and banners of his army. After becoming emperor, and desiring the continued favor of Jesus over his rule, Constantine stopped the Roman persecution of Christians and began to show preference for Jesus over the ancient gods of Rome. He built elaborate church buildings, and convened church councils to settle doctrinal disputes. Future developments after Constantine continued to favor the church. In 380, the Emperor Theodosius I issued an edict declaring Christianity to be the only lawful religion in the Roman Empire.

Chapter 6

DIFFERING INTERPRETATIONS OF JESUS

Doctrinal Conflict

Scriptural Canon

Creedal Confessions

Apologists

Responding to Heresies

Common Denominators of Error

Chapter 6

DIFFERING INTERPRETATIONS OF JESUS

Doctrinal Conflict

Over a time span of three centuries, the Christian church rose from targeted persecution aimed at extermination to supreme status as the official religion of the Roman Empire. Once peace was attained in church and state relations, another kind of warfare broke out. Controversy emerged within the arena of the church's fundamental teachings and doctrines. This is not to imply that the church had ever been free from struggles over correct doctrine. From New Testament times onwards, the church has been faced with the task of identifying and exposing false teachers and false teachings that seek to alter the foundations of Christian truth.

Movements in the early stages of development are particularly vulnerable to the corruption of their basic teachings because they are in a process of doctrinal stabilization. This means that authoritative guidelines of belief such as scriptural content, creedal confessions and doctrinal standards are in a process of resolution. In the case of the Christian church, the rise of aberrant teachings served a positive purpose of helping to stimulate the church to solidify her standards of truth.

Scriptural Canon

This is not to say that the scriptural writings ultimately constituting the twenty-seven books of the New Testament were not present and in use by the churches from the late first century onwards. When the New Testament finally was canonized in 397 A.D., the Council of Carthage was performing a perfunctory but necessary task of officially ratifying the books already recognized as scripturally authoritative for many years.[17] Yet to have a closed Scriptural canon of authorative status like the New Testament, linked with the Old Testament to form the Christian Bible, represented a milestone in the vital pursuit of preserving truth.

Creedal Confessions

Other than the Apostle's Creed, an early baptismal confession, the major creedal confessions of the early church were formulated in the heat of battle in response to specific doctrinal challenges threatening the church. They were the products of special councils attended by bishops of local congregations throughout the Roman Empire and convened under the auspices of the Roman emperor. Creedal confessions had a binding effect upon the churches of Christendom in that they were upheld by the force of Roman law. Bishops unwilling to comply with official creedal confessions were banished from their churches.

Apologists

Creedal confessions were not the only protection against false teachings. In pivotal times of doctrinal disturbance, church leaders have risen to the occasion by producing influential writings[18] in defense of Christian truth. Apologetical writings have helped to expose and discredit perpetrators of false teaching, and bring truth into a clearer light among the faithful. Although intent upon exposing the errors of specific heresies within a specific historical context, major apologetic writings have served an enduring purpose. Old errors have a way of resurfacing in different disguises in subsequent generations. Leaders who have familiarized themselves with ancient apologetical defenses are more likely to detect the same or similar errors seeking to deceive new generations of Christians.

Responding to Heresies

Over a period of 350 years, the Christian church was bombarded by a series of heresies threatening to dislodge her from her ancient foundations. Beginning in approximately 170, and extending to the year 529, the very survival of the church depended upon several key leaders who were willing to confront the rising tide of false teaching and to take a gallant stand for truth. During that span of time, seven significant heresies sought to infiltrate the church and spread corrupt teaching, any of which would have perverted the sacred foundations necessary for the church's survival. All of these heresies were potentially destructive precisely because they challenged the very cornerstone of truth, i.e., the true knowledge of the person of Jesus and His work of salvation. If the cornerstone is removed, the foundation sags, and the entire structure becomes unstable. Had any one of these doctrinal errors gained lasting credibility in the church, the house, devoid of her treasure, would have been without value. The apostle John makes this point abundantly clear. "Any one who goes too far and does not abide in the teaching of Christ, does not have God; …" (II John 9) Any mistaken identity concerning Jesus is a fatal error.

Common Denominators of Error

Among the seven heresies, doctrinal errors can be reduced to three common denominators. The three are the denial of the true humanity of Jesus, the denial of the true deity of Jesus, and the rejection of the all-sufficiency of God's grace in Jesus. These factors represent essential bulwarks of Christian truth, without which Christianity becomes reduced to nothing more than religious futility and superstitious fantasy. If there were a diabolical head of all evil, and surely there is, he would vent his final, futile efforts in the attempt to subvert the absolutely essential truths upon which the church stands, the doctrines concerning the identity of Jesus and the nature of His grace.

Chapter 7

SON OF GOD:
Recovery Of The Old Testament Messiah

Salvation Must Come From God

Messiah Must Be Divine As Well As Human

Expected Messiah Need Not Be God

A Divine Messiah Blasphemous

Static View of Monotheism Challenged

Messiah Must Be Savior God

Messiah Must Be Eternal God

Chapter 7

SON OF GOD:
Recovery Of The Old Testament Messiah

Salvation Must Come From God

The fatal flaw during Jesus' lifetime was to misidentify Him as being merely a human person, while failing to recognize His divine origin. The Old Testament conclusion was that no mere human had been able to please God and thereby serve as a vehicle for rescuing the rest of the human race. God would have to bare His own right arm and come Himself to redeem His fallen creatures. The prophet Isaiah rightly envisioned the human predicament leading to God's self-intervention. "Now the Lord saw, and it was displeasing in His sight that there was no justice. And He saw that there was no man, and was astonished that there was no one to intercede; then His own arm brought salvation to Him; and His righteousness upheld Him." (Isaiah 59:15-16)

Messiah Must Be Divine As Well As Human

The mystery Jesus sought to unravel, first for the Jewish people, then for humankind, was that the expected Messiah would be of divine as well as human origin. No mere human could qualify as the world's Savior. The Psalmist had said, "No man can by any means redeem his brother, or give to God a ransom for him." (Psalms 49:7) Jesus understood that the Messiah must be unique. He must be from above, from the eternal being of God, while having human nature in kind with His brother men. As the Galilean walked and talked, ate and drank, awakened and slept, and laughed and wept, no one disputed His real humanity. In contrast, Jesus' affirmations of deity failed to register, except among His close followers and a few others.

Expected Messiah Need Not Be God

Jesus' claims to be the Divine Messiah met rejection from the religious establishment on two fronts. For one, they did not believe that He was their promised Messiah of Scripture. As has been noted, Jesus did not fit their stereotypic image of a Messiah king of the Davidic lineage, a warrior possessing great military/political prowess, able to rally support for a liberation movement potent enough to win Israel's independence from Rome. From their conceptual framework, the Messiah needed only to be an exceptional human leader, not God. Granted, He would be God's chosen leader, but certainly not God Himself.

A Divine Messiah Blasphemous

So, on the second front, Jesus distanced Himself even further from the authorities by presenting Himself as the **Divine** Messiah. Since Jesus was God's Son from above sent on a messianic mission, He was merely telling the truth about His unique nature and purpose. But such claims were perceived by the Jews to be absolute anathema. On just such an occasion, Jesus declared before the Jewish leaders, "'I and the Father are one.' The Jews took up stones again to stone Him. Jesus answered them, 'I showed you many good works from the Father; for which of them are you stoning Me?' The Jews answered Him, 'For a good work we do not stone You, but for blasphemy; and because You, being a man, make Yourself out to be God.'" (John 10:30-33) On another occasion, Jesus declared

Himself the great "I AM," a name reserved in scripture for Jehovah God. Jesus said, "'Your father Abraham rejoiced to see My day; and He saw it, and was glad.' The Jews therefore said to Him, 'You are not yet fifty years old, and have You seen Abraham?' Jesus said to them, 'Truly, truly, I say to you, before Abraham was born, I AM.' Therefore they picked up stones to throw at Him; ..." (John 8:56-59)

Static View of Monotheism Challenged

Monotheism was a bedrock truth of the Jewish faith. Jesus did not challenge the monotheism of the Old Testament, but confronted the static view of monotheism held by most of His contemporaries. Seeing themselves as the keepers of traditional monotheism, Jewish leaders failed to see in their own scripture clear indications that the God of Abraham, Isaac and Jacob could be relationally constituted. The Jewish establishment held to an undifferentiated Godhead, whereas Jesus revealed that God is multi-dimensional, made up of a communion of Divine Persons (Father, Son and Holy Spirit) sharing the same eternal essence.

Theologian Donald Bloesch has noted, "The most frequent appellation for God in the Old Testament, the Hebrew word, *Elohim*, connotes a divine plurality in unity." [19] An obvious reference is found in the creation story from the Pentateuch. As God contemplated the creation of the first humans, He made this statement. "Then God said, 'Let **us** make man in **our** image, according to our likeness; ...'" (Genesis 1:26) A first century Christian apocryphal writing,[20] *The Epistle of Barnabus*, although not a New Testament book, nonetheless sheds interesting light on this Genesis passage.[21] The context is a conversation between the Father and the Son, as they work together to create humanity. In another Old Testament passage, the prophet moves freely from singular to plural cases in reference to God. "Then I heard the voice of the Lord, saying, 'Whom shall I send, and who will go for **Us**?' Then I said, 'Here am I. Send me!'" (Isaiah 6:8)

Messiah Must Be Savior God

The Old Testament does not hesitate to connect the messianic figure with attributes of eternal divinity. Already introduced early in this chapter is the truth that only God can bring salvation to His fallen human creatures. No mere human can save himself, nor can he save his fellow creatures. Jesus' contemporaries were looking for the coming of a great human leader, but Jesus knew that the Messiah must be God. Only divine intervention from above could redeem the people from their sins. Old Testament prophets declared that only God could be humanity's Savior. "Yet I have been the Lord your God since the land of Egypt; and you were not to know any god except Me, for there is no savior besides Me." (Hosea 13:4) "I, even I, am the Lord; and there is no savior besides Me." (Isaiah 43:11) Isaiah further implies that no savior will appear who is not God Himself. "A righteous God and a Savior; there is none except Me." (Isaiah 45:21)

Messiah Must Be Eternal God

Other Old Testament messianic passages connect the Messiah with attributes of eternality, which can only apply to One who is God. The prophet Micah gives an example. "But as for you, Bethlehem Ephrathah, too little to be among the clans of Judah, from you One will go forth for Me to be ruler in Israel. His goings forth are from long ago, from the days of eternity." (Micah 5:2) Another familiar messianic passage explicitly links the child to be born and the son to be given with the divine names Mighty God and Everlasting Father. "For a child will be born to us, a son will be given to us; and the government will rest on His shoulders; and His name will be called Wonderful Counselor, Mighty God,

Eternal Father, Prince of Peace. There will be no end to the increase of His government or of peace, on the throne of David and over his kingdom, to establish it and to uphold it with justice and righteousness from then on and forevermore." (Isaiah 9:6-7) This passage explicitly reveals a coming Messiah of human birth who is also divine in nature.

Chapter 8

SON OF GOD:
The New Testament Witness

Birth Announcement and During Jesus' Earthly Life

Post Ascension Testimony

Doctrine of the Incarnation

Jesus' Pre-existence in the New Testament

Chapter 8

SON OF GOD:
The New Testament Witness

The early church identified Jesus to be both Messiah and Son of God. So incontestable was the apostolic confession of Jesus' messiahship that this title was appended to His name. The New Testament honors Jesus with the name **Jesus Christ**. The title, **Christ**, literally means, **Messiah**. And equally significant for the early Christians was the belief that their Messiah was of divine origin and nature.

Birth Announcement and During Jesus' Earthly Life

As He entered human history, authoritative writings surrounding His birth and life provide resounding and incontrovertible testimony that Jesus is the Christ (Messiah), the eternal Son of God.

1) When **the angel Gabriel** announced Jesus' coming birth to Mary, His Mother, these affirmations of His deity and messiahship were spoken. "And behold, you will conceive in your womb, and bear a son, and you shall name Him Jesus. He will be great, and will be called the Son of the Most High; and the Lord God will give Him the throne of His father David; and He will reign over the house of Jacob forever; and His kingdom will have no end." (Luke 1:31-33)

2) **John the Baptist** confessed to Jesus' divinity. "And I have seen, and have borne witness that this is the Son of God."

(John 1:34)

3) **Father God Himself** witnessed in audible voice on various occasions that Jesus was His Son. One occasion was following Jesus' submission to John's baptism. "…and behold, a voice out of the heavens, saying, 'This is My beloved Son, in whom I am well-pleased.'" (Matthew 3:17)

4) As Jesus was assembling **His band of disciples,** their willingness to abandon their jobs and homes to follow Him hinged primarily upon their conviction that they had found the Messiah. When Andrew told his brother, Simon (Peter) about Jesus, his first words were, "We have found the Messiah." (John 1:41) An amazing event occurred when Jesus walked on the water and also enabled Peter to step out of a boat and walk. The event inspired the disciples to worship Jesus. "And those who were in the boat worshipped Him, saying, 'You are certainly God's Son'" (Matthew 14:33)

5) The events surrounding Jesus' death on the cross struck fear in the heart of **a Roman centurion** and others keeping guard over Jesus, moving them to exclaim, "Truly this was the Son of God!" (Matthew 27:54)

6) After Jesus rose from the dead on the third day, **His disciple Thomas** was struggling to believe reports of Jesus' resurrection. After Jesus appeared to him and others, and allowed Thomas to touch the crucifixion wounds, he became a believer. "Thomas answered and said to Him, 'My Lord and my God!'" (John 20:28) Jesus did not forbid Thomas' worship of Him. And worship is reserved for God alone. Earlier, Jesus Himself had resisted Satan with the words of the Old Testament Law, "You shall worship the Lord your God, and serve Him only." (Matthew 4:10, quoted from Deuteronomy 6:13)

Post Ascension Testimony

After Jesus' ascension into heaven, New Testament writers continued to offer abundant evidence of Jesus' eternal deity. Belief that Jesus is God's Son was an essential point of early church belief and doctrine.

1) Soon after the dramatic conversion of **Saul (Paul)**, "he began to proclaim Jesus in the synagogues, saying, 'He is the Son of God.'" (Acts 9:20) Later in Paul's ministry, in a letter to the Colossian church that he founded, he declared, "For in Him (Jesus) all the fullness of Deity dwells in bodily form, …" (Colossians 2:9)

2) In another instance, an early church deacon (one who assisted the apostles), **Phillip**, explained the Gospel of Jesus to an Ethiopian man. His receptivity to the message led him to exclaim to Phillip, "'What prevents me from being baptized?' And Phillip said, 'If you believe with all your heart, you may.' And he answered and said, 'I believe that Jesus Christ is the Son of God.' …and he (Phillip) baptized him." (Acts 8:36-38)

3) The apostle **John** affirmed consistently in his writings that, without the belief that Jesus is the Son of God, there is no relationship with God or inheritance of God's eternal life. In John's Gospel, he reveals his primary purpose in writing his account of Jesus' life and ministry. "Many other signs Jesus also performed in the presence of the disciples, which are not written in this book; but these have been written that you may believe that Jesus is the Christ, the Son of God; and that believing you may have life in His name." (John 20:30-31) In one of John's epistles, he lays down the New Testament standard. "Whoever confesses that Jesus is the Son of God, God abides in Him, and he in God." (I John 4:15)

Doctrine of the Incarnation

The church's belief concerning the Deity of Jesus as God's Son developed into what became known as the doctrine of the Incarnation. Implied in this belief is recognition of His pre-existence. Jesus existed as God's eternal Son prior to His human birth to Mary in Bethlehem. The apostle John testifies to Jesus' divine nature. In the following passage, John identifies Jesus with the divine Logos (Word). The New Testament describes Jesus in His pre-existence both as God's Word and God's Son. John states, "In the beginning was the Word, and the Word was with God, and the Word was God." (John 1:1) Jesus, as the Word, chose to become incarnate, in order to free humanity from sin. In the act of Incarnation, the Logos assumed into His divine nature the nature of humanity, without ceasing to be God. John succinctly describes this event. "And the Word became flesh and dwelt among us, ..." (John 1:14)

In space and time, God became human. Upon this mysterious, supernatural occurrence rests the entire superstructure of Christian belief. The apostle Paul states, "But when the fullness of the time came, God sent forth His Son, born of a woman, born under the Law, ..." (Galatians 4:4) Mary struggled to comprehend the angel Gabriel's message to her, that she would give birth to "the Son of the Most High." "'And behold, you will conceive in your womb, and bear a son, and you shall name Him Jesus.' ...And Mary said to the angel, 'How can this be, since I am a virgin?' And the angel answered and said to her, 'The Holy Spirit will come upon you, and the power of the Most High will overshadow you; and for that reason the holy offspring shall be called the Son of God.'" (Luke 1:32, 31, 34-35)

The circumstances surrounding Jesus' conception were unique in human history. A virgin became a mother. Possessing a seed mysteriously supplied by the divine person of the Holy Spirit, Mary was fertilized by that seed, producing a conception in her womb, resulting in what otherwise would be a natural pregnancy and birth. When the baby boy, Jesus, was born, He was an individual person possessing both a divine and a human nature. His divine nature came from above, and pre-existed within the Godhead as God's Son and Word. His human nature came from Mary, and was like that of other human creatures.

Jesus' Pre-existence in the New Testament

As Jesus conversed with Nicodemus, He revealed His pre-existence. "And no one has ascended into heaven, but He who descended from heaven, even the Son of Man." (John 3:13) Also in John's Gospel is Jesus' confession, "before Abraham was born, I AM." (John 8:58) In a prayer to His heavenly Father, Jesus made reference to His prior existence within the Godhead. "And now, glorify Thou Me together with Thyself, Father, with the glory which I ever had with Thee before the world was." Jesus continues His prayer by saying, "for Thou didst love Me before the foundation of the world." (John 17:5, 24)

In summation, the biblical writers affirmed that Jesus is the incarnate Son of God. For the sake of the human race, Jesus descended from His place of intimacy with Father God in heaven to assume human nature into His own divine being. He lived within the limitations of finite humanity, yet never violated the Mosaic Law as had all other humans. His death on Calvary's cross in substitution for the sinful race purchased justification and forgiveness for the alienated creation and its creatures. His resurrection brought regeneration and the promise of eternal life for all believing humanity. His ascension and baptism of the Holy Spirit upon the church empowered believers to spread the Gospel message worldwide with supernatural enablement. These accomplishments represent the work of Jesus the Christ, eternal Son of God.

Chapter 9

SON OF GOD:
Christian History And The Threat Of Arianism

Arius' Teachings

False Protector of Monotheism

Constantine and the Council of Nicaea

Arians and Semi-Arians

The Nicene Creed

Christendom Divided

The Triumph of Athanasius and the Creed

Homoousios – Key to Victory

Athanasius' Brilliant Defense

Chapter 9

SON OF GOD:
Christian History And The Threat Of Arianism

    A brief early history of the church has been ventured previously. Christianity eventually permeated the Roman Empire, emerging from obscurity and harsh persecution to the place of becoming the official religion of that same Empire. Belief in Jesus' divine identity continued without serious challenge until the fourth century.[22] Within the second decade of the fourth century, a presbyter from Baukalis, Egypt, in the shadows of the highly regarded Alexandrian church, began spreading an erroneous opinion of Jesus' divinity that eventually divided Christendom.

    The man's name was Arius. He once rivaled Alexander for the bishop's office of Alexandria. Returning in defeat to the obscurity of Baukalis, he sought notoriety by disseminating novel doctrine.[23] Alexander, now Arius' superior as bishop of Alexandria, was the first to detect heresy[24] in Arius' teachings. In personal conferences, Alexander sought to correct Arius' errors, and warned him to cease in the propagation of his views. However, Arius, to the contrary, accelerated his efforts, even gaining some noteworthy adherents to his perspective, such as Eusebius, the bishop of Nicomedia.

Arius' Teachings

Before the story progresses too far, we should pause to make mention of the substance of Arius' teachings about Jesus. Arius did not explicitly deny Jesus' divinity, but the manner in which he qualified the divinity had the effect of challenging the normative belief that Jesus shared the Father's essential deity. Arius accepted the church's belief in Jesus' pre-existence, even agreeing with Scripture that Jesus was the divine agent used by God to create the world. Yet Arius stopped short of affirming that Jesus divinity was eternal. Only the Father's divinity was eternal. Jesus possessed a created divinity, unlike the Father's eternal divinity. For Arius, God was not always Father. When He created the Son, prior to creating the universe, He then became Father. Prior to the creation of the Son, God was alone.

This meant that Arius fabricated two levels of deity, created and uncreated divinity. Only God the Father was eternally, thus essentially, divine. Jesus was not divine in the way that divinity is understood, as possessing God's eternal being. For Arius, Jesus was viewed as a lesser god, used by the eternal God as an agent in creation and redemption. Arius' Jesus was semi-divine, whereas eternal deity is reserved only for Father God.

False Protector of Monotheism

Arius believed that his teachings served to protect the monotheistic tradition of the Judeo-Christian heritage. Somehow, he imagined that monotheism would be best preserved by refusing to give Jesus the same status of divinity as the eternal, transcendent God. As presbyter of the Baukalis church, Arius continued to baptize in the name of the Father, the Son, and the Holy Spirit. Yet in doctrine, he attributed to the Son and Spirit a creaturely divinity wholly unlike the eternal divinity reserved only for Father God. How ironic it was that the self-professed champion of monotheism, by failing to allow the Son and Spirit to share the eternal deity of the Godhead with the Father, inadvertently introduced a polytheistic[25] principle within Christian doctrine. As Arius' dangerous teachings managed to gain widespread popularity, the church's established beliefs about Jesus would face a severe test of survival.

Constantine and the Council of Nicaea

As Constantine became Roman emperor, the persecution of Christians was stopped and the church enjoyed the favor of the state. It was during Constantine's reign when Arius' teachings began to gain popularity. Those who adopted Arius' teachings were known as Arians, and their movement, Arianism. Constantine became concerned as Arians began to divide the church into rival factions. Failing in his efforts to bring unity by personal negotiation, Constantine called for a conference of the church's bishops to be held in the year 325, in the town of Nicaea near his imperial residence. Including presbyters and assistants who accompanied the 318 bishops responding to the emperor's invitation, somewhere between 1500 and 2000 persons attended the Council of Nicaea. The bishops engaged in deliberations for approximately six weeks. The major issue at hand was the need to reach agreement over the doctrinal issues raised by Arianism.

Arians and Semi-Arians

The Arian contingency first presented their creedal confession before the assembly of bishops. The bishops could not tolerate the Arian position in its precise definition, and the Arian creed was soundly rejected. Another group, representing what has been labeled the semi-Arian party, presented to the Council a modified form of Arianism. Its subtle wording smoothed over the harsh edges of Arius' teachings, but it leaned too far in compromise to orthodoxy.[26] The wording of the semi-Arian creed did not clearly differentiate between the Arian and non-Arian positions, thus it offered no resolution to the controversy at hand.

The Nicene Creed

Constantine was determined to break the stalemate between the bishops. At the advice of his consultant, he ordered that the semi-Arian confession be amended by adding the Greek word, *homoousios*, into the document at the appropriate place. Alexander, the Alexandrian bishop, was called upon to carry out the editing work. Athanasius, his brilliant young assistant, who would succeed him as bishop of Alexandria in 328, assisted him. Alexander and Athanasius did more than amend the creed. Their work represented a major revision. And their employment of the term, *homoousios*, artfully worded into the document, struck a clear dividing line between the contrary parties. This confession became the Nicene Creed, and, unmasking all subtlety, forced Arianism out into the open. Constantine backed the Nicene Creed with the force of Roman law, banishing from the churches of the Empire any bishops who refused to support it. As a result, the vast majority of the bishops ratified the Creed.

Christendom Divided

With nearly unanimous support, the Nicene Creed initially appeared to be the instrument that would unite the Empire's churches under a common doctrinal confession. Constantine hoped that Arianism simply would go away. But Arianism was far from finished. After Nicaea, Arius continued his furious campaign to promote his teachings. Other bishops who had voted for the Creed aggressively continued to propagate Arian doctrine. Three years after Nicaea, when Athanasius took office as bishop of Alexandria, he found Christendom more divided over the Arian issue than ever. Athanasius had been Alexander's assistant from the beginnings of the confrontations between Alexander and Arius. He knew the theological issues at stake, and the formidable threat posed by Arianism to the church's spiritual health and prosperity.

Conditions went from bad to worse after Constantine's death, as a succession of emperors took opposite stands regarding Arianism, thus leading the church on a wild roller-coaster ride of confusion. When emperors favoring Arianism came to power, the church suffered upheaval as orthodox bishops were banished from their posts. Athanasius was banished from Alexandria five times during the struggle. Throughout this fiercely contested battle, Athanasius was using his gifted pen, producing an arsenal of articulate and authoritative doctrinal writings in opposition to Arianism.[27]

The Triumph of Athanasius and the Creed

The Arians hated Athanasius, and schemed to falsify his reputation and to turn emperors and empire against him. At one point, a particular slogan gained prominence, "Athanasius contra mundum," a Latin phrase which meant, "Athanasius against the world." But after a struggle of more than fifty years, the truth of the Gospel began to prevail. The orthodoxy of the Nicene Creed eventually triumphed over the error of Arianism. The Nicene Creed[28] has endured over centuries of time to remain a unifying doctrinal standard of Christendom. All three major branches of Christianity today (Roman Catholicism, Eastern Orthodoxy, and Protestantism) support the Nicene Creed.

Homoousios – Key to Victory

The secret of the Creed's triumph, the use of the word *homoousious*, needs further explanation. This Greek word, properly translated, simply means "same substance, essence or being." Referring to the Son's relationship with the Father, the *homoousios* identifies the Son as **having the same substance, essence and being** as the Father. The semi-Arians stretched to the limit their view when they supported the term *homoiousios*, which meant **of like or similar essence**. They admitted that the Son had a similar essence with the Father's divinity. However, *homoousios* was totally unacceptable to them. They refused to acknowledge that the Son shared **the same essence** as the Father's divinity.

Alexander and Athanasius recognized this subtle but critical difference. They perceived that only *homoousios*, not *homoiousios*, was essential to preserve the orthodox faith. As Athanasius' writings revealed, the superstructure of Christian doctrine depended upon the foundational truth that Jesus' divinity shares **the same** eternal essence as the Father's. Otherwise, even if his godlike qualities are **similar** to the Father's, He must be viewed as other than God Himself. Only *homoousios* reveals the truth. Jesus and the Father's divine essence are **the same**, thus Jesus is eternal God. Athanasius reasoned that if Jesus is not God, then the scriptures are invalidated, and those who believe in Jesus are without redemption. Salvation must be from God, not from a being created by God. Only God Himself can pardon sins and bestow eternal life.

Athanasius' Brilliant Defense

Athanasius' refutation of Arianism established a standard of theological defense against any adversary of the eternal deity of Jesus that may rise up against the Christian church. His apologetic can be summarized in two key premises.

I. FIRST PREMISE. To deny that the Son of God shares the same eternal divinity as the Father's logically requires that He be viewed as a creaturely being, even if some level of divine status is attributed to Him.

A. LOGICAL CONCLUSIONS.

1. If God created Jesus, His Son, then God is not an eternal Father. He became Father when He created the Son.

2. If God created Jesus, His Son, yet Jesus is regarded as being god in some sense, then Christianity has been reduced to a form of heathen polytheism.

3. If God created Jesus, His Son, then He must also have created the Holy Spirit. Three gods have now been postulated, leaving open the possibility that more gods may yet be added to this pantheon.

4. Only if God is triune in being, eternally existing as Father, Son and Holy Spirit, can monotheism be preserved. Each member of the Trinity may be worshipped as eternal God.

II. SECOND PREMISE. If God created Jesus, His Son, even if he is regarded in some sense as God, then the historical Jesus was only a "middle-man," while God Himself remains transcendent and unknowable to humanity.

B. LOGICAL CONCLUSIONS.

1. Since our encounter with the historical Jesus was with a secondary being, we have no assurance that his ministry to us was reliable. We have no way of knowing if he accurately represented the will of God. We have no assurance of our salvation.

2. If our encounter with the historical Jesus was with a secondary being, then we did not relate to God when we related with Jesus. We have yet to know God relationally. God remains unknown to us.

3. If our so-called "mediator" was a creature like ourselves, and not God Himself, then he must find one who can mediate for

him. If Jesus' mediator is not God, then his mediator must also find a mediator. The conclusion is an infinite progression of mediators, never successfully leading us to God Himself.

The Fall of Arianism

Athanasius' profound critique spelled the doom of Arianism as an influential movement. Although the triumph of the Nicene Creed was not totally secured at the time of Athanasius' death in 373, the victory was sealed in 381 at the Council of Constantinople. There, the bishops reinforced the Nicene confession, while incorporating into orthodoxy the truth of the essential, eternal divinity of the Holy Spirit.

Arianism had mounted the first major threat to the church's belief in Jesus' full divinity, but other challenges would arise through the centuries. However, no serious threat would encompass the distinctives of the Arian heresy. Arius was a dangerous pretender, in that he recognized pre-existent deity in Jesus. His error was to withhold from Jesus the status of eternal deity held by the Father. In so doing, Arius postulated for Jesus a kind of created deity lacking the authenticity of the truly divine.

Chapter 10

SON OF GOD:
Christian History And The Threats Of Nestorianism And Liberalism

Nestorianism
Theotokos
No Incarnation
Union of Wills
Son of God By Promotion
Classical Adoptionism
Cyril's Refutation - Anhypostasis
Jesus, A Divine-Human Being
Kenosis
Liberalism
Jesus Reduced to a Human Ideal
Barth's Critique
The Epistle to the Romans
Neo-Orthodoxy
Final Thoughts

Chapter 10

SON OF GOD:
Christian History And The Threats Of Nestorianism And Liberalism

Nestorianism

Other threats to Jesus' true divinity would arise in Christian history, manifesting heresy in a different disguise. Approximately 100 years after Arius' appearance, a new threat to Jesus' deity arose in the person of Nestorius. Nestorius became bishop of the prestigious church of Constantinople in 428. His erroneous teachings concerning Jesus had not been obvious until his appointment to Constantinople. Coming into the limelight, his views gained attention and speedily aroused alarm.

Theotokos

Nestorius' opinions were called into question initially as he publically opposed the traditional title for Mary, Jesus' mother, i.e., *theotokos*. The translation of this Greek word is "God bearer." Nestorius opposed the notion that in giving birth to Jesus, Mary was giving birth to God. Nestorius preferred the title, *Christokos*, meaning, "Christ bearer." He could tolerate the idea that Mary had given birth to Christ, the Messiah, but he would not agree that she had given birth to God.

No Incarnation

This controversy signaled that underlying problems lurked under the surface concerning Nestorius' view of Jesus. His protective stance regarding Jesus' true humanity led him to embrace an excessively extreme interpretation of Jesus' deity. Although Nestorius recognized Jesus' unique birth from a virgin, he failed to acknowledge Jesus' pre-existence as the Son of God. For Nestorius, Jesus was not divine by nature, but merely human. God made provision for Jesus to be conceived supernaturally, in that He was able to foresee that Jesus would be a fit vessel for His purposes. At Jesus' conception, the divine logos, or the "Christ from above" indwelt him. This meant that during Jesus' earthly life, He was essentially and totally human, yet indwelling him was the divine *logos* from God. He was not God incarnate, but a man indwelt by the divine.

Union of Wills

Furthermore, Nestorius taught that the relationship between the indwelling logos and the man Jesus was moral only, and not a substantial, inseparable union of the divine and human. Nestorius believed that Jesus' personhood as a man possessed its own independence apart from the logos, and maintained unity with the divine purely as an act of His human will. At any time, Jesus could have willed to be separated from the logos and His messianic mission. Should that have occurred, he would have been just another Jewish man, walking around Galilee.

An analogous illustration of this view of Jesus' relationship with the divine is the marriage relationship. Two individual persons become one by their willingness to enter into the marriage covenant. Should one or the other partner violate the covenant agreement, resulting in divorce, the unity of the marriage relationship becomes dissolved by an act of the will. Nestorius viewed the union of the human and the divine in Jesus as just such a relationship.

Son of God By Promotion

Although Nestorius relegated Jesus' essential nature to be merely human, yet he devised a way to attribute to him the status of Son of God. Jesus was not Son of God by nature, but earned the title as a result of His sinlessness and successful fulfillment of His redemptive mission. God resurrected Jesus from death, and conferred divinity upon him at His ascension into heaven.

Classical Adoptionism

Nestorius did not invent this pattern of doctrinal interpretation. This perspective has been generally classified as "adoptionism" throughout Christian history. Perhaps the earliest propagator of adoptionistic teaching was Paul of Samosata (third century). The adoptionist who helped shape the views of Nestorius was Theodore of Mopsuestia (350-428). Adoptionism in its classic form views Jesus essentially as a man, whose virtuous life culminates in His "adoption" to divine status as the Son of God. Nestorius was not the first heretic, nor would he be the last, to advocate adoptionistic opinions of Jesus' divinity. Yet because of the timing and position of Nestorius as bishop of Constantinople, the church took swift and decisive action against his heresy. When the church condemned Nestorianism at the Council of Ephesus in 431, she was making a conclusive statement against all adoptionistic denials of Jesus' eternal divinity.

Cyril's Refutation - Anhypostasis

The theologian of note most instrumental in exposing the errors of Nestorianism was Cyril, bishop of Alexandria. Cyril, the most highly regarded theologian of his time, was urged by his contemporaries to address in writing the issues at stake in this controversy.[29] Cyril effectively utilized two Greek words to disassemble the Nestorian heresy. Cyril applied the first word, *anhypostasis*, in reference to the humanity of Christ. This compound word is translated thusly: *an* = without; *hypostasis* = independent personal existence. Cyril asserted that Jesus' humanity is *anhypostasis*, i.e., without independent personal existence. This meant that Jesus' humanity never possessed independence apart from His deity. Cyril explained that the two natures of Jesus came together indivisibly at His conception in Mary. Jesus was not a human person, indwelt by the divine. His personhood is wholly unique, consisting of two separate natures indivisibly and inseparably united in His miraculous conception.

Jesus, A Divine-Human Being

Cyril held that Jesus pre-existent, eternal divinity as God's Son was resident in His divine nature, imparted into Mary's womb by the Holy Spirit. There, it was inseparably united to His human nature, supplied by His mother. Thus, Jesus was uniquely constituted. He was not a divine being per se, in that He also had a human nature. Yet neither was He merely a human being, since the divine nature was present. **He was a divine-human being.** Jesus is one indivisible person, the union of human and divine natures. Cyril pinpointed Nestorius' basic error, i.e. to reduce the essence of Jesus to humanity only. Even if "adopted" to become Son of God, His essence remains mere humanity. In addition, having the title Son of God does not invalidate His creaturely, finite origins. A finite human cannot be transformed into infinite God. Nestorius' Jesus could never be God in His essential being. In being, he was human only.

Kenosis

Cyril also utilized the word *kenosis* in his refutation. In the New Testament, Paul effectively uses *kenosis* to describe the action of the Incarnation, in which the divine Son submits to the process of becoming human. Paul relates that Jesus "although He existed in the form of God, did not regard equality with God a thing to be grasped, but **emptied Himself**, ...being made in the likeness of men." (Philippians 2:6-7) The Greek word for "emptied" in this passage is *enkenosen*, a form of the word *kenosis*.

Cyril rightly understood Paul's use of 'emptied,' not in the literal sense, as being emptied from one receptacle to another. Rather, it meant utter abasement in the Son of God's willingness to live within the finite limitations and boundaries of lowly humanity, without dependence upon the infinite glory of His divine nature. In short, the Son of God denied Himself the use of all divine capacities that would compromise the integrity of the humanity that He assumed in His Incarnation. The act of emptying Himself of divine prerogatives was an act of love for the fallen race that He came to save. The Son of God became human, without abandoning His divine identity and status.

Cyril knew that the vital link between *kenosis* and Incarnation spelled the ruin of Nestorius' view of Jesus. Cyril reasoned that, for Nestorius, there could be no *kenosis* of the Son of God. One who was a human being in essence cannot lower himself to become what He already is. Nestorius' Jesus was a man aspiring to be elevated to divine status. Cyril indicted Nestorius for substituting indwelling for the church's doctrine of the Incarnation. A mere man, even though indwelt by God, cannot save. He needs one to save him.

Liberalism

The church's belief in the eternal deity of Jesus withstood the fourth century challenge of Arianism and the fifth century challenge of Nestorianism. The standard of orthodoxy had been set, and no serious threat appeared for nearly 1400 years.[30] With the rise of biblical criticism in European academic circles in the nineteenth century came a major attempt to restructure the theological orthodoxy of the Christian church. The father of this movement, driven to reshape the Gospel into cultural "relevancy" at the expense traditional orthodoxy, was Frederick Schleiermacher (1768-1834).

The most dangerous facet of this movement, known as Liberalism, was its subtle reinterpretation of essential biblical doctrines, leaving its gullible followers with only a human Jesus. In the process of "demythologizing" the scriptures, Liberals striped away from the Testaments all supernatural events. No longer was Jesus the incarnate Son of God. His miracles were explained away. Even the sacred doctrines of the resurrection and ascension of Jesus were renounced.

Jesus Reduced to a Human Ideal

The Liberals were content to reduce Jesus to an ideal of human "God consciousness." Jesus was a mere man who epitomized the ultimate experience of God. Other Liberal theologians expanded the original concept to a collective and ethical consciousness. Jesus' exemplary life culminated in His sacrificial death, leaving us to find our salvation by emulation. Liberalism spiraled to its logical conclusion in Ernst Troeltsch's religious relativism. Once Jesus' ideal of "God consciousness" was realized, Jesus as an historical person became expendable. Jesus' ideal is attainable by all cultures, yet no culture may impose its religious norms upon others. Christians have Jesus as their model, while other cultures and religions must tread their own pathway without Him.

Barth's Critique

Because European theological schools bought into the Liberal agenda, generations of Liberal pastors filled the pulpits of churches for nearly a century. The status quo was rocked by the devastation brought on by World War I, awakening many to the shallowness of Liberalism in the face of human suffering. Change erupted when a young Swiss pastor, schooled under the Liberal system, began to test the shaky foundations of the prevailing worldview. Karl Barth (1886-1968) found that his theological preparation was lacking as he sought answers to the troubling questions of life posed by his parishioners. His quest led him to a fresh reinterpretation of the Bible. Barth helped rescue European Christianity from a powerless human Jesus whose death had no atoning efficacy for sinful humanity.

The Epistle to the Romans

Barth's publication in 1919 of his book *The Epistle to the Romans* sent shockwaves throughout the theological world of the Liberals. Barth pointed out that the God of the Bible was not a reflection of human idealism, but a sovereign God who related to His human creatures according to His own will. Furthermore, Jesus was not simply a human model of virtuous living, but God's eternal Son sent into the world to redeem the human race from sin. Barth baffled his opponents by utilizing some of their own critical tools of biblical interpretation to demolish Liberal presuppositions and to recover for the church the sound orthodoxy of her ancient faith.

Neo-Orthodoxy

Barth's Neo-Orthodoxy produced a new wave of theologians and pastors for twentieth century Europe, strong in their commitment to Jesus' deity, the atoning efficacy of the cross, and of His resurrection triumph over sin and its bondage. For Christianity at large, Barth demonstrated that the intellectual honesty demanded by the modern world need not be sacrificed by those who refuse to compromise the essential doctrines of the faith. The church must not jettison essential beliefs such as Jesus' pre-existent, eternal deity in the name of cultural relevance, for her authority and authenticity are at stake.

Final Thoughts

Our comfort as Christians rests in the truth of our confession that Jesus is the Son of God. He eternally has been the Son, while the Father has always been His Father. The Godhead is triune in essence. God the Father, God the Son and God the Holy Spirit are relationally differentiated, yet of One Divine Essence. When the Son willed to become flesh and dwell in history, for the sake of our redemption, He did not cease to be God. All of our dealings with Jesus are wholly trustworthy and reliable. God the Father initiated all of Jesus' words and works. Because Jesus forgave us of our sins, we are forgiven. Because Jesus won redemption for all who believe, then we can be assured of our eternal salvation.

Chapter 11

SON OF MAN:
Old Testament Backround

Messiah is Son of Man

The Son of God is Son of Man

Two Sonships

Son of David

Jesus David's Offspring

Bethlehem, the City of David

Jesus' Sinlessness

Sinless Sacrifice

Chapter 11

SON OF MAN:
Old Testament Backround

During the thirty-three years of Jesus' earthly life, the issue of His true humanity was not in dispute. Only after Jesus was no longer physically present with His church, having miraculously ascended to the throne of His Father in heaven, did questions emerge as to whether His humanity had been truly authentic. The challenge Jesus faced during His lifetime was not convincing people that He was human, which was not doubted, but rather attempting to establish that He was also divine. Among the throngs of people whom He regularly encountered, no one had cause to question Jesus' human identity.

Messiah is Son of Man

Messianic prophecy in the Old Testament revealed the coming of a divine Savior who also would be human. One of the descriptions that emphasize the human origins of the Messiah is **Son of Man**. Jesus appropriated the designation **Son of Man** for Himself, and it became a description prominently used for Him in the New Testament. The prophet Daniel experienced a vision of the coming of the Son of Man. "I kept looking in the night visions, And behold, with the clouds of heaven **One like a Son of Man** was coming, And He came up to the Ancient of Days and was presented before Him. And to Him was given dominion, glory and a kingdom, that all the peoples, nations, and men of every language might serve Him. His dominion is an everlasting dominion which will not pass away; And His kingdom is one which will not be destroyed." (Daniel 7:13-14) Daniel's prophetic vision of a coming Son of Man is clearly messianic.

The psalmist Asaph provides another Old Testament link between the coming Messiah and Son of Man." Let Thy hand be upon the man of Thy right hand, upon the **Son of Man** whom Thou didst make strong for Thyself." (Psalms 80:17) Here, "the man of Thy right hand" is the One who holds the highest place of honor, namely, the Father's own Son. The Father's Son is also known as the **Son of Man**.

The Son of God is Son of Man

Jesus took command of the description Son of Man, and applied it to Himself. Numerous times in the Gospels, Jesus refers to Himself as Son of Man. Here are a few examples to illustrate this point. "Now when Jesus came into the district of Caesarea Philippi, He began asking His disciples, saying, 'Who do people say that the **Son of Man** is?' ...And Simon Peter answered and said, 'Thou art the Christ, the Son of the living God.' And Jesus answered and said to him, 'Blessed are you, Simon Barjona, because flesh and blood did not reveal this to you, but My Father who is in heaven.'" (Matthew 16:13, 16-17) Notice that Jesus identifies Himself as the Son of Man, yet commends Peter's response to His question, that He also is "the Son of the living God." Jesus' reinforced His dual sonships, as Son of Man and Son of God.

Another instance finding Jesus referring to Himself as Son of Man, He is speaking of His coming crucifixion when He will be "lifted up" on the cross of Calvary to die for the sins of humanity. "And no one has ascended into heaven, but He who descended from heaven, even the **Son of Man**. And as Moses lifted up the serpent in the wilderness, even so must the Son of Man be lifted up; that whoever believes may in Him have eternal life." (John

3:13-15) Notice that in the same passage, Jesus calls attention to His pre-existence in heaven. He speaks of His descent from heaven, and predicts His coming ascent back to His Father's throne. Jesus continues to make references to His dual natures, for the One who is Son of Man is also Son of God.

In another passage, Jesus miraculously gave sight to a man born blind. Jesus addressed the man, now able to see. "'Do you believe in the **Son of Man**?' He answered and said, 'And who is He, Lord, that I may believe in Him?' Jesus said to him, 'You have both seen Him, and He is the one who is talking with you.' And he said, 'Lord, I believe.' And he worshiped Him." (John 9:35-38) Here, Jesus both invited the healed man to believe in Him, as Son of Man, and permitted worship of Himself. Without question, Jesus saw no inconsistency in assuming the dual roles of God's Son and Man's Son.

Two Sonships

In summation, the New Testament identifies Jesus as having two distinct sonships: He is simultaneously Son of Man and Son of God. His identity is not complete if one or the other designations is not recognized. It was foreordained and revealed in prophetic scripture that the Messiah be both. His saving mission required that He be both. Two seemingly antithetical entities, deity and humanity, are combined in one person. He is a person with dual origins: uncreated in His eternal deity, and created in His humanity. Skeptics may be hard-pressed to reconcile how divinity and humanity can co-exist in one person. Yet scripture presses upon us its own logic, leaving no room for deviation. The Jesus of scripture is a person of dual identities. He is Son of Man and Son of God.

Son of David

Another important scriptural designation evidencing the humanity of the Messiah is **Son of David**. In Israeli history, David had been a king who had followed God with all his heart. (I Kings 14:8) As a result, God had covenanted with David to establish his seed forever and his throne throughout all generations. (Psalms 89:3-4) God promised David, "And your house and your kingdom shall endure before Me forever; your throne shall be established forever." (II Samuel 7:16) And from David's seed, house, city and kingdom would come forth Israel's Messiah. "For a child will be born to us, a son will be given to us; And the government will rest on His shoulders; and His name will be called Wonderful Counselor, Mighty God, Eternal Father, Prince of Peace. There will be no end to the increase of His government or of peace, **on the throne of David and over his kingdom**, to establish it and to uphold it with justice and righteousness from then on and forevermore. The zeal of the Lord of hosts will accomplish this." (Isaiah 9:6-7)

Jesus David's Offspring

Jesus took His rightful place on the throne of David His father. As the apostle Paul stated in his sermon at Pisidian Antioch, "From the offspring of this man (King David), according to promise, God has brought to Israel a Savior, Jesus." (Acts 13:23) Elsewhere, Paul spoke of Jesus' human origins through David, "who was born of the seed of David according to the flesh."[31] (Romans 1:3) In the angel Gabriel's announcement to Mary that she would have a son, he told her, "He will be great, and will be called the Son of the Most High; and the Lord God **will give Him the throne of His father David**; and He will reign over the house of Jacob forever; and His kingdom will have no end." (Luke 1:32-33)

Bethlehem, the City of David

Even Jesus' birth in Bethlehem is significant, in that Bethlehem is the city of David. The Gospel of Luke records the angel's message to nearby shepherds of the birth of the Messiah, "for today **in the city of David** there has been born for you a Savior, who is Christ the Lord." (Luke 2:11) Although Jesus is known by the city in which He grew up (Jesus of Nazareth), Mary and Joseph were in Bethlehem at the time of His birth because of the census registration required at that time by the Roman emperor. They journeyed to Bethlehem because Joseph "was of the house and family of David." (Luke 2:4) This aligned the place of Jesus' birth with prophecy concerning the location of Messiah's birth. "But as for you, Bethlehem Ephrathah, too little to be among the clans of Judah, from you One will go forth for Me to be ruler in Israel. His goings forth are from long ago, from the days of eternity." (Micah 5:2)

Since Jesus grew up in Nazareth of Galilee, most of His adversaries did not know that Bethlehem was His place of birth. Yet they knew that Bethlehem was the scriptural place of Messiah's birth. Jesus' opponents used their misinformation to stir up controversy by disclaiming the possibility that Jesus could be the Messiah. "Others were saying, 'This is the Christ.' Still others were saying, 'Surely the Christ is not going to come from Galilee, is He? Has not the Scripture said that the Christ comes from the offspring of David, and from Bethlehem, the village where David was?' So there arose a division in the multitude because of Him." (John 7:41-43)

Yet Jesus possessed the appropriate scriptural ancestry to be the Messiah. The Gospel of Matthew begins with this statement, "The book of the genealogy of Jesus Christ, the son of David." (Matthew 1:1) Jesus' birthplace in Bethlehem and His ancestry through Joseph linked Him with the family of David. Jesus' case for messiahship was substantiated by His credentials, in that He met the scriptural qualifications to be son of David. And, as Son of David, Jesus' historical ancestry corroborated His earthly origins, undergirding His identity as Son of Man.

Jesus' Sinlessness

Another dimension of Jesus' messiahship that highlights His true humanity is His **sinlessness.** Jesus was a type of the sacrificial lamb, offered regularly in the Old Testament system of worship as an atonement for the sins of the people. God's instructions to His priests on this point were clear and nonnegotiable. The lamb or other animal must be **"without defect."**[32] "And you shall provide a lamb a year old without blemish for a burnt offering to the Lord daily; morning by morning you shall provide it." (Ezekiel 46:13)

For Jesus to be the ultimate and final lamb offered in sacrificial, atoning death for sins, His life must have been without blemish or defect. This meant that the moral quality of Jesus' life must have been untarnished by sin. The Apostle Peter notes, "…you were …redeemed …with precious blood, as of a lamb unblemished and spotless, the blood of Christ." (I Peter 1:18-19) The author of Hebrews also affirms that Jesus, through the shedding of His blood, "offered Himself without blemish to God." (Hebrews 9:14) For the animals, to be unblemished was a trait of natural breeding. For Jesus, to be unblemished was a moral accomplishment. "For we do not have a high priest who cannot sympathize with our weaknesses, but one who has been tempted in all things as we are, yet without sin." (Hebrews 4:15)

Sinless Sacrifice.

Jesus' value as a sin offering would have been nullified had He Himself been a sinner. No human could rightly claim to be the Messiah whose own sins would link Him with the sins of the humanity that He came to deliver from sin and its power. Not only was Jesus the offering for sin, but also He was the High Priest representing the people. Yet His priesthood stood in contrast to the Levitical priesthood of the Hebrews. The Levites were sinners like all the people, offering sacrifices that also covered their own sins. They, too, awaited a coming Messiah who would offer a perfect atonement for sins. Jesus was that Messiah, and His sacrificial role as an atonement for sins was for others, not for Himself. He was the High Priest without sin, whose offering was acceptable to God on that basis. "For it was fitting that we should have such a high priest, holy, innocent, undefiled, separated from sinners and exalted above the heavens; who does not need daily, like those high priests, to offer up sacrifices, first for His own sins, and then for the sins of the people, because this He did once for all when He offered up Himself." (Hebrews 7:26-27)

Chapter 12

SON OF MAN:
New Testament Witness

The Word Became Flesh

Jesus Incarnate in Our Flesh

Flesh Not Just Physical

Jesus' Obedience in Our Flesh

True Humanity Cause For Praise

Self-limitation of the Incarnation

The Holy Spirit Assisted Jesus' Humanity

Chapter 12

SON OF MAN:
New Testament Witness

Jesus' amazing moral accomplishment, to live an entire lifetime perfectly free from sin, is not appreciated as it should be. I believe that this lack of appreciation is due to a severe misperception of Jesus' true humanity. Christians generally place a disproportionate emphasis upon Jesus' deity, at the expense of His real humanity. Although most Christians profess to believe that Jesus is human, they do not give His humanity its proper place because they lack understanding of the significance of Jesus' Incarnation and its implications.

The Word Became Flesh

The apostle John announces the Incarnation event in clear and meaningful terms. "And the Word became flesh, and dwelt among us." (John 1:14) The term "Word" (*logos* in Greek) is important, in that the subject of this statement is the eternal *Word* or *Son* of God who became incarnate. The term "flesh" (*sarx* in Greek) is significant, in its description of the nature of the humanity the Word assumed in His Incarnation. The "flesh" normally is thought of as the physical, bodily part of a person. But sarx (translated flesh) in its biblical usage is **the sphere of earthly, human life in its totality.** Sarx embraces the whole of human existence, including its bodily and intellectual functions.

"Flesh' also is often misunderstood as having an evil tenor. However, sarx in its biblical context does not carry that meaning. States biblical scholar Eduard Schweizer, "...the flesh is not a sphere which is to be differentiated from other earthly things and which is intrinsically bad or especially dangerous. It becomes bad only when man builds his life on it."[33] Schweizer adds, "But the world acquires its sinful character only through unbelief, not through the sarx."[34]

Jesus Incarnate in Our Flesh

This discussion of "flesh" is necessary because many Christians, unmindful of the biblical material, consider the "flesh" of the incarnate Jesus to be different than the "flesh" of common humanity. Some Christians are uncomfortable accepting that Jesus' "flesh" was identical with our common humanity. Perhaps they have difficulty believing that Jesus could have prevailed over sin had He really shared our common nature and temptations.

Flesh Not Just Physical

In their attempt to resolve this dilemma, they find it expedient to reduce the "flesh" of Jesus to the purely physical realm. They reason that the Incarnation was about Jesus' taking a body like ours, as if He were putting on a physical garment of "flesh" to cover His otherwise divine being. Those who reason in this manner not only duplicate the ancient Apollinarian heresy (which we will cover in a coming chapter), but also set themselves at odds with the biblical revelation. Schweizer's findings again are helpful in this regard. He states that when Jesus' assumed our human nature, He "did not merely bear it as a vesture but became identical with it."[35] Those who reduce Jesus' humanity to His physical constitution have selectively redefined "humanity" for Jesus, compromising His incarnate purpose to identify fully with Adam's race as our Brother Man.

Jesus' Obedience in Our Flesh

The most troubling part of this scenario is that it robs Jesus of His magnificent moral victory over sin. Our salvation is dependent upon Jesus being obedient to the will of His Father as Son of Man. He had to reverse the pattern of disobedience initiated by Adam. "For as through the one man's disobedience the many were made sinners, even so through the obedience of the One the many will be made righteous." (Romans 5:19) Yes, it is right to emphasize the culmination of Jesus' obedient life when He surrendered Himself to death on the cross. But Jesus' sacrificial death had meaning because Jesus' was faithful to His Father's will over a lifetime of suffering to resist sin's temptations. The author of Hebrews declares that Jesus "learned obedience from the things which He suffered." (Hebrews 5:8) What made Jesus' flesh "special" was not its substance, but in keeping His flesh in continuous obedience to His heavenly Father's will. His moral obedience was not a sham, done only in the guise of humanity, and really accomplished by His divine prowess. Far from it. Jesus' flesh was identical to the flesh of Adam's race when He lived out His life in complete obedience to the will of His Father. Glory be to Jesus!

True Humanity Cause For Praise

When the reality of Jesus' true humanity is recognized, then the magnificent accomplishment of His sinlessness may be emphasized, giving cause for our honor, praise and worship. We, indeed, can rejoice that Jesus did not have "special" flesh, unlike the common flesh of Adam's race. We can be thankful that Jesus was morally upright, even though He was limited by our human nature and realm. The Incarnation was complete. Hebrews records, "since then the children share in flesh and blood, He Himself likewise also partook of the same, that through death He might render powerless him who had the power of death, that is, the devil; for assuredly He does not give help to angels, but He gives help to the seed of Abraham. Therefore, **He had to be made like His brethren in all things**, that He might become a merciful and faithful high priest in things pertaining to God, to make propitiation for the sins of the people. For since He Himself was tempted in that which He has suffered, He is able to come to the aid of those who are tempted." (Hebrews 2:14-18)

Self-limitation of the Incarnation

The purpose of the Incarnation was to redeem Adam's fallen race. The flesh that had become corrupted and alienated from God had to be cleansed from its sin and reconciled with God. This redemptive motive led the Son of God to leave His place of majesty and glory in heaven and descend to earth to take within Himself the lowly flesh of Adam. This kenosis (self-emptying) of His deity was not an abdication of His divine nature, but rather a self-limitation to live within the boundaries of finite humanity.

The Holy Spirit Assisted Jesus' Humanity

Throughout His incarnate life, Jesus chose not to exercise His divine prerogatives, but consented to live as a man, though a man in complete dependence upon the Father's provision of the Holy Spirit. Through the sanctifying presence of the Holy Spirit, Jesus kept His common, human flesh in absolute holiness. His flesh was fully temptable to sin, as is the common flesh of humanity. The author of Hebrews plainly declares, our High Priest "has been tempted in all things as we are, yet without sin." Sharing the same flesh with all humanity, our Priest can "sympathize with our weaknesses." (Hebrews 4:15) The Athanasian Creed declares that Jesus' humanity is "of the substance of His mother."[36] Although Mary lived an exemplary life in the favor of God, the stuff of her humanity was like that of every human, i.e., mortal and corruptible.

We must learn not to shy away from Jesus' sinlessness in mortal, corruptible humanity, but glory in it. Humanity achieved eternal victory in Jesus' moral triumph against sin. Because of it, our fallen nature is now restored before the Father. We are accepted and justified with our holy God because Jesus took our nature and made it sinless.

Chapter 13

SON OF MAN:
The Gnostic Challenge To Jesus' True Humanity

John's Apostolic Authority

The Spirit of Anti-Christ

The Gnostic Heresy

Gnosticism is Syncretistic

Infiltrated the Church

Gnostic Beliefs

Gnostic Redemption

Denial of Jesus' Humanity

No Incarnation, Atonement or Resurrection

Anti-Gnostic Father Irenaeus

Recapitulation

Doctrinal Errors Exposed

Other Failures

Docetism

The New Age is Neo-Gnosticism

New Age Misappropriates Jesus

Narcissism

Jesus Delivers Us From Narcissism

Chapter 13

SON OF MAN:
The Gnostic Challenge
To Jesus' True Humanity

John's Apostolic Authority

Controversy surrounding Jesus' dual identities as Son of Man and Son of God surfaced early in church history, even in biblical times. The apostle John made Ephesus his home, a hotbed city for doctrinal diversity and aberration. John exercised his apostolic authority to confront Christological errors and to keep the church on a straight course. John was the ideal figure for such a task, being one of the chief shapers of biblical doctrine. He recognized that properly considering the person of Jesus and His redemptive mission was foundational for right thinking about all other Christian doctrines. John took a firm, unwavering stance against Christological heretics. "Anyone who goes too far and does not abide in the teaching of Christ, does not have God; the one who abides in the teaching, he has both the Father and the Son." (II John 9)

The Spirit of Anti-Christ

At the close of the New Testament era, the apostle John addressed a false conception of Jesus that had surfaced in the early church. There were those who were contending that Jesus had not come in real human flesh. "For many deceivers have gone out into the world, those who do not acknowledge Jesus Christ as coming in the flesh. This is the deceiver and the antichrist." (II John 7) This Christological error so forcefully confronted by John represented a specific expression of a broader religious worldview that has challenged Christian truth at other times. It bears closer examination.

The Gnostic Heresy

The erroneous opinion addressed by John can be traced to an ancient cosmological dualism generally called Gnosticism. Sectarian Jewish movements, even before the time of Christ, were known to have espoused Gnosticism. Another form of it reappeared to threaten early Christianity, as we have observed from John's writings. Then in the second century, various Gnostic groups infiltrated the church, challenging the essential doctrines of the Christian faith. Certain church fathers such as Irenaeus and Tertullian exposed the errors of Gnosticism and helped free the church of its deception.

Gnosticism is Syncretistic

Our focus will be on the second century expression, in that it posed the first serious threat to the integrity of essential Gospel truths. The Gnostics were not a monolithic movement, but represented a variety of doctrines and practices. Although the details of Gnostic teachings varied, a pervasive religious worldview typical of all Gnostic advocates can be detected. Generally, Gnosticism was syncretistic, in that their teachers sought to utilize Christianity as a focal point to unify and harmonize various religious and philosophical sensibilities. They sought to absorb a variety of religious ideas and practices into one system in an effort to provide a holistic religious worldview. They utilized cosmogonies (theories of the origin of the universe) to attempt to offer answers to questions not addressed specifically in the Christian scriptures.

Infiltrated the Church

Gnostics circulated an abundance of private writings, attempting to gain credibility by falsely claiming their writings to have originated from Jesus, the apostles and other early writers. Some Gnostic teachers, such as Marcion (110-160), founded an organization outside of the established church, but most stayed within the church and sought to penetrate the establishment with their teachings. The Gnostics disdained common Christians, and sought to proselytize the church by holding separate meetings apart from the regular services where their secret doctrines and practices could be propagated. The most important Gnostic systems of the times were those of Basilides, Valentine and his disciples (Heracleon, Ptolemaeus and Theodotus in the Italian school), the Ophites, Kainites, Perates, Sethians, Justin, and the Naasenes. Representatives of the ultra-Gnostics were Marcion and Carpocrates.

Gnostic Beliefs

All Gnostic teachers believed that the universe is governed by opposite, dualistic forces. The realm of the spirit is good, and the realm of the material is evil. In between these opposite extremes, beginning with the spirit realm, is a descending continuum of levels of reality, permeated by multiple gods and emanations from those gods. At the lowest level of the continuum is the created universe, whose origin is a result of a cosmological accident wrought by an evil god. The only good part of humanity is an uncreated, spiritual part of the soul. The soul is trapped within a material body and environment that is wholly evil.

Gnostic Redemption

The only redemptive hope for humankind is intellectual enlightenment. The name "Gnosticism" is derived from the Greek word *gnosis*, meaning "knowledge." The answer to the human dilemma is self-knowledge, leading to a state of enlightenment allowing the entrapped soul to escape its evil material environs. Although final release from evil comes at death, Gnostics believe that when enlightenment occurs in this life, liberty from responsibility is a present reality. Lifestyle among the enlightened generally went in one of two directions. Some Gnostics lived in strict self-denial, starving the appetites and awaiting their ultimate escape through death. Other Gnostics viewed their liberty as an occasion for self-gratification. They reasoned that having an enlightened soul guaranteed their spiritual destiny, and granted them the license to engage in any form of self-indulgence in this life. Since the material, historical realm will ultimately self-destruct, they believe that their actions within this vanishing world are not accountable.

Denial of Jesus' Humanity

Jesus, the Gnostic Savior, comes into the picture as the Master Teacher. Since self-knowledge brings the desired state of enlightenment, Jesus' essential purpose is to teach the proper self-knowledge, leading to enlightenment. Jesus did not participate in matter, but came to free entrapped spiritual beings from their material baggage. The Gnostics believe that Jesus' emanated from the realm of the spirit, and has no constitution or association with evil. He is a pure spirit, being completely divine in nature, with no vestige of humanity in His being. Jesus' human appearance was merely camouflage, disguising His purely spiritual substance. The Gnostic denial of a real humanity and a true physical body is their way of protecting Jesus from participation in the evil realm of materiality.

No Incarnation, Atonement or Resurrection

For the Gnostic, Jesus' body was "phantom flesh." Jesus had no human nature or physical body, which was an explicit denial of the biblical doctrine of the Incarnation. Crucifixion had no meaning for the Gnostic, since Jesus' body was immaterial and thus could not die. They had one of two explanations of the crucifixion narrative. One group believed that the soldiers mistakenly crucified Simon the Cyrenian instead of Jesus, the man who helped carry Jesus' cross. Another group held that Jesus mystically separated Himself from His "phantom body," and observed from a distance the crucifixion proceedings with mocking disdain. Gnostics, therefore, denied the value of Jesus' blood atonement on the cross for the sins of humanity. The Gnostics also denied Resurrection, since Jesus experienced no death. Resurrection had no meaning in their system of thought, since being restored to materiality is merely to be reconstituted into the evil realm. The ultimate goal of the Gnostic is escape, not resurrection. For the enlightened, the good part of the soul will one day be returned to the realm of the purely spiritual. All else will be given over to annihilation.

Anti-Gnostic Father Irenaeus

Emerging in the mid-second century, the Gnostic threat was too early to have been dealt with by a major church council such as those convened after Constantine became emperor. However, Gnosticism appeared at a time when two church fathers of considerable theological wisdom were on the scene. These two leaders were Irenaeus of Lyons (France) and Tertullian of Carthage (North Africa). In particular, Irenaeus (130-203) devoted himself to the study of Gnosticism, familiarizing himself with the variety of Gnostic teachers and their specific teachings. His findings were compiled in a massive treatise, *Against Heresies*. This definitive refutation of Gnostic doctrinal errors proved to be a major factor leading to the demise of Gnosticism. Tertullian (160-220) contributed an influential refutation of the teachings of the ultra-Gnostic, Marcion, and his movement (Marcionism).

Recapitulation

Irenaeus refuted Gnosticism by organizing his ideas around the biblical theme of *recapitulation*. This theme reflects the insight revealed in Ephesians 1:10, as Paul depicts the drama of Jesus' redemptive work in "the summing up of all things in Christ, things in the heavens and things upon the earth." The Greek word, translated "summing up," is *anakephalaiomai*. The Latin translation is *recapitulatio*, thus is derived Irenaeus' theme of recapitulation. This theme emphasizes the divine purpose of the Son's Incarnation, as He took upon Himself the common nature of humanity. By taking our nature and entering into our experience, He brought redemption, restoration and recovery to Adam's race. Adam's fall into sin thwarted God's plans, but Jesus' mission in entering the world as the Second Adam was to recapitulate all things into loving harmony with God and His original design. The first Adam fell into disobedience with God's will, thus plunging the entire race into sinful alienation from God. It was needful that the Second Adam take on the true nature and conditions of fallen humanity, yet offer unto the Father perfect obedience, in order to undo the work of the first Adam (Romans 5:19). Christ's sinless obedience, culminating in His submission to the cross of Calvary, resulted in His triumphal defeat of all the enemies common to humanity (sin, Satan, and death). Because Jesus is the Second Adam, the Brother Man of all members of the race, He is capable of recapitulating to the Father all who place their trust in Him. R.P.C. Hanson augments this discussion of recapitulation: "whereby Christ retraced all the stages of Adam's experience and all the process of Adam's transgression, at each stage and each act obeying where Adam had disobeyed."[37]

Irenaeus' portrayal of the divine drama of redemption relies heavily upon an accurate understanding of the doctrine of the Incarnation. It was necessary for the fulfillment of God's redemptive purpose for the eternal Son of God to become fully human in the Incarnation event. His human nature and conditions must have been common to all of humanity for His obedience to be authentic. His human nature and body must have been authentic for His sacrifice on the cross to be vicarious (done or acting for another) and thus effectual for the redemption of Adam's race.

Doctrinal Errors Exposed

By clarifying the significance of the doctrine of the Incarnation, Irenaeus ruled out Gnostic interpretations of Jesus. The Gnostic Jesus is not human, thus to offer an obedient life to the Father is not possible or even desirable. Death is not possible for a divine Jesus who is not mortal. Nor is death necessary in Gnostic teaching, for the Gnostic Savior does not die to atone for sins, but simply transmits knowledge. The resurrection of the body is a vital Christian doctrine denied by the Gnostics. The transformation to immortality and incorruption for Christian believers is a future occurrence associated with the time of Jesus' Second Coming. With no resurrection, death becomes final. As the apostle Paul declares, "For if the dead are not raised, not even Christ has been raised; and if Christ has not been raised, your faith is worthless; you are still in your sins. Then those also who have fallen asleep in Christ have perished." (I Corinthians 15:16-18)

Other Failures

In addition to these central doctrinal issues, other failures of Gnosticism were detected by Irenaeus' analysis. He exposed the error of positing a creator other than God Himself. He demonstrated the foolishness of postulating multiple gods, emphasizing the monotheistic character of the Christian Gospel. He revealed that the root human problem is not ignorance, but sin. He established that humanity, materiality and history are not evil in themselves, but were created good and were restored to their original goodness in Jesus' redemption. Irenaeus demonstrated that the starting point for Christian knowledge is God's self-revelation in history through His Son, and not in philosophical speculation.

Docetism

The Gnostic denial of Jesus' true humanity emphasized a pattern of doctrinal error that has tended to resurface in various forms throughout the history of the Christian church. This pattern of Christological heresy has been identified as *docetism*. **Docetism is a pattern of thought that denies or devalues the true humanity and/or the true human body of Jesus.** Docetism found expression in early Christianity not only in Gnosticism, but in two other major heresies which will be considered later, Apollinarianism and Eutycheanism. Gnosticism itself, although dead in its ancient expression, has reemerged within history in slightly different variations of the original to pose new threats to the doctrine of Jesus' true humanity.

The New Age is Neo-Gnosticism

The New Age movement, originating in the twentieth century, is a contemporary school of thought displaying many similarities to ancient Gnosticism. Not all New Age thought concerns itself with Jesus. Teachings that include Jesus pay only scant attention to Him as an historical figure. New Age thought is more concerned with an archetypal image of Jesus considered to be imprinted into the soul of every human person; often called "the Christ within." This inner Christ is an eternal, uncreated spark of divinity in all persons that must be "discovered" through self-knowledge if one is to experience the full potential of life. Most New Agers contend that the Jesus of history was a real person who exemplified the quest for authentic self-discovery. Jesus was just one example among others of those who have discovered on a high level the "Christ within." Buddha and Gandhi would represent other historical examples of persons achieving their true human potential through realizing the "Christ within." Jesus Himself is not the Savior of humankind. What "saves" in New Age thought is an "esoteric Christ" portrayed as an archetypal imprint of divinity residing in every person. He must be awakened or activated if life's potential is to be realized.

New Age Misappropriates Jesus

New Age thought is guilty of misappropriating the authentic Jesus of the Bible. While acknowledging a Jesus of history, they deny His unique, exclusive identity as Son of God and Savior of the world. Instead, their emphasis is upon the "Christ within," a divine spark present in all humanity. In summation, New Age thought plunges its adherents into Narcacistic self-worship, the very antithesis of the Christian invitation to self-surrender to Jesus and His cross.

Narcissism

The Narcissistic self indulgence of New Age thinking is reminiscent of ancient Gnosticism. Even among the Gnostics who practiced strict self-denial, their motive was self-protection and isolation from the world. Gnostic thought promotes escape from the responsibility of relationships. If physical, historical existence is viewed as evil, then retreat from life's relationships is to be preferred rather than involvement.

Jesus Delivers Us From Narcissism

The Christian Gospel presents a radical alternative to Gnosticism. Jesus promises forgiveness from sin and its self-absorption. He invites persons to love God first, and their neighbors as they love themselves. Delivered from the power of sin, Christians are free to experience the goodness of God's creation, and to share the richness of God's love in all of life's relationships. The Jesus of the Scriptures was not ashamed to take our humanity into His own divine being, in order to restore true humanity and true human relationships to all people. The Gnostic Jesus only promises retreat into self-absorption until death's final escape from life's tyranny and bondage.

Chapter 14

SON OF MAN:
The Apollinarian Challenge To The True Humanity Of Jesus

The Rise of Apollinarianism

Jesus Human in Body Only

The Divine Logos Constituted Jesus' Rational Soul

Humanity is More Than a Body

Apollinarianism – To Be Human Is To Be Sinful

The Church Responds

"The Unassumed Is The Unredeemed"

Incarnation and Redemption At Stake

Apollinarianism Justly Condemned

Apollinarianism Today

Jesus' Complete Humanity Is Not an Optional Doctrine

Chapter 14

SON OF MAN:
The Apollinarian Challenge To The True Humanity Of Jesus

The pattern of denying or devaluing Jesus' true humanity, known as docetism, achieved its classic expression in Gnosticism. For the Gnostic, there was absolutely nothing human about Jesus. Jesus' apparent humanity was a disguise, covering His pure divinity. Yet this strict denial of Jesus' humanity was not the only form of docetism that the church would face in her history. Other manifestations of docetism appeared in early Christianity, deviating from the classic expression and thus more subtle in their challenge to Jesus' true humanity.

The Rise of Apollinarianism

At the outset of his ministry, Apollinaris (310-392) was a respected bishop of Laodicea. He was a gifted intellectual, and a strong defender of the Nicene Creed, thus a champion of Jesus' eternal divinity. Yet his teachings concerning Jesus' humanity drew suspicion early on, soon after his appointment to the bishophric of Laodicea in 360. Finding his teachings condemned by local councils, Apollinaris removed himself from the church in 375. He became a sectarian, forming his own organization and ordaining his own bishops. Recognizing Apollinarianism to be a dangerous heresy, the church formally condemned and anathematized this teaching at the Council of Constantinople in 381. Emperor Theodosius I exerted the force of Roman law against Apollinarianism following the 381 Council.

Jesus Human in Body Only

Apollinarianism was not a complete denial of humanity in Jesus, but limited His humanity to His physical body. Technically, Apollinaris also granted to Jesus a sensitive soul. Yet this proved to be an inconsequential concession in light of his definition of humanness. Apollinaris' trichotomy of human nature included a) the physical body, b) a closely connected sensitive soul, and c) a rational soul (consisting of the will, mind and spirit). In this scheme, the sensitive soul was simply a part of the body's functioning. The real control center of the human personality Apollinaris believed to be the capacity of free will, a part of the rational soul. Here, Apollinaris' problems began. He assumed that possessing a free will necessarily implicated the person in sin. Therefore, to protect Jesus from participation in sin, Apollinaris denied Jesus' a rational human soul.

The Divine Logos Constituted Jesus' Rational Soul

Apollinaris recognized that he must find a way to attribute personality to Jesus, having withheld from him a rational soul. In order to complete Jesus' personhood, Apollinaris posited that the rational soul was contributed by the divine *logos* or Word. The soul and spirit of Jesus was from His divine nature, while His body was human. Utilizing this formula, Apollinaris was satisfied that he had explained how Jesus had maintained a sinless life. Jesus had attained sinlessness by having only a body that was human. His will, mind and spirit were divine. Apollinarian arithmetic was simple: 2/3 deity + 1/3 humanity = the one person, Jesus Christ.

Humanity is More Than a Body

What apparently was a logical solution for Apollinaris concerning the composition of Jesus' personhood raised glaring suspicions among his contemporaries. The most obvious question surfacing in the wake of the Apollinarian formula is this. Does the physical body constitute the whole of human personhood? The Scriptures clearly attribute to Jesus the full range of capacities and characteristics common to humanity, including a human will, mind and spirit. This is aptly illustrated as Jesus prayed in the Garden of Gethsemane prior to His crucifixion. In His humanness, and desiring to avoid the ordeal of the cross, Jesus prayed to His Father, "'Father, if Thou art willing, remove this cup from Me; yet not My will, but Thine be done.' …And being in agony He was praying very fervently; and His sweat became like drops of blood, falling down upon the ground." (Luke 22:42, 44) Here, it is proven that Jesus had a human will of His own separate from the divine will. Furthermore, Jesus' prayer was not a sham, for appearance sake. His personal agony is obviously genuine.

Apollinarianism – To Be Human Is To Be Sinful

By denying Jesus a rational human soul, Apollinaris in effect was negating real humanness in Jesus. Apollinaris mistakenly reasoned that if Jesus were fully human, He would not have been able to avoid sin. And as a sinner, Jesus could not be our Savior. This false presupposition, i.e., that to be human is to be sinful, is the root of the Apollinarian error.

The Church Responds

The Apollinarian error surfaced at a time when some very wise and astute Christian leaders were on the scene. They saw danger in the Apollinarian Christology, and they dedicated themselves to careful study and apologetic discourse in order to expose and discredit this heresy. The Cappadocian Fathers led the charge against Apollinarianism. Two of the Cappadocians were brothers, Gregory of Nyssa and Basil the Great, while the third was a lifelong friend, Gregory of Nazianzus. Athanasius, a vital force in refuting Arianism, also played a role in countering Apollinarianism.[38]

"The Unassumed Is The Unredeemed"

Gregory of Nazianzus' brief treatise, *Epistle 101*, proved to be the most effective refutation of Apollinarianism. This work was canonized at the Council of Chalcedon in 451 as being one of the most crucial defenses of orthodox Christology written in early Christian history. A phrase from *Epistle 101* emerged as the rallying cry against the Apollinarian heresy. **"For that which He has not assumed He has not healed."** Referring to the Incarnation event, Gregory reasoned that the portion of humanity assumed by the Son of God in the Incarnation represented the portion of humanity that qualified to be healed and restored by Jesus' redemptive work. He most certainly was implying that the Son of God took our complete humanity so that the salvation that He purchased for us would be complete.

Incarnation and Redemption At Stake

In *Epistle 101*, Gregory continued by stating, "If only half Adam fell, then that which Christ assumes and saves may be half also; but if the whole of His nature fell, it must be united to the whole nature of Him that was begotten, and so be saved as a whole." Gregory recognized that the church's doctrine of the Incarnation was at stake. When Apollinaris restricted Jesus' humanity to His physicality only, he was betraying an incomplete Incarnation. And an incomplete Incarnation meant an incomplete redemption for the human race. Gregory reasoned that if the Son assumed a human body devoid of a rational human soul, then Jesus' atoning sacrifice on the cross was not effectual for the whole human person. Only our bodies are redeemed.

Apollinarianism Justly Condemned

Furthermore, the Cappadocians contended that the scriptural statement, "And the Word became **flesh**," (John 1:14) was misrepresented by Apollinaris. Apollinaris held that **flesh** (*sarx* in the Greek New Testament) is purely the physical, material component of humanity. The Cappadocians noted that the more accurate meaning of **flesh** (*sarx*) included the totality of all that is essential to humanity. Apollinaris' lack of biblical awareness resulted in a false conception of the Son's Incarnation, and a Jesus who was not really human at all. If Jesus' rational soul was divine and not human, then we are left with a Christology no better than Gnosticism. The Apollinarian Jesus, devoid of a human mind, a human will, and a human spirit, does not qualify to be human by any logical definition. Apollinaris' profession of humanity in Jesus was only a pretense. The bishops at Constantinople in 381 took a necessary step in defense of Christological orthodoxy when they condemned and anathematized Apollinarianism.

Apollinarianism Today

The type of docetic heresy represented by Apollinarianism continues to plague Christendom. The doctrine of the Incarnation in some Christian circles continues to be de-emphasized and misconstrued. Many have little awareness of the direct connection between Incarnation and redemption. The Incarnation becomes an afterthought of seasonal reflection at Christmastime, rather than an essential staple of regular instruction in the church's preaching and teaching agenda. I once heard a highly educated pastor of a large Protestant church, during a Christmas message, explain the Incarnation as the event in which the divine son "was clothed with a physical body." This was a glaring example of Apollinarian heresy.

Jesus' Complete Humanity Is Not an Optional Doctrine

Few Christians understand Gregory's profound statement, "That which He has not assumed, He has not healed." The scriptural logic of redemption is that the object of the Son's Incarnation must include the totality of human identity. If the Son did not become what we are as the Second Adam, then that which He did not assume in His Incarnation remains under the curse of sin. Jesus took all that we are so that reconciliation, redemption and relationship with the Father could apply to our whole humanity. Not only did Jesus have to pay sin's penalty by shedding His blood on the cross, but also it was needful that He offer the Father a lifetime of true human obedience. For Jesus' obedience to be authentic, His rational soul must be authentically human. Christians naively dismiss the significance of Jesus' humanity, thinking that overemphasis upon Jesus' deity at the expense of His humanity is a virtuous exchange. Few realize that our redemption is null and void if Jesus is not fully human as well as fully divine.

Chapter 15

SON OF MAN:
The Eutychean Challenge To The True Humanity Of Jesus

The Rise of Eutycheanism

Divinized Humanity

Not of the Same Substance

Council of Robbers

New Emperor and Empress

The Chalcedonian Definition of Faith

Distinct Natures Maintained

The Heresy of a "Changed Flesh" Christology

Classic Heresies Concluded at Chalcedon

Monophysites

A 19th Century Version of Eutycheanism

Eutychean Groundswell Against Edward Irving

Modern Eutychean Notions

No Apologies For Being Human

Jesus Needed No Unfair Advantage

Chapter 15

SON OF MAN:
The Eutychean Challenge To The True Humanity Of Jesus

The condemnation of Apollinarianism in 381 did not end the church's warfare against docetic challenges to Jesus' true humanity. Another threatening heresy arose in the mid-fifth century named Eutycheanism that temporarily gained the approval of the Roman Empire. It took a major church council, meeting at Chalcedon in 451, to subdue the Eutychean Christology and reestablish orthodoxy in the land.

The docetism found in Apollinarianism reduced Jesus' humanity to nothing more than His physical body, which is not humanity in the full sense. The docetism represented by Eutycheanism acknowledged Jesus to be human, but viewed His humanity to be so altered when united with His deity that it lost all resemblance to humanity as we know it. Eutycheanism presented us with a Jesus having a "changed" or "divinized" flesh that was different than our common human nature.

The Rise of Eutycheanism

Eutycheanism appeared on the scene in the midst of a power struggle between rival churches in the Eastern realm. Alexandria and Antioch were known for different emphases in their Christological interpretations. It is difficult today for us to relate to the reality of the fifth century, in which differing doctrinal interpretations were issues of national interest and discussion. Alexandria tended to stress Jesus' divine nature, and Antioch emphasized Jesus' human nature. When Christian leaders of integrity and theological stability were in control, the differing views of these two churches tended to compliment one another and promote theological balance. When poor leaders were in charge, a bitter, unhealthy competition erupted producing a climate of extremism and error.

Eutycheanism surfaced when the unscrupulous Dioscorus rose to power as bishop of Alexandria. He was politically rather than spiritually motivated, and would stop at nothing to advance his Alexandrian church above Antioch. Dioscorus gained a huge advantage by being able to manipulate the weak Roman emperor Theodosius II (died 450). Dioscorus was not theologically inclined, but he sought an extreme expression of Alexandrian Christology to use as a weapon against the Antiochean position. He chose the Christology of Eutyches (384-454) for his purposes. Eutyches was a monk living in monastic seclusion, far removed from the struggles of ecclesiastical and imperial politics.

At this juncture, a more complete picture of Eutychean Christology is in order. Eutyches placed an exaggerated emphasis upon Jesus' divinity, and gave only scant attention to Jesus' humanity. He is known for the saying, that there were "two natures before the Incarnation, but one after." Eutyches admitted that two natures were involved in the Incarnation of the Son, one divine and the other human. But at the moment of Jesus' conception in Mary, a radical change took place. The divine nature from above so overpowered and dominated the human nature, that the person of Jesus produced by this mysterious union was essentially one divine nature. After the union of natures at conception, only the divine nature was distinguishable.

Divinized Humanity

Technically, Eutyches admitted that Jesus had human nature after conception, but he held that the human attributes were absorbed into His divinity upon contact. Another way to explain what happened in Jesus' conception was that the human nature became "divinized," thereby losing its distinctly human attributes. Eutyches used the illustration of a drop of vinegar (representing Jesus' human nature) being dropped into the ocean (representing Jesus' divine nature). The drop of vinegar, although chemically present in the ocean, became so widely diffused within the vastness of the ocean that it was no longer distinguishable.

Not of the Same Substance

In application, this meant that traits such as mortality and corruptibility characteristic of Mary's humanity were altered as they came into union with the divine seed. At conception, they were transformed into the traits of immortality and incorruptibility. Human traits were "divinized," so that Jesus' nature and experience were not common to the race that He came to save. Eutyches admitted that Jesus' body was not *homoousios* (Greek word employed in the Nicene Creed, meaning "same substance, essence and being") with our human bodies. His words were, "This body of Christ's was not of the same substance (*homoousios*) with ours."

Council of Robbers

Returning now to the historical context, Dioscorus sought to utilize Eutycheanism to unfair advantage against the Antiocheans. He convinced Theodosius II to convene a council that would officially establish Eutycheanism as the orthodox doctrine of the churches, and to banish by law all bishops who disagreed. Theodosius hastily called the Council of Ephesus in 449, so that many bishops favoring Antiocheanism would not be able to attend. Opponents of Eutycheanism in attendance were roughly treated by Roman troops, so that the Eutychean Christology was forcibly installed as the orthodox doctrine of Christendom. Emperor Theodosius II ratified the Council's conclusions. History has not looked favorably upon the proceedings of the Council of Ephesus (449). Its unethical character has resulted in its name being remembered as the "Council of Robbers," in that Dioscuros temporarily succeeded in robbing the church of her orthodox Christology. This council is not recognized among the eight great ecumenical councils of the Christian church.[39]

New Emperor and Empress

An unexpected event played a big role in the resolution of this controversy. When circumstances looked bleak for the Antiocheans, a tragic accident suddenly turned the tide in their favor. In 450, emperor Theodosius II fell from his horse and died. Next in line to rule the Roman Empire was his sister, Pulcheria. The new empress and her husband, Marcian, favored Antiochean Christology. In 451, they called for a new council to consider fairly the issues. More than 500 bishops constituted the Council of Chalcedon. No single church leader rose to the occasion as a major figure in the deliberations. Although not present at the council, Leo I, bishop of Rome, contributed a significant Christological treatise that gained the council's approval. The writings of the now deceased Cyril of Alexandria also played a major role in the council's conclusions.

The Chalcedonian *Definition of Faith*

Although supportive of the Nicene Creed, the council found it necessary to formulate a new confession, known as the *Definition of Faith*, in order to summarize the refutation of heresies arising after the Council of Nicaea in 325. The main item on the agenda at Chalcedon was to reach a conclusion regarding the Eutychean Christology. The council condemned as heretical the doctrine of Eutyches, and carefully worded its *Definition of Faith* to exclude Eutycheanism. A significant statement from the *Definition* was worded as follows: "...our Lord Jesus Christ, ...consubstantial (*homoousios*) with the Father as to His Godhead, and consubstantial (*homoousios*) also with us as to His manhood: like unto us in all things, yet without sin; ..." Here, the council reinforced the Nicene faith by affirming that Jesus' deity was of the same substance as the deity of the Father. In addition, they took aim at Eutyches by applying *homoousios* also to Jesus' humanity. The council declared that Jesus' humanity was of the same substance as our humanity. Eutyches had refused to concede that Jesus' humanity and human body shared the same substance with us.

Distinct Natures Maintained

In a carefully worded statement, the *Definition* affirmed that no alteration of substance occurred when the human and divine natures of Jesus were united in Mary's womb. The two natures of Jesus were "without confusion, without change, ...the distinction of the natures being in no wise abolished by their union, but the peculiarity of each nature being maintained." This meant that the distinctly human attributes of Jesus were not confused or changed when contact occurred with His divinity. The humanity maintained its own distinct qualities after the union, and the divine nature maintained its distinct qualities. Distinctly divine and distinctly human attributes co-existed together in the person of Jesus. That which was taken from Mary did not change when brought into union with the Son's divinity at conception.

The Heresy of a "Changed Flesh" Christology

In summation, Eutyches was wrong to present Jesus with a "changed flesh," i.e., a human nature different from the substance of Mary His mother.[40] The orthodox faith of the Christian church affirms that it is proper to attribute to Jesus two complete and distinct natures, inseparably united and co-existing together within His unique personhood. His divine nature must not be considered in such a way that it negates or minimizes His humanity. His human nature must not be considered in such a way that it negates or minimizes His deity. Jesus is a complete person, with two complete natures constituting His personhood. According to Chalcedon, it is correct to consider Jesus as a divine/human person, possessing both a divine and a human nature. It is incorrect to consider Him to be a divine person or being. It is also incorrect to consider Jesus to be a human person or being. He is both, in one unique person. Jesus is a God/Man. As scripture reveals, Jesus is both Son of God and Son of Man.

Classic Heresies Concluded at Chalcedon

The Council of Chalcedon represents a watershed in the historical development of Christian doctrine. It was the fourth of the major ecumenical councils of the church, each of them dealing with various heretical challenges to the scriptural identity of Jesus Christ. Four more ecumenical councils would be convened within early Christianity, but Chalcedon was the last council whose deliberations centered upon Christological themes. The *Definition of Faith* produced at Chalcedon has proven to be a significant confessional document, in that it sets certain boundaries for orthodox Christology that must not be transgressed. The *Definition* also explicitly rejects the classic heresies that threatened early Christology, thus setting a standard for future generations. The *Definition* specifically targeted the heretical systems of Arianism,

Apollinarianism, Nestorianism, and Eutycheanism. Christological heresies in any age usually can be classified as having basic similarities with one of these classic expressions. Over the centuries, all three major branches of Christendom (Roman Catholicism, Eastern Orthodoxy, and Protestantism) have demonstrated their support for the orthodox truth concerning Christ's person embedded in the *Definition of Faith* framed at Chalcedon in 451.

Monophysites

In the aftermath of Chalcedon, Eutychean bishops were banished from their churches, including Dioscuros. Although no longer a serious threat to orthodoxy, a remnant party of Eutycheans has survived throughout the centuries within Eastern Orthodoxy. They are known as the monophysite party (mono = one; physite =nature). Thus, they persist in the heretical opinion that Jesus has only one nature, and that being a divine nature.

A 19th Century Version of Eutycheanism

As Christian history has progressed, lingering Eutychean opinions have resurfaced at various times to plague the church. A flagrant expression of Eutychean Christology permeated the established churches of Britain in the early nineteenth century. The preaching of Edward Irving, a noted Scottish pastor serving in London, attracted a backlash of opposition from mainline church leaders displaying classic Eutychean sensibilities. Irving's Christology stressed the Incarnational themes common to the Early Church Fathers and Protestant Reformers.[41] Irving had not anticipated controversy. But as his preaching continued to emphasize Jesus' redemptive victory won by His obedient life and death accomplished in our common Adamic humanity, a flurry of opposition was aroused. Henry Cole, the initiator of opposition against Irving, espoused in blatant terms the Eutychean

Christology. Cole argued that Jesus' body "was ever pure and free from all mortality, -ever adorably immortal."[42] Other churchmen joined Cole in attacking Irving, not recognizing that they were opposing orthodoxy.

Eutychean Groundswell Against Edward Irving

Irving held the position that when the Word became flesh (John 1:14), the substance of His humanity was from Mary, in the state of mortality and corruptibility. Irving held that possessing mortal flesh did not implicate Jesus in sin. To the contrary. Jesus' sinless human obedience while having our common nature and environment gives us cause for honoring Him with our highest praise. Irving produced several Christological writings in defense of His position, but overwhelming opposition from the religious world led to his deposition from the ministry of the Church of Scotland in 1833. Although his life was cut short at the age of 42, Irving continued to minister in independent circles until his death in 1834.

Modern Eutychean Notions

Much confusion is evident in today's church regarding the nature of Jesus' humanity. Many well-meaning believers think that they are bringing glory to Jesus by minimizing or even denying His distinctly human attributes. A theory is in circulation today that the blood Jesus shed on Calvary's cross was not human blood, but "God's blood." Certainly, Jesus is fully God as well as being fully human, so, in that sense, His blood is God's blood. But the meaning behind this contemporary usage implies that Jesus did not possess human blood at all, which is a Eutychean error. Scripture expressly asserts that the flesh and blood of Jesus was "the same" as the flesh and blood of common humanity. (Hebrews 2:14) Jesus' blood was part of His physical constitution, a part of what makes Him human. And the shedding of His blood was a part of His physical death, authenticating His mortal humanity. Had Jesus not shed the blood of Adam's race, then the children of Adam would still be excluded from the Father's presence because of sin. Because the blood of Jesus was "without blemish," being the blood of sinless yet mortal humanity, the door of salvation has been opened to Adam's race, among those who place their faith in Jesus. The Father accepted Jesus blood, not because it was naturally, inherently divine, but because it was blood of moral purity. We will forever be praising Jesus that He took our humanity, including our physical constitution, and made it holy and acceptable to the Father by the quality of His life and His death.

No Apologies For Being Human

The Christian church will move to a new level of maturity and faith when we allow ourselves to be delivered from an unhealthy, negative complex about humanity. It is a serious, unscriptural mistake to equate our humanity, which was created good, with evil and sin. The problem with the human race is not that we are humans, but that we are sinners. Jesus came to deliver us from sin and its power, so that we can be reconciled to God, others and ourselves. He came that we may enjoy abundant life, which includes the full, creative potential of our humanity. Jesus epitomized that abundant, human life. He assumed the same human nature that we possess, and lived His life within the same environment and conditions that we face. And His life was full of joy. He showed us that we can live free from sin and its power, through the indwelling, sanctifying life of the Holy Spirit. The believer who knows His standing in Christ does not have to apologize for being human. We know that we are the temple of the Holy Spirit.

Jesus Needed No Unfair Advantage

Docetic Christologies rob us of our hope of being free from the domination of sin. They make Jesus' humanity different than ours. They give Jesus unfair advantage against sin by attributing His sinlessness to divine capacities not available to us. The standard line is, "Sure Jesus didn't commit sin. He was God. We sin because we are just humans." Yet Jesus needed no unfair advantage. The writer of Hebrews restores our hope. He reveals the authentic Jesus, who "had to be made like His brethren in all things." (Hebrews 2:17) Jesus had all the power of divinity at His disposal, yet He refused to compromise the integrity of His humanity. He needed to win the victory as man, that His brother men might reap the rewards of His conquest. The only advantages that Jesus had are advantages available to every believer: our intimate relationship with Father God, and the indwelling presence of Jesus through the Holy Spirit.

Chapter 16

JESUS: FIRST GIFT, THEN EXAMPLE
Christology and the Grace of God

Luther's Insight

Jesus: Indescribable Gift!

Human Helplessness and God's Love

Gracious Alternative

Gracious Exchange

Faith: Acceptance of the Gift

Faith is Not a Work

Luther's Personal Pilgrimage

Luther's Breakthrough

Recovery of Augustine

Chapter 16

JESUS: FIRST GIFT, THEN EXAMPLE
Christology and the Grace of God

Luther's Insight

Sixteenth century Protestant Reformer Martin Luther identified Jesus as "first gift, then example."[43] He was calling attention to the futility of attempting to follow the example of Jesus' lifestyle without having first received Him as gift. Jesus lived His life as a model of human virtue and fulfillment, but His example is completely unattainable where sin dominates the human condition. Therefore, Jesus' exemplary role is secondary to His redemptive purpose. Only because Jesus was successful in the fulfillment of His redemptive mission is it possible for Adam's race to emulate Jesus' lifestyle. Redemption became possible when Jesus rose triumphantly from the grave, and breathed upon His disciples to receive the Holy Spirit (John 20:22). Since that time, salvation has been available for all people who are willing to receive Jesus as Savior. Only those recipients, i.e., the company of redeemed humanity, are in a position to live according to Jesus' example. The Holy Spirit that Jesus imparts to every believer provides the enabling power to follow Jesus' example of abundant living. Humanity devoid of the Holy Spirit is powerless to emulate the lifestyle Jesus modeled.

Jesus: Indescribable Gift!

Luther's insight, that Jesus is "first gift, then example," provided a necessary critique to late Medieval Catholicism's burdensome system of conditional standards of human performance required for salvation. Luther sought to educate people concerning the priority of receiving Jesus as gift, thus eliminating performance as a condition for salvation. Luther's discovery restored to the Gospel its liberating power, and reestablished salvation as a gift of God's grace. Most of all, it exalted Jesus in His rightful place as God's "indescribable gift!" (II Corinthians 9:15)

Human Helplessness and God's Love

The biblical doctrine of salvation is logically founded upon the premise that Jesus is gift. The most basic salvation passage in the Bible affirms this. "For God so loved the world, that **He gave** His only begotten Son, that whoever believes in Him should not perish, but have eternal life." (John 3:16) God, in His tripartite being as Father, Son and Spirit, is pure love. The plan of salvation was born in the heart of God. God, motivated by compassion for the sinful, alienated race of humanity, designed and implemented a plan whereby His creatures could be redeemed and restored to relationship with Himself. The salvation of humanity is solely an accomplishment of God, and is a result of His love, mercy and grace. The opportunity for salvation became a reality when humanity was absolutely helpless. No prerequisites or qualifications on the human side were taken into account in the origination of God's plan. By its very nature, salvation is a gift from God to the human race.

Gracious Alternative

Rather than separate Himself eternally from His fallen creatures, God exercised His mercy. He chose to provide a gracious alternative to the punishment and judgment deserved by every creature. Not that He would simply overlook the reality of sin and its consequences. His justice required that sin be punished and judged. But love motivated Him to bear the full consequences of sin upon Himself, so that He might extend pardon and life to those who deserved His judgment.

Gracious Exchange

By definition, "grace" means **unmerited favor**. Salvation has its source in God's grace, apart from any consideration of merit on the part of potential recipients. Jesus, God's Son, came into the very place where sin abounded, taking into His own person the human nature entrapped by sin, bringing reconciliation and righteousness into the arena formerly under sin's control. Jesus, in His own person, abolished the wall of sin dividing Holy God from sinful humanity. He substituted obedience for disobedience, thus healing the humanity that sin had dominated by removing its condemnation. He also substituted His own freedom from suffering and judgment due to His sinlessness for the punishment sinful humanity deserved. As the apostle Paul clarifies, "He made Him who knew no sin to be sin on our behalf, that we might become the righteousness of God in Him." (II Corinthians 5:21) This gracious exchange, enacted by Jesus, is the basis of human salvation.

Faith: Acceptance of the Gift

No biblical passage better describes the dynamics of salvation, with its characteristic emphasis upon the graciousness of God coupled with the helplessness of humanity, than a segment of Paul's letter to the Ephesians. "For by grace you have been saved through faith; and that not of yourselves, it is the gift of God; not as a result of works, that no one should boast." (Ephesians

2:8-9) Paul tells the Ephesian Christians that their salvation is a result of God's graciousness. For salvation to become actualized for the individual, it must be appropriated by faith. Faith is simply the individual's acceptance of the gift of salvation. Faith is the means of transmission, whereby salvation is conveyed from God to humanity. Faith conveys specifically to the individual the salvation won by Jesus generally for all humankind.

Faith is Not a Work

Paul wants to be sure that the reader does not confuse the faith that appropriates salvation with a human work considered necessary to be performed in exchange for salvation. If any work, even faith, is regarded as a human requirement for salvation, then salvation ceases to be a gift and can no longer be attributed to the graciousness of God. Earlier in his Ephesian letter, Paul extols the blessings coming to the believer through Jesus' redemption, ascribing it "to the praise of the glory of His grace, which He freely bestowed on us in the Beloved." (Ephesians 1:6) The faith to receive Jesus and His salvation must never be considered a work on our part, something done to earn our salvation. That would leave room on our part for boasting that we had contributed to our own salvation. Paul approves of boasting only in God, whose graciousness solely is responsible for our salvation. "And what do you have that you did not receive? But if you did receive it, why do you boast as if you had not received it?" (I Corinthians 4:7)

Luther's Personal Pilgrimage

Martin Luther's sixteenth century rediscovery of these basic biblical truths, allowing him to conclude that Jesus is "first gift" before He can be viewed in any sense as an example for human behavior, came to him after years of personal struggle. Luther's personal theological pilgrimage led him to a fresh understanding of the Pauline doctrine of "justification." Justification relates to "the state of being made right by God." Justification is not a determination of humanity. Only God has the prerogative to justify. Luther rightly saw himself as a sinner, condemned by God and deserving to spend eternity in hell. A product of late Medieval Catholicism, Luther sought justification with God through the prescribed avenues of conduct set before him. He sought to live a holy, penitent life. Yet his conscience tormented him. He was aware of evil motives behind even his best behavior, and found no escape from the anger and wrath of God.

Luther's Breakthrough

A crisis experience during his university years led Luther to a drastic conclusion. He decided to enter a monastery and become a monk and priest. He reasoned that the way to justification would not be denied him if he dedicated himself to a lifetime of monastic devotion. Yet years of religious achievement did not move him any closer to salving his troubled conscience before God. Luther's breakthrough eventuated as he undertook teaching duties at the University of Wittenberg. As Bible lecturer, Luther became immersed in scriptural study, climaxing in personal theological discovery of God's grace revealed in Jesus. Luther's sense of sinfulness was swept away as he recognized justification as a gift of God's grace won by Jesus' righteousness, and without any works or merits on the part of humanity. As Luther centered his life and ministry upon the theme of "justification by grace through faith," and the practical implications of this doctrine in the church, a Reformation was born that completely altered the course of Western civilization.

Recovery of Augustine

Luther concluded that all efforts to live a virtuous and religious life after the pattern of Jesus are futile without first receiving

Jesus as the gift of God's grace. Good works are not the **root** of righteousness, but the **fruit** of a life inhabited by Jesus though the Holy Spirit. Yet Luther did not claim originality in his "reformation discovery." He saw himself merely as a product of a rich biblical heritage, epitomized by the Apostle Paul's definitive teachings concerning our justification by grace. Luther was also a product of the teachings of perhaps the most influential of the Western Church Fathers, Saint Augustine. Known as the "Church Father of God's Grace," Augustine helped revive the fifth century church with a fresh understanding of "justification by grace" when threatened by the Pelagian heresy. As an Augustinian monk, Luther was familiar with Augustine's writings and keenly aware of the issues at stake in the Augustinian-Pelagian controversy. A careful look at this ancient controversy not only will shed additional light on Luther's Reformation discovery, but also will accentuate our exploration of the identity of Jesus. Our awareness will be deepened in the truth that Jesus is God's "indescribable gift!"

Chapter 17

JESUS: FIRST GIFT, THEN EXAMPLE
Jesus As Gift: The Challenge of Pelagianism

The Rise of Pelagianism

Salvation By Works

"Primary Grace" is Free Will

Pelagianism Condemned at the Council of Ephesus (431)

Augustine's Refutation

Gratia Christi

Salvation is God's Work of Grace

Grace From Start to Finish

Pelagianism: Moral Perfectionism

Pelagian Jesus: Assists in Self-Help

Justification is Based upon the Righteousness Obtained by Jesus

The Council of Ephesus (431) Upheld the Gospel

Liberal Protestantism: Pelagianism Revisited

Jesus Reduced to the Guru of Self-Help

Chapter 17

JESUS: FIRST GIFT, THEN EXAMPLE
Jesus As Gift: The Challenge of Pelagianism

The Gospel of our Lord Jesus Christ is "good news" precisely because the redemption that Jesus purchased for humanity is a free gift. Redemption is available to all persons, and cannot be earned or merited. Although all are sinners, all who receive the gift of God's grace in Christ automatically are considered by the Father to be righteous. No amount of personal works by the sinner can attain righteousness. Receiving Jesus allows righteousness to be transferred as a gift to the believer's account. This glorious truth is the only means for human salvation, and represents the very essence of the Christian Gospel. Historically, the most direct challenge to the truth of the Gospel, i.e., that redemption is a free gift in Jesus Christ, was contrived by Pelagius in the fifth century. He remains the archenemy of the grace of God.

The Rise of Pelagianism

Pelagius (360-431) was a British monk who visited Rome early in the fifth century. Pelagius was shocked at the expression of Christianity that he witnessed in Rome, being alarmed particularly by what he judged to be the declining moral standards of the church. He traced the root of the problem to what he believed to be a state of "theological passivity" among Christians, spawned by the teachings of none other than the influential bishop of Hippo, North Africa, St. Augustine. Pelagius viewed Augustine's emphasis upon God's sovereignty as promoting a passive fatalism among believers, leading to moral indifference. Pelagius saw it as his place to provide the church with an alternative to Augustinianism. He developed a doctrinal stance in contrast to Augustine, and attracted a band of proselytes who traveled with him to spread this novel teaching.

Salvation By Works

Pelagius assumed that the best way to encourage the church to embrace a strict moral standard is to emphasize human responsibility in the salvation process. He taught that the Mosiac Law was an obtainable standard of human behavior, even without God's provision of redemption accomplished by Jesus. He believed that numerous biblical characters, both from the Old and New Testaments, lived without sin and therefore gained salvation as a result of their own obedience to the Law. Such teaching, of course, ignores the doctrine of original sin and contradicts Paul's assertion that "all have sinned and fall short of the glory of God." (Romans 3:23)

Even more dangerous is Pelagius' belief that salvation can be obtained without Jesus and His redemptive triumph. Pelagius did not deny Jesus' work on the cross and His resurrection, but viewed the redemption won by Jesus as a "secondary grace" to be utilized only if sin is committed. Jesus comes into the Pelagian picture only when sin is committed. His grace is available to provide forgiveness and restoration. Once the sinner is restored, Jesus fades out of the picture. Righteousness remains a matter of one's adherence to the Law. In the final analysis, God's verdict of righteousness is based upon the righteous deeds of the believer, not by faith in Jesus' righteousness.

"Primary Grace" is Free Will

Pelagius presupposed that all humans are created good, based upon the "primary grace" of free will every person receives when they are conceived. Having evidence of God's grace in the functional capacity to freely choose, every person is expected by God to live in perfection according to His holy Law. Every person is born in a state of neutrality, just as with Adam and Eve before they sinned. Pelagius denied that the sin of Adam and Eve resulted in a "fall" of the human race. Since no "fall" occurred, the descendants of Adam and Eve did not inherit "original sin" or a "sin nature." The first sin in the Garden was an isolated act. Every person approaches each new circumstance with a clean slate, just as Adam and Eve faced the choice of eating the forbidden fruit without proclivity to sin. God expects total obedience. When sin is chosen, the "secondary grace" of Jesus is brought into play. Once forgiveness is obtained, restoring neutrality, the cycle begins again. Jesus is set aside, and the individual returns to dependence upon the "primary grace" of one's own free will. In the end, the goal of Pelagianism is a lifetime of unbroken righteous actions that ultimately gain promotion to heaven.

Pelagianism Condemned at the Council of Ephesus (431)

Pelagius proved to be an illusive nemesis for the fifth century church. He stayed on the run. Remaining in one location only long enough to plant a small cadre of adherents, and, as opposition surfaced, escaping before he could be apprehended, only to plant another seed of heresy elsewhere, Pelagius dotted the landscape with pockets of festering doctrinal disease that troubled Christendom for a season.

Recognizing the danger lurking beneath the disguise of Pelagius' apparent "moral revolution," Augustine was the leading authority in the church's refutation and repression of the Pelagian heresy. Augustine's compelling and brilliantly insightful writings against Pelagianism brought to the surface the erroneous nature of this movement, discrediting its appeal. A year after Augustine's death, as the bishops of the church convened at the Council of Ephesus in 431, Pelagianism was officially condemned. Pelagianism in its ancient doctrinal formulation ceased to be a serious threat to the Gospel of Jesus Christ.

Augustine's Refutation

Augustine's refutation of Pelagianism refreshed the fifth century church with the priority and absolute necessity of God's grace in Jesus for the salvation of humankind. Augustine taught that an actual "fall" occurred in the Garden of Eden, separating a holy and loving God from His sinful creatures. Adam's fall into sin altered the nature of humanity. Adam's original nature was inclined towards the good. With Adam's sin came the fall of the human race. Adam and all his posterity became infected with "original sin" and hereditary guilt. Human nature after the fall is inclined towards evil. All of humanity, therefore, stands under the judgment of God, for the sinful nature inherited by all inevitably results in the committing of actual sins against God. For Augustine, sinful humanity is faced with an irresolvable dilemma with no way of escape.

Gratia Christi

Since humanity was helplessly alienated from Creator God, the only possible remedy must come from God Himself. Augustine taught that human sin did not stop God's love for His fallen creatures. God responded to fallen humanity by exercising His grace. He enacted a plan of salvation, involving the costly sacrifice of His own Son as an offering for the sins of the people. Augustine linked God's grace with the gift of Jesus Christ (*gratia Christi*). Without the gracious gift of His Son, Jesus, there is no possibility for human salvation.

Salvation is God's Work of Grace

Augustine contended that no ethical or religious behavior on the part of humanity could earn right standing with God. Even the faith to believe in Jesus' redemption is a product of God's grace, and is not to be viewed as an independent work of merit deserving God's favor. In human salvation, the initiative always comes from God. Humanity can only respond. All glory and credit, therefore belongs to God.

Grace From Start to Finish

From Augustine's perspective, God's grace works progressively in the human condition. Within the family of God, children are presented for baptism. The seed of Jesus is imparted to the infant, beginning a journey of progressive transformation through God's gracious initiative. Outside the church, the conversion process begins with **prevenient grace**, as the Holy Spirit draws the individual to the knowledge of Jesus. A longing for redemption is imparted. Next, **operational grace** creates faith in the individual, resulting in a union between Jesus and the human soul. **Cooperational grace** does its work of transforming and emancipating the human will to bring forth fruits of faith. **Perfecting grace** produces perseverance in the individual, leading to eternal life and the perfect state. The work of perfecting grace does not reach completion until the believer is resurrected with Jesus. Augustine viewed salvation as a process, with God's grace involved at every level from start to finish.

Pelagianism: Moral Perfectionism

Augustine's explication of salvation, involving God's gracious initiative through Jesus on every level, served to uproot the shaky foundations of Pelagian doctrine. The most serious, dangerous error of the Pelagian system is to deny the necessity of human salvation through the gift of Jesus Christ. If God's grace was imparted at creation, endowing humanity with the ability to live righteously and earn eternal life, then the Gospel itself and the costly sacrifice of Jesus Christ is rendered unnecessary. If Jesus' saving work is reduced to nothing more than a roadside recovery for those who temporarily falter in life's journey, but the final reward at the end of the line is a product of human moral achievement, then the Gospel itself has been jettisoned and replaced by a humanistic system of moral perfectionism.

Pelagian Jesus: Assists in Self-Help

Pelagianism contends that the goal of human life is moral perfectionism according to the Mosaic Law of the Old Testament. All persons will be judged according to their adherence to the Law. Eternal life is based upon righteous conduct. The appearance of Jesus in history primarily is to provide forgiveness for those who lapse into sin. His forgiveness does not bring eternal life, but removes the sin, thus restoring the individual to a previous state of neutrality. Complete adherence to the Law remains the basis of eternal life. It must be said that Pelagius allowed for an additional role to be contributed by Jesus. The perfectionism of Jesus' life is meant to inspire emulation and instruction in righteous conduct. In the end, however, eternal life must be merited by righteous works performed by the individual. At best, Jesus contribution is to assist the individual to attain righteousness. He is not a factor in the final judgment. Each individual must stand or fall according to his own righteousness.

Justification is Based upon the Righteousness Obtained by Jesus

Augustinianism turned the tables on Pelagianism by asserting that no person can achieve eternal life based upon their own merits of righteousness. Every person stands condemned before God because of sin. The only solution for sinful humanity is God's gracious choice to provide salvation as a free gift through His Son. For those willing to receive salvation through faith, salvation and eternal life are provided freely without merit. Justification with God is not based upon human moral accomplishment, but upon the righteousness attained by Jesus and transferred undeservedly and without merit as a gracious gift to the recipient. Faith in the living Jesus and His redemptive work actualizes the transfer.

The Council of Ephesus (431) Upheld the Gospel

The Council of Ephesus (431) confirmed Augustine's refutation of Pelagianism. The Council officially condemned Pelagius' teachings as heretical. Augustine's writings against Pelagius represent a landmark of defense against any attempt to base the salvation of the Gospel upon any system of ethical and/or religious works. The Christian Gospel must always be founded upon justifcation through the merits of Jesus' righteousness, graciously given without condition to all who receive by faith. We all are sinners, and cannot help ourselves. God Himself has made possible our relationship with Him, and Jesus is the door to that relationship. Jesus is God's gracious gift, and our life now and eternally with God is through Him.

Liberal Protestantism: Pelagianism Revisited

The most serious reappearance in Christian history of the Pelagian type of heresy is the Liberal Protestantism that swept across

Europe in the nineteenth century. This pervasive movement that sought to reinterpret essential biblical doctrines in accordance with Enlightenment presuppositions displayed striking similarities with the Pelagian worldview. Liberalism denied the reality of "original sin" in the human condition, and cast Jesus in the role primarily of inspirational example of the religious and ethical ideal of human achievement. Going beyond Pelagianism, Liberalism denied Jesus' deity and the atoning value of Jesus' shed blood. Pelagius, however, misapplied these facets of orthodoxy, leading him to similar conclusions later embraced by Liberalism. Both movements reduced Jesus' primary role to that of moral/religious example, and robbed Him of His redemptive triumph at Calvary, in that they advocated the inherent moral perfectibility of humanity apart from Jesus' atonement.

Jesus Reduced to the Guru of Self-Help

Liberal Protestantism did a major disservice to Western society at large by attempting to legitimize an unorthodox version of Christianity catering to "modern" sensibilities. The "demythologization" of the Gospel resulted in a "modernized" culture positive about moral and religious perfectibility through educational acquisition. Knowledge is power, and abundant methods of self-help release the vastness of human potential for every person who possesses the will-power to succeed. In this model, Jesus becomes the "guru" of self-help, whose loving and giving lifestyle and willingness to lay down His life for others represents a larger-than-life model for self-giving. Such accommodation permits modern humanity to be moderately religious and altruistic, while steering clear of Gospel essentials such as sin, the Cross, blood atonement, new birth, resurrection, the supernatural, and final judgment.

Chapter 18

JESUS: FIRST GIFT, THEN EXAMPLE
Jesus As Gift: The Challenge of Semi-Pelagianism

Attack on the Giftedness of Salvation
A Variation of Pelagianism
Last Writings of Augustine
Official Condemnation
Worldview Has Persisted
Definition
Initiative Belongs to God

Chapter 18

JESUS: FIRST GIFT, THEN EXAMPLE
Jesus As Gift: The Challenge of Semi-Pelagianism

Prefacing this chapter with a brief historical summary of a heresy is not without purpose. Semi-Pelagianism, as it came to be known, followed closely on the heels and is a direct offspring of Pelagianism. Both shared the same threatening characteristic. Each represented an attack upon the foundational Scriptural revelation that Jesus Christ is the supreme gift of God's grace to humanity, and to receive Him as such is the only way to salvation.

Attack on the Giftedness of Salvation

As an historical movement, semi-Pelagianism was short-lived and only regionally influential. As the church gained awareness of the subtle errors contained in this theology, a consensus of bishops decisively condemned the doctrine. Yet as a system of thought, semi-Pelagianism has wormed its way into the presuppositions and beliefs of several generations of Christians throughout history. It parades itself as a doctrine giving due honor and recognition to human responsibility, but its true character is to siphon over into the resume' of human merit some of the glory due to God alone for the gift of Jesus Christ and His salvation, thus compromising the very nature of Christian salvation as a pure gift from a gracious God.

A Variation of Pelagianism

Sympathizers of Pelagius' teachings were formulating a compromise position even before the church's pronouncement of heresy against Pelagianism became official in 431. Pelagius' disregard for the necessity of Jesus' redemptive work in human salvation could not be tolerated, but Pelagian adherents concluded that a subtle variation of this theme held the promise of gaining widespread sympathy.

Last Writings of Augustine

This compromise perspective, initially known as Massilianism and later labeled semi-Pelagianism,[44] made its early headway in southern France. The doctrine had gained enough attention by the early fifth century that news reached Augustine of its existence during the waning years of his life. Finding cause for concern, Augustine managed to pen the final two writings of his illustrious career[45] in an effort to repel the advancement of this dangerous doctrine.

Augustine's corrective efforts were not enough to slow the growing momentum of semi-Pelagian doctrine, and its influence continued to spread after Augustine's death in 430. Throughout the fifth century, semi-Pelagianism dominated the theology of the French church, yet not without strong resistance from Augustinian sympathizers.[46]

Official Condemnation

Three decades into the sixth century, resistance solidified noticeably and the bishops rallied together to take official action against this aberrant theology. Convening in 529, the bishops of the Second Council of Orange concluded that the semi-Pelagian doctrine failed to meet the standards of Christian orthodoxy. The Council's refutation involved the formulation of twenty-five articles affirming truths of Scripture and milder aspects of Augustinian theology while repudiating points of semi-Pelagian doctrine. The condemnation of semi-Pelagianism gained additional support in 530 when the bishop of Rome, Boniface II, ratified the decisions of the Council of Orange. After the Orange proceedings, the movement never really flourished again.

Worldview Has Persisted

Yet semi-Pelagianism as a system of thought did not disappear. At various junctures within Christian history, semi-Pelagian presuppositions have resurfaced to cloud the vision and distort the way for generations of Christians. Our task through the remainder of this chapter will be to identify the basic presuppositions of semi-Pelagianism, expose its doctrinal errors (particularly as they affect the orthodox doctrine of Jesus Christ and His redemptive work), and to explore historically and practically the continued influence of semi-Pelagianism in the development of Christianity.

Semi-Pelagians shared the basic worldview of the Pelagians, in that they were opposed to Augustinian theology, particularly his predestination theory. They believed that an emphasis upon predestination stifled moral responsibility, producing in persons a sense of passivity towards life and fatalism for the future. Yet semi-Pelagians believed that Pelagius went too far in his attempt to counterbalance Augustinianism. Pelagius held that good works were the sole qualification for human salvation. The atoning blood of Jesus served only to give a fresh start for those who failed, but final acceptance from God came purely through human attainment of righteousness.

The semi-Pelagians disagreed with their mentor in their rejection of the notion of the moral perfectibility of natural humanity. They concurred with Scripture (and Augustine) that humans inevitably sin and stand in need of the grace of God. Yet in their desire to emphasize human responsibility in the salvation process, the semi-Pelagians erroneously introduced a synergistic dynamic to the Gospel formula that nullified the very nature of the grace that they espoused.

Definition

Historian Philip Schaff accurately defines the semi-Pelagian system of belief. "Its leading idea is, that divine grace and human will jointly accomplish the work of conversion and sanctification, and that ordinarily man must take the first step."[47] Admitting the role of God's grace in Christ, both in the dimensions of conversion and sanctification, the semi-Pelagians in effect contradict the nature of grace by requiring initial human conditions to be fulfilled before God's grace becomes available.

Scripture does not fail to emphasize human responsibility in the act of receiving the gift of salvation, but more than human responsibility is required to bring the sinner to a place of being able to benefit from the salvation that has been provided freely for all. God has taken the initiative through His grace and the Holy Spirit's intervention to prepare the sinner for conversion. Likewise, sanctification is not the result of the believer's initiative to take independent steps that merit the intervention of the Spirit's sanctifying presence. The initiative is God's, to draw the believer into deeper levels of sanctification.

Initiative Belongs to God

The semi-Pelagians failed to see that the essence of human responsibility is in responding to the divine initiative, not in being the initiator. Initiative, which means 1) first step, origination; and 2) power or right to begin something, is the prerogative of the Giver, not the receiver. Even Jesus did not initiate the words and deeds that constituted His earthly life. As Son of Man, He submitted Himself to the human role of recipient of grace from the Father, even though He was the Giver of all life as Son of God. "I can do nothing on My own initiative," He stated in John 5:30. In John 8:28, Jesus said, "I do nothing on My own initiative, but I speak these things as the Father taught Me." The original sin was prompted by the adamic desire to step out of the responsive role as creature, in an attempt to become the Initiator, the Creator. The semi-Pelagians failed to see that authentic human responsibility is to respond to the Creator's initiative, not to seize the initiative. The initiative belongs to God, both in conversion and in sanctification.

Chapter 19

JESUS: FIRST GIFT, THEN EXAMPLE
Semi-Pelagianism and Conversion

No Prevenient Grace

Sinners Have Capabilities

The Council's Ruling

Grace Prior to Conversion

Joel's Prophecy

Dual Outpourings of the Spirit

New Testament Conversion

Sinners Are Drawn to Christ

Semi-Pelagianism Adds Works to Grace

Chapter 19

JESUS: FIRST GIFT, THEN EXAMPLE
Semi-Pelagianism and Conversion

No Prevenient Grace

In this chapter, the conversion experience specifically will be isolated in order to highlight the conditionality injected by the semi-Pelagians into the Gospel of grace. Right from the beginning, we should notice that the semi-Pelagians wanted no part of the initial stage of the operation of God's grace as identified by Augustine, the stage known as prevenient grace. Prevenient grace is the theory that the grace of God resulting from Christ's redemptive work is actively drawing the human race to a saving knowledge of Jesus Christ prior to any conscious awareness on the part of the recipient. Prevenient, or preventing, refers to the initiative of divine grace that prevents human control of the process until grace has completed its preparatory work to bring the sinner to a possible saving encounter with Christ. God's grace does not force conversion, but overpowers the resistance of natural humanity until a decision is rendered either for or against Christ's saving love.

Sinners Have Capabilities

Disregarding the notion of prevenient grace, the semi-Pelagians viewed optimistically the capacity of natural humanity to take prerequisite, conditional steps that would move God to release His grace for the purpose of actualizing the conversion experience. The semi-Pelagians admitted that grace alone actualizes conversion, but they believed that humans in the natural state were capable of meeting the conditions of repentance and faith that God required in order to release His saving grace. Thus, sinners were seen to be capable of achieving the conditions of repentance and faith without the aid of grace.

The Council's Ruling

The Council of Orange condemned such teaching. Several of the official articles of the Council recognized that preliminary actions by the sinner leading to the conversion experience are not performed apart from the process of God's grace. Prior to conscious awareness, the sinner has been the object of the Holy Spirit's loving, wooing and drawing influence, brought to the very precipice of the conversion experience by the purposive operation of God's grace. Canon 7 from the Council of Orange highlights the position that the sinner can take no positive action in the direction of conversion without the Holy Spirit's influence.

> If anyone affirms that we can form any right opinion or make any right choice which relates to the salvation of eternal life, as is expedient for us, or that we can be saved, that is, assent to the preaching of the gospel through our natural powers without the illumination and inspiration of the Holy Spirit, who makes all men gladly assent to and believe in the truth, he is led astray by a heretical spirit, and does not understand the voice of God who says in the Gospel, "For apart from me you can do nothing" (John 15:5), and the word of the Apostle, "Not that we are competent of ourselves to claim anything as coming from us; our competence is from God" (2 Corinthians 3:5).

Grace Prior to Conversion

The biblical doctrine of conversion makes full allowance for the entrance of grace prior to conversion. The Holy Spirit, God's agent of conversion, visits the sinner with the gracious influence of the Gospel prior to the actual conversion experience. Recognizing that the natural capacity of sinful humanity is incapable of any level of self-help, the Holy Spirit comes to the aid of the sinner, enabling the sinner to respond appropriately to the initiative of the Gospel. Faith and repentance, components of conversion, are responses that can be made only through the Spirit's influence and enablement. God's gracious initiative must invade the life of the sinner, releasing the Spirit's presence and power, for conversion to be actualized.

Semi-Pelagianism fails to acknowledge, at this critical point in the conversion process, the Holy Spirit's role of positively influencing the sinner in the direction of the Gospel before the occurrence of new birth. The sinner is expected to improve his standing before God by virtue of his natural human efforts, thereby meriting the grace of God. Such naïve optimism inappropriately glorifies sinful humanity and compromises the sufficiency of God's grace in human conversion.

Joel's Prophecy

Joel prophetically envisioned the advent of the "last days," to be initiated by the momentous event of the Spirit's outpouring upon all humankind. Peter, preaching to the crowd of onlookers on the Day of Pentecost, did not hesitate to connect the "tongues of fire" manifested by the disciples that day with the fulfillment of Joel's ancient prophecy. He stated, "For these men are not drunk, as you suppose, for it is only the third hour of the day; but this is what was spoken of through the prophet Joel: 'And it shall be in the last days,' God said, 'that I will pour out My Spirit upon all mankind;'" (Acts 2:15-17 NAS) Peter recognized that the Spirit's power being poured out upon the church was but a fraction of the universal measure of the Spirit's outpouring then descending upon the earth's inhabitants. Human history has never been the same since that day.

Dual Outpourings of the Spirit

The significance of the Day of Pentecost events cannot be overestimated. We find the resurrected, triumphant Jesus, now ascended to heaven, fulfilling His promise to baptize His church with the Holy Spirit, while simultaneously pouring out the Spirit upon all living flesh. A common purpose links these dual outpourings. While Jesus was empowering His church to "go into all the world and preach the gospel to all creation," (Mark 16:15) He was also facilitating the evangelistic mission by releasing the Holy Spirit upon all human flesh.

Thus, from the Day of Pentecost onwards, the Holy Spirit has been released both to empower the church and to encounter every human creature. The Scriptures do not make it clear just how the earth's inhabitants are impacted by the Spirit's visitation. However, the New Testament is definite about the Holy Spirit's vital connection with the risen Jesus and His Gospel message. A primary mission of the Holy Spirit is to glorify Jesus (John 16:14) and to bear witness of Him (John 15:26). God's grace was demonstrated in the accomplishment of redemption through the finished work of Jesus, and God's grace continues to be manifest through the Holy Spirit's outpouring upon the peoples of the earth, glorifying Jesus and testifying of Him.

New Testament Conversion

Peter's interpretation of Joel's prophecy provides the New Testament rationale for the church's evangelistic enterprise. The doctrine of conversion cannot be rightly formulated without factoring in the "Pentecostal" perspective. Peter's sermon leads us to conclude that no one is converted to Jesus independent of the saving influence of God and His grace. Jesus' death for the sins of the world was not an isolated event, but was a pivotal point in world history. As Jesus stated in John's Gospel, "'And I, if I be lifted up from the earth, will draw all men to Myself.' But He was saying this to indicate the kind of death by which He was to die." (John 12:32-33) The Holy Spirit has been poured out upon all of humanity, and the message of Jesus' cross conveyed by the Spirit carries with it the power of salvation. (I Corinthians 1:18)

Sinners Are Drawn to Christ

God the Father also works through the Spirit's influence to draw lost humanity to His Son and His redemption. John's Gospel relates Jesus' words, "No one can come to Me, unless the Father who sent Me draws him; and I will raise him up on the last day." (John 6:44) Everyone who is privileged to share in Jesus' resurrection in the last day has been drawn to Him by Father God. Semi-Pelagians fail to understand the means whereby persons are converted to Jesus. No one makes oneself a candidate for conversion by their own actions independent of the grace of God. Each member of the Triune God (Father, Son and Holy Spirit) participates in the work of preparing sinners to receive the Gospel of grace.

Such a scenario suggests questions of utmost seriousness concerning the nature of the Semi-Pelagian "gospel." Does God dispense the grace of His salvation according to the performance of certain merits demonstrated by lost humanity? Is God's grace conditioned upon the satisfactory completion of prerequisites, preparing potential converts to be worthy of salvation? Semi-Pelagianism answers "Yes" to these questions. The church, however, must counter with a resounding "No" to both, unless we are prepared to sacrifice God's grace on the altar of human performance.

Semi-Pelagianism Adds Works to Grace

Semi-Pelagianism reduces salvation to a system of works plus grace. Yet the church's proclamation of the Gospel maintains its integrity precisely because it is a Gospel of grace, irrespective of any human prerequisites, merits or works. Jesus states clearly that "apart from Me you can do nothing." (John 15:5) Jesus and His grace are not held at bay until we present evidence that we deserve His visitation. Paul remarks that we were both "helpless" and "ungodly" when Jesus took decisive action to die for us (Romans 5:6). How dare we presume that we must perform satisfactorily as sinners before God's grace is made available to us. Semi-Pelagianism clings to a standard of human performance precluding the entrance of grace, thus it represents a rejection of the very essence of the Christian Gospel.

Chapter 20

JESUS: FIRST GIFT, THEN EXAMPLE
Semi-Pelagianism and Sanctification

Semi-Pelagian Sanctification

Jesus Not in Control

Faith a Performance

Minimizes the Bible's Worth

Augustine and Faith

Authentic Faith

God Controls the Process of Sanctification

The Sin of Presumption

Presumption From the Old Testament

Presumptuous Living

Presumption is Heresy

Chapter 20

JESUS: FIRST GIFT, THEN EXAMPLE
Semi-Pelagianism and Sanctification

Semi-Pelagian Sanctification

Recalling Philip Schaff's astute observations from Chapter 17, semi-Pelagianism not only denies the exclusiveness of divine grace in the conversion experience, but also introduces a synergism of grace and the human will in sanctification. And in each dimension of Christian experience, humanity must take the first step. Our purposes in this chapter are to explore why such errors regarding sanctification are fatal to the Gospel, and to counter with considerations of sanctification more faithful to the Biblical witness.

For clarification purposes, sanctification is to be defined as the Holy Spirit's work in the life of the believer, leading to increasing conformity with the holy humanity of Jesus Christ. God wills for all Christians to progress in sanctification. Jesus, the Lord of believers and the church, controls the sanctification process, and has given the Holy Spirit to fulfill this task.

Jesus Not in Control

Semi-Pelagians misunderstand Christian sanctification. They assume that Christians control the process. They falsely assume that the sanctifying presence of the Holy Spirit only operates when believers initiate actions that invoke the Spirit's intervention. In essence, they think that God's grace is apportioned according to successful human performance. This erroneous belief injects into the equation an unwarranted weight of burden for the Christian not set forth in Scripture.

Although semi-Pelagians view Jesus as the supreme Lord of history, yet they see Him as having voluntarily restricted the activity of His Holy Spirit until the church takes the appropriate steps to "trigger" His intervention. So who is really Lord of history, if Jesus and the activity of His Spirit are under the control of human initiative? The semi-Pelagian scheme requires that human works precede and regulate the operation of God's grace in Christ.

Faith a Performance

For instance, semi-Pelagians are guilty of abusing the Biblical doctrine of faith. They view faith as a capacity within the believer capable of being expressed without the enablement of Christ and the Spirit. The believer must first express the appropriate measure of faith before Jesus allows the Spirit to intervene. God's grace and corresponding benefits are conditionally rewarded only as the believer exhibits proper faith. In each display of the believer's faith, God evaluates the level of performance as a basis for determining the nature of His involvement and the measure of benefits to be imparted. Since every performance must measure up, believers are pressured to seek various techniques expected to elevate their faith.

Not only faith, but other types of legitimate Christian activity such as prayer, fasting, giving and other forms of service suffer similar abuse when transformed into tools of self-interest. When these activities are allowed to deteriorate in significance to become spiritual techniques meant to solicit special privileges and benefits from God, then they have lost their connection with the Gospel of Jesus Christ.

Minimizes the Bible's Worth

This reduction of the Gospel to a performance agenda often causes believers to minimize the true worth of the Bible, making it a repository of benefits promised by God to His people if certain behavioral conditions are satisfied. Faith becomes the behavioral norm that, when performed successfully, releases the benefits of God. This perspective conditions God's activity, based upon the accomplishments of His people both to acquire knowledge of His benefits as specified in the Bible, and to demonstrate the appropriate measure of faith warranting His intervention.

Augustine and Faith

Historically, the issue of faith was a pivotal factor in the resolution both of the Pelagian and semi-Pelagian controversies. What made the difference was Augustine's dramatic reversal of opinion, leading him to reject the notion that Biblical faith is a human work. He came to a conclusion after much deliberation that faith should not be considered an independent human work, but rather a gift from God. This conclusion later proved to be a hedge of doctrinal defense against the subtlety of Pelagian and semi-Pelagian errors. A verse from the Pauline book of *I Corinthians* sealed Augustine's position on this issue. "And what do you have that you did not receive? But if you did receive it, why do you boast as if you had not received it?" (I Corinthians 4:7) As Augustine came to see, even the faith to believe in the Gospel of Jesus and to live dependently upon Him is not to be considered a work of merit, but a gift of God's grace.

Authentic Faith

When faith is viewed rightly as a product of God's grace, then the authentic Gospel is preserved. This truthful presupposition necessarily excludes the view that faith is a product of the believer, independent of divine enablement. Faith should not be viewed as a qualifying work on the part of believers meant to control God's gracious intervention. God is gracious in His innermost being, and does not depend upon the performance of His children to be gracious in all of His ways. The gift to humanity of Jesus Christ and His salvation demonstrates fully that God is gracious to the highest level. God is gracious, and desires that His children respond positively to His initiatives. Yet He is not depleted of grace when His children fail to reciprocate. The grace of God is bigger than the believer's lapses into sin, and the Holy Spirit uses both failures and successes in a delicate process of weaving all the experiences of every Christian into a beautiful tapestry of sanctification (Romans 8:28).

God Controls the Process of Sanctification

Christian sanctification is a lifelong process under God's control, and must not be reduced to a succession of performance initiatives exercised by believers, as semi-Pelagians contend. Believers are "new creatures" in Christ (II Corinthians 5:17), and are no longer dominated by fleshly behavior, but live by the Spirit of God (Romans 8:9). Yet fleshly behavior remains a possibility, when Christ's cross and Lordship are not applied continuously in Christian living.

The Sin of Presumption

A disastrous aspect of semi-Pelagianism is its tendency to sanction fleshly behavior, over against Spirit-led behavior, by advocating that initiative is the prerogative of the believer. The Bible identifies this type of error as the sin of presumption. King David prayed that he be guarded from presumptuous sins (Psalms 19:13). One of the four temptations Jesus resisted in the wilderness was the sin of presumption. Satan took Jesus to the pinnacle of the temple, and challenged Him to jump off, citing God's promises of angelic protection. Jesus detected the flaw in Satan's use of Scriptural promises. He countered by quoting a different Scripture: "You shall not tempt the Lord your God." Jesus' words may also be rendered, "You shall not put the Lord your God to the test." The essence of this temptation was to challenge Jesus to initiate a course of action not directed by God, yet to utilize a Scriptural promise in an attempt to force God to intervene. God is not a pawn, to be controlled by the whims of His people. God honors submission to His initiative, but does not respond to presumptuous efforts to manipulate His will.

Presumption From the Old Testament

An Old Testament example of the sin of presumption is represented by the children of Israel under Moses' leadership, as they experienced their first opportunity to take the Promised Land. The twelve spies, with the exception of Joshua and Caleb, brought back a negative report relating to the difficulty of occupying the land of Canaan. The negative report had the effect of discouraging the children of Israel from obeying God and responding to His promise of victory and conquest. Instead, they refused to follow God's command to take the land. In view of the disobedience of God's children, God withdrew His promise of victory and sent His people back into the wilderness to wander for another forty years.

When faced with the sentence of more wilderness wandering, a faction of the people changed their mind and decided to march into battle to take the land. This presumptuous move was their own plan, for God had withdrawn His promise of successful conquest. God refused to back them, and they went into battle on their own strength. The result predictably was disastrous. Moses summarized the outcome. "So I spoke to you, but you would not listen. Instead you rebelled against the command of the Lord, and acted presumptuously and went up into the hill country. And the Amorites who live in that hill country came out against you, and chased you as bees do, and crushed you from Seir to Hormah." (Deuteronomy 1:43-44)

Presumptuous Living

Semi-Pelagianism condones presumption as the proper course of action for Christians. Rather than living as responders to the Spirit's initiative, believers are challenged to act on their own initiative, presuming that God will get involved as a result of their performance. Semi-Pelagians advocate that Christians live every day with such a sequence of behavior. God begins as a spectator, waiting for the believer to initiate a course of action presumed to be a precondition meriting His intervention. If the action is successfully performed, God graciously comes on the scene and manifests His benefits. As this sequence is repeated over the course of a lifetime, the believer grows in sanctification as a result of God's system of rewards for good behavior.

Presumption is Heresy

The Council of Orange in 529 rejected this semi-Pelagian view of sanctification. Canon 6 addresses the false assumption that the intervention of God and His grace is a reward of Christian performance.

"If anyone says that God has mercy upon us when, apart from his grace, we believe, will, desire, strive, labor, pray, watch, study, seek, ask, or knock, but does not confess that it is by the infusion and inspiration of the Holy Spirit within us that we have the faith, the will, or the strength to do all these things as we ought; or if anyone makes the assistance of grace depend on the humility or obedience of man and does not agree that it is a gift of grace itself that we are obedient and humble, he contradicts the Apostle who says, 'What have you that you did not receive?' (I Corinthians 4:7), and, 'But by the grace of God I am what I am.' (I Corinthians 15:10)"

The bishops at Orange also noted from Jesus' teachings that the life required to produce fruit does not come from the branch, but from the Vine. Fruit is not the reward for the branch's performance, but is the result of an abiding relationship with the Vine. Canon 23 refutes the Performance/Spectator motif of semi-Pelagianism.

> "Concerning the branches of the vine. The branches on the vine do not give life to the vine, but receive life from it; thus the vine is related to its branches in such a way that it supplies them with what they need to live, and does not take this from them. Thus it is to the advantage of the disciples, not Christ, both to have Christ abiding in them and to abide in Christ. For if the vine is cut down another can shoot up from the live root; but one who is cut off from the vine cannot live without the root (John 15:5ff)."

In Scripture, no separation or distance between the believer and the Holy Spirit is indicated, nor is the believer expected to perform "for God." Jesus desires willing and loving submission from His people. Intimate relationship is the means that He guides His children into the further reaches of His purpose. How preposterous and arrogant is the notion that we manipulate Jesus to grant our wishes by using His Word as a legal contract to force His hand to act. Jesus has His own timing and way to orchestrate history, and our total submission to His Lordship better prepares us to know and yield to the direction of His Spirit.

Chapter 21

JESUS: FIRST GIFT, THEN EXAMPLE
Semi-Pelagianism to the Present Day

Semi-Pelagianism Permitted
Flesh Allowed to Dominate the Spirit
Catholic Toleration
Luther's Alternative
Opportunity Lost
Protestant Beginnings
Council of Trent: Bastion of Semi-Pelagianism
Protestantism After Luther
Evangelical Error
The Spirit's Influence
Faith and Repentance
The Performance Trap
Legalism in Galatia
Led by the Spirit

The Tendency to Resist God's Grace
Trying to Compete With God
Total Glory to the Lord

Chapter 21

JESUS: FIRST GIFT, THEN EXAMPLE
Semi-Pelagianism to the Present Day

Semi-Pelagianism Permitted

Although condemned as heresy by the Council of Orange in 529, semi-Pelagian doctrine managed to resurface at various times throughout the church's history in varied disguises to challenge the essential truth of the unconditional nature of God's grace in Jesus Christ. Ancient semi-Pelagianism was not able to generate universal support, yet advocates of this doctrine in some cases not only avoided the censorship of heresy, but managed to maintain general respect within Christendom. This represents an enigma that seems to characterize semi-Pelagianism. In spite of the undisputed sentence of heresy levied against the ancient expression, new forms of this doctrine have navigated beneath the church's radar screen without detection, jettisoning its destructive cargo among the faithful.

When semi-Pelagian presuppositions capture the thinking of a generation of Christians, a "Pharasaic" style of Christianity enshrouds the church. Human traditions begin to infiltrate Christian beliefs and practices, submerging believers in a sea of performance activities not initiated by the Spirit of God.

Numerous expressions of semi-Pelagianism have surfaced within Christendom after the Council of Orange. By failing to take a stand against this heresy, the church's toleration has had the effect of sanctioning its presence. All three major branches of Christendom, whether Catholic, Protestant or Eastern Orthodox, have allowed semi-Pelagian beliefs to coexist peacefully with established orthodoxy. As a result, Gospel truths have been weakened and in some cases corrupted as a result of compromise.

Flesh Allowed to Dominate the Spirit

The gravest danger of semi-Pelagianism is its subtle attack upon the truth that God's grace through the gift of Jesus Christ is the only basis for knowing God. In times when the church tolerates the presence of this heresy, human actions are allowed to rival the work of God's grace both in conversion and in sanctification, with human initiative controlling the process. When semi-Pelagian tendencies dominate, fleshly activities masquerade in Christian disguise while the legitimate operations of the Holy Spirit suffer decline.

Catholic Toleration

Late Medieval Catholicism is a prime example of a church easily misled by semi-Pelagian presuppositions. As the dominance of Scholasticism subsided after Thomas Aquinas, tendencies towards semi-Pelagianism increased. Even Thomas, in unguarded moments, seemed to invite misinterpretation. A case in point is the following discussion: "…man of himself, and without the external help of grace, can prepare himself for grace. Further, man prepares himself for grace by doing what is in him to do, since, if man does what is in him to do, God will not deny him grace."[48] In other instances, Thomas legitimated the need for human merits, both prior to conversion and in the sanctification process. After Thomas, the theologies of William of Ockham and Gabriel Biel further fortified the presence of semi-Pelagianism in late Medieval theology.

Luther's Alternative

Martin Luther's troubled conscience reacted adversely to the established dogma of sixteenth century Catholicism precisely because the church under semi-Pelagian influence applauded human merit unaided by divine grace. Luther instinctively knew that even his best efforts were corrupted by sin. As he pored over the Scriptures in preparation for his university teaching assignments, his explorations led to the discovery of the essential content of the doctrine of justification. Put simply, our relationship with God is purely the product of divine grace through the gift of Jesus Christ.

As a Catholic priest, monk and professor, Luther's developing theological insights had the potential of bringing renewal to a church that had lost touch with the Gospel. Yet an unforeseen set of circumstances thrust Luther into unavoidable conflict with the Catholic establishment, closing the door on any real possibility of mutual communication.

Opportunity Lost

Luther's 1517 academic critique, the Ninety-five Theses, directed at abuses he detected in Pope Leo X's Jubilee Indulgence, unexpectedly seized the attention of the entire Holy Roman Empire. Luther's bold criticisms captured the imagination of a populace already intensely disenchanted with the Roman church and her internal corruptions and lack of spiritual power. Luther probably had no knowledge when he posted his theses that the Pope and a leading Archbishop of the church had major financial investments that were dependent upon the success of the Jubilee Indulgence. As public attention turned to Luther's criticisms, the success of the campaign suddenly became jeopardized. The church viewed Luther as an expendable commodity to be silenced before irreparable damage was done. Luther only wanted a hearing, to defend his views. Instead, after refusing to recant his position, he found himself excommunicated from the only Christian church in the Empire.

Prior to his excommunication, Luther had devoted his efforts to helping his church rediscover the doctrine of justification, rejecting performance based approaches in favor of grace only through the gift of Jesus Christ. Having been cast out of that church, Luther was forced to redirect his focus upon the formidable task of formulating a new ecclesiological structure for himself and others who had been alienated from Catholicism.

Protestant Beginnings

As Luther was thrust in the role of starting a new Christian movement, he maintained remarkable consistency in grounding all doctrines and practices in the foundational truth that justification is a product of God's grace alone, and no human works other than those accomplished by Jesus Christ contribute in any way to the reconciliation freely extended to the human race. In the Lutheran model, even the good works of Christians are not to be viewed as initiatives from the human side intended to merit God's grace and favor, but rather are to be seen as Spirit influenced responses to the grace and favor of God already bestowed through Jesus Christ. Now having the luxury of looking back upon the development of Protestantism, we would be hard pressed to find any period of theological history more free of semi-Pelagian influence than in the early days of Luther's leadership of the Protestant movement.

Council of Trent: Bastion of Semi-Pelagianism

The Catholic Church had not been predisposed to pay heed to Luther's views while he served as a Catholic priest, so it hardly needs to be said that they were unwilling to give him a hearing now that he had become the dominant voice of a rival ecclesiastical body outside their official boundaries. As the Counter Reformation of the Catholic Church took shape at the Council of Trent (1545-1563), acquiescence to Protestant doctrinal challenges was not a consideration. The Catholic bishops were bent on ratifying a status quo doctrinal and practical agenda heavily laden with semi-Pelagian assumptions.

Most revealing was Trent's explication of the doctrine of justification. Catholic theology codified its synergistic orientation by asserting that works of love must accompany the gift of God's grace for justification to be validated. Faith alone in the redemptive triumph of Jesus Christ is not enough. Furthermore, the cooperative venture between human works of charity plus God's grace must result in an acquired, inherent righteousness in the believer, necessitating that justification be viewed as a lifelong process. Eternity with God is not assured until the final judgment, when the righteous works of the believer must meet the ultimate test of the holiness of God.

Trent represents a model case study of the semi-Pelagian error. Any formula for justification that attempts to add performance oriented merits to the grace of God as a basis for God's ultimate acceptance logically contradicts the very essence of God's grace. The apostle Paul clarifies the only valid doctrine of justification. Grace must stand alone. "But if it is by grace, it is no longer on the basis of works, otherwise grace is no longer grace." (Romans 11:6) And assurance must be of the very essence of faith, for justification is a gift based upon the past accomplishments of Jesus Christ, completed on the cross of Calvary. Human works can neither add nor take away from the finished work of Jesus Christ on the cross. Justification is based solely upon the victory that was finished on the cross, and it is actualized in the individual simply by believing in the accomplishment of Jesus.

Protestantism After Luther

Catholic theology remained oblivious to her semi-Pelagian bedfellow long after Trent's permissive sanction of a works based doctrine of justification. Luther detected the Catholic problem, but found no acceptance from the mother church to make a positive difference. An outcast, he charted a new course on the secure foundation of Pauline theology, enhanced by Augustinianism. Yet after Luther's promising beginnings, later generations of Protestants departed from his founding vision. Semi-Pelagian views infiltrated various Protestant groups, compromising the doctrinally sound beginnings of the movement.

Protestantism has progressed into the modern era naively harboring the subtly of semi-Pelagian influence. Few periods have escaped the corruption of this pestilent heresy. The presence of semi-Pelagianism can be detected in Calvinism after Calvin, in Lutheran Pietism, in the Wesleyan movement and Methodism, in the American Awakenings, in European Liberalism, and in American Evangelicalism. The Pentecostal and Charismatic movements of the twentieth century are no exception.

Evangelical Error

American Evangelicalism, riding upon revivalist practices characteristic of colonial and early American Awakening movements, views conversion in a semi-Pelagian fashion. Evangelicals generally recognize conversion as a work of divine grace, made available to humanity exclusively through the redemptive work of Jesus Christ. Yet the grace that actualizes conversion is portrayed as being locked up and inaccessible until prerequisite actions on the part of the sinner are performed. The sinner must perform acts of repentance and faith, without divine assistance, in order to qualify for the activation of grace and the Holy Spirit's converting work.

Evangelistic appeals aimed at converting sinners challenge individuals to repent, that is, to turn away from their sinful practices, and to make a personal commitment to Jesus Christ. Some preachers attempt to move the emotions, some appeal to the intellect, while others try to move the will of the hearer. In any case, the common assumption is that sinners must take the first step, satisfying God's conditions of repentance and faith, before He takes reciprocal action by imparting His grace to actualize the conversion experience. Furthermore, such a mindset assumes that sinners are capable of repenting and having faith in their natural, sinful state, apart from the presence and influence of God's grace.

The Spirit's Influence

Evangelicals who embrace these beliefs probably are unaware that they are operating from a semi-Pelagian rather than a Scriptural model. The Scriptures reveal that God is graciously working in the lives of sinners prior to any conscious acknowledgment of such actions. Peter indicated that the Holy Spirit had been poured out upon "all flesh" on the Day of Pentecost, soon after Jesus' ascension to heaven. (Acts 2:16-17) Speaking of His crucifixion for the sins of the whole world, Jesus said, "And I, if I be lifted up from the earth, will draw all men to Myself." (John 12:32) God the Father graciously orchestrates this drawing influence administered through Christ and by the Holy Spirit. Jesus stated, "No one can come to Me, unless the Father who sent Me draws him; and I will raise him up on the last day." (John 6:44) Those who come to Christ in the new birth, in reality, are revealing that their actions are not totally their own, but have been "wrought in God" from the beginning. (John 3:21)

Faith and Repentance

Another common Evangelical error related to conversion deserves treatment here, for its roots are semi-Pelagian. This view holds that repentance precedes conversion. The logic follows that sinners must reject their sinful practices so that they will be presentable to Christ. Once sin is abandoned, faith in Jesus becomes the final step from the human side. He rewards those who have satisfactorily performed the preparatory action He deems worthy of redemption, and releases His grace to finalize the process.

Reformer John Calvin insightfully dismissed such non-Scriptural thinking in his *Institutes of the Christian Religion*. States Calvin, "There are some, however, who suppose that repentance precedes faith, rather than flows from it, or is produced by it as fruit from a tree." "Now it ought to be a fact beyond controversy that repentance not only constantly follows faith, but is also born of faith."[49] (III.3.1) The instant that the sinner receives Jesus as Redeemer, the gift of faith is produced, actualizing the new birth of the sinner. The Holy Spirit now inhabits the new believer, empowering that one to take steps of genuine repentance. In the light of Christ's presence, the believer is able to distinguish the darkness of sin and turn away from it. Without faith already being present through a living encounter with Christ, true repentance is impossible. The sinner, unaided by divine grace, does not have the discerning ability or the power to turn away from sinful practices.

The Performance Trap

Semi-Pelagian errors related to the sanctification process are evidenced in many groups. These Christians fall into the trap of performance oriented living. They think that because they lived for the devil prior to being born again, now they have to compensate by living for Jesus Christ, as if He is now a spectator in heaven evaluating Christian behavior. Performance that pleases

Him, He rewards with His divine sanction and blessing. Sub-par performance, He disciplines. Believers desiring superior blessings and manifestations think that they must demonstrate higher levels of faith. They take upon themselves the challenge of initiating spiritual practices sure to qualify them for uncommon supernatural impartations.

This orientation becomes a trap, because prayer, fasting, Bible reading and meditation, speaking in tongues, praise and worship, etc., are legitimate activities never meant to be used as merits offered to God to solicit His manifest presence and supernatural privileges. Such favors are not to be purchased by works, but are to be appropriated as gifts of Christ's presence already indwelling every believer.

Legalism in Galatia

Performance oriented Christianity at its root is a fleshly version of the Gospel similar to the problematic perspective plaguing the Galatian church in the days of the apostle Paul. Chastising the Galatians for their legalistic mentality, Paul asserts, "Are you so foolish? Having begun by the Spirit, are you now being perfected by the flesh?" (Galatians 3:3) The Galatians had begun well, gaining their freedom by simple faith in response to Paul's proclamation of the Gospel of grace. But certain Judiazers were threatening to rob them of their freedom by attempting to force them to obey the Mosaic Law as a condition to maintain God's presence and blessings. Paul declared to the Galatian church, "It was for freedom that Christ set us free; therefore keep standing firm and do not be subject again to a yoke of slavery." (Galatians 5:1) Paul explained that Christians are called to abide in Christ and walk in faith by the Holy Spirit. To depend on external standards of performance, whether the Law of Moses or any formula of good works, when employed as a conditional step to acquire God's presence and benefits, is a falling away from God's grace into a fleshly scheme of working for God.

Led by the Spirit

The Gospel counters the semi-Pelagian performance orientation by affirming two critical truths. 1) Faith is not a performance, but a continuous submission to the initiative of the Holy Spirit, directing our lives according to the Lordship of Jesus Christ. 2) Christians do not live **for** Jesus, but rather, have died to self life and have become **vessels of the indwelling Christ** through the Spirit's presence. Earlier in his letter, Paul brought together all of the essential elements of living in the freedom of the Gospel of grace. "I have been crucified with Christ; and it is no longer I who live, but Christ lives in me; and the life which I now live in the flesh I live by faith in the Son of God, who loved me, and delivered Himself up for me." (Galatians 2:20) Jesus' presence, blessings and power are not external goals to be acquired by superior spiritual performance, but are freely bestowed giftings that accompany Christ's presence. The Spirit does not respond to the believer's works, but leads the believer to respond to the works of Christ in His continuing mission in the earth.

The Tendency to Resist God's Grace

Modern Christians continue to fall prey to the trap that has ensnared multitudes of believers since the days of Paul. We have trouble really believing that our Gospel is a Gospel of grace. Rather than gratefully receiving Jesus Christ and the full endowment of giftings and benefits associated with His baptism in the Spirit, we are tempted to fall back into carnality by attempting to do something for God to reciprocate for our good fortune. We want to demonstrate to God, to others, and to ourselves, that He made the right choice when He selected us. We are repelled at the thought of being objects of charity, chosen purely out of His desire to show mercy rather than because of something within us that merited His favor.

Trying to Compete With God

Yet when we fail to accept our status of freedom in Christ solely on the basis of His gracious will, we quickly nullify our freedom by becoming slaves again to fleshly self-centeredness. By trying to add our accomplishments to the incomparable story of God's redemptive triumph in Christ, we only succeed in detracting from His success and revealing that we don't really comprehend that our position in Christ was sealed for us while we were absolutely helpless. When Christians are found to be trying to impress God, to measure up, to do something for God, or to obtain the blessings of the abundant life by spiritual performances, they are displaying symptoms of immature, fleshly behavior. Paul demolishes the performance orientation of semi-Pelagianism: "For I will not presume to speak of anything except what Christ has accomplished through me, ..." (Romans 15:18)

Total Glory to the Lord

Those liberated by the Gospel give no place for self glory. They recognize the handiwork of God in all good things, and delight in giving Him exclusive and total glory. The Psalmist understood the basic truth. "For I will not trust in my bow, nor will my sword save me. ...In God we have boasted all day long. And we will give thanks to Thy name forever." (Psalms 44:6, 8) Again, we turn to Paul for definitive revelation of the need for the believer to give due recognition for every part of the abundant and eternal life imparted through God's grace in Christ Jesus. "But by His doing you are in Christ Jesus, who became to us wisdom from God, and righteousness and sanctification and redemption, that, just as it is written, 'Let Him who boasts, boast in the Lord." (I Corinthians 1:30-31)

Chapter 22

JESUS: FIRST GIFT, THEN EXAMPLE
Jesus as Example: Spirit Dependency

Exercise in Futility

The Law: Built-in Failure

Death to the Natural Way

Failure of the Liberal Ideal

Jesus: Temporary Amnesia

Jesus: Natural Human Development

The Source of Jesus' Divine Life

Real Humanity, Real Obedience

Sinless Humanity is Submitted Humanity

The Holy Spirit: Jesus' Source and Ours

Authentic Human Living Requires the Supernatural

Spirit Control Opens Up the Supernatural Dimension

Jesus Unique as Incarnate God and Savior

We Emulate Jesus in His Total Submission to the Father

Chapter 22

JESUS: FIRST GIFT, THEN EXAMPLE
Jesus as Example: Spirit Dependency

Proceeding to the second part of Luther's statement, "Christ is first gift, then example," we direct our attention to the truth that Jesus is our example. Some readers may doubt that a biblical basis exists for such an affirmation. From the apostle Peter, we find solid evidence. "For you have been called for this purpose, since Christ also suffered for you, leaving you an example for you to follow in His steps, …" (I Peter 2:21) The apostle John offers additional reinforcement. "…the one who says he abides in Him ought himself to walk in the same manner as He walked." (I John 2:6) John continues, "…as He is, so also are we in this world." (I John 4:17) But Jesus is not a dead hero, whose teachings and lifestyle are to be followed as a model for contemporary inspiration and emulation. Because of His resurrection and impartation of the Holy Spirit, Jesus is the only dead hero who has come back to life to indwell and direct the lives of His people.

Exercise in Futility

After exposing the fallacy of semi-Pelagianism in previous chapters, it should be beyond question that persons relying solely upon their own natural resources, without the presence and enablement of the Holy Spirit, have no possibility of following Jesus' example. Even to attempt such an endeavor is an exercise in futility. Had Jesus Himself attempted to live the life set before Him without the indwelling of the Spirit provided by His Father,

He would have failed miserably. In His humanity, Jesus was never without the fullness of the Holy Spirit (John 3:34-35). The Holy Spirit was the source of His ability to speak the words and do the works of His heavenly Father. His absolute yieldedness and total dependency upon the Holy Spirit enabled Jesus to fulfill completely His personal mission and destiny.

The Law: Built-in Failure

A parallel illustration can be found in the dilemma faced by the Jews as they were presented with the obligation to live by the standard of conduct specified by the Mosaic Law. God's commandments regulated every area of human life, and no one was able to comply perfectly with its statutes. The Law aroused mixed reactions for the Jew. Although God's glory was revealed through the Law, yet the Law also magnified human sin (Romans 3:20). The Law was given for a dual purpose. It was given to reveal something of God's character and of His behavioral obligations to be followed in covenant relationship among His people. Yet beyond its purpose as a code of conduct, the Law was given to reveal the finitude, futility and failure of fallen humanity to please God apart from His provision of a Messiah. Failure was built into the Jewish system of worship, in that animal sacrifices were necessary as a sacrificial atonement for human sin. Such atoning sacrifices foreshadowed the coming of the Messiah, whose own blood was shed as a permanent sacrifice and atonement for the people's sins. The Mosaic Law brought human sin to light, and confronted Jews with the realization that their only hope of attaining the righteousness of God would be through their dependency upon the gift of Messiah, God's own Son.

Death to the Natural Way

When Jesus the Messiah died on the cross of Calvary, all attempts by natural humanity to attain personal righteousness and gain the favor of God met their death. After Calvary, the only acceptable way to experience relationship with God is to abandon all efforts of personal initiative, and surrender to God's gracious initiative. God has provided no other way of entering into relationship with Himself than to accept freely the gift of His only Son Jesus. The moment that Jesus is received, the Holy Spirit comes to dwell in the life of the believer. Of all who receive Him, Jesus stakes His claim as Lord of that life, and begins the process of exercising His initiative to gain and maintain full control. The personal mission and destiny of the life of the individual believer can be achieved only as the Holy Spirit is given freedom to enforce the Lordship of Jesus in every facet of thought and action.

Failure of the Liberal Ideal

Particularly in the context of Liberal Protestantism in 19th century Europe, the biblical revelation of Jesus was replaced by an image of Jesus as a romantic idealist who modeled love for God and concern for His fellow humans. Jesus was portrayed as a cross-cultural embodiment of universal love for all people, and a general model of how everyone should love God and others. Sin was simply the absence of loving concern, which could be remedied by modeling the love that Jesus exemplified. Such lofty idealism certainly inspired a temporary sense of good will and altruism, but ultimately left in its wake the decidedly bitter taste of discouragement and defeat. Ideals unsupported by the solid foundation of Truth crash and crumble in the face of the frontal attacks of sin. Jesus' lifestyle of consistent love stands as a definitive indictment against fanciful humanistic prescriptions oozing with positive intentions and pious resolutions. Sin must be crucified by the cross of Jesus, and life regenerated by the invasion of the Holy Spirit.

Jesus: Temporary Amnesia

Part of the humiliation of the Incarnation for the Son of God was His voluntary, although temporary, surrender of the privileges and prerogatives of His Godhead position. For our sakes and for our salvation He willingly limited Himself to the conditions of incarnate humanity. The apostle Paul captures the depth of condescension willingly endured by the Son of God. "…although He existed in the form of God, did not regard equality with God a thing to be grasped, but emptied Himself, taking the form of a bondservant, and being made in the likeness of men." (Philippians 2:6-7) Memory of His previous life within the Godhead was temporarily unavailable to Him. This could legitimately be called a state of temporary amnesia. When He assumed His new identity as Son of Man, He did not continue to be engaged in the consciousness and experience of His divine nature. Certainly He maintained His divine identity. A big part of His redemptive mission was to communicate to a skeptical world that He was God's Son. But His divine nature and experience was not available to Him as He took on His human identity as Jesus of Nazareth.

Jesus: Natural Human Development

As Jesus of Nazareth, He fully entered into life as a human, developing naturally within the conditions of finitude. As Luke reveals, "And the Child continued to grow and become strong, increasing in wisdom; and the grace of God was upon Him. … And Jesus kept increasing in wisdom and stature, and in favor with God and men." (Luke 2:40, 52) Although His inherent nature was divine, He voluntarily restricted His access to the resources of His divinity in order to be true to the realm of His humanity. Consciously, He knew that He was Son of God, but He had no memory of His life and experience as a member of the Godhead. His only conscious memories were His life as Mary's son. He knew that He had an identity beyond His human life and experience, but He gave up His natural access to His divine identity from conception to the grave.

While developing within His human identity, Jesus was "dead" to His divine nature. Jesus spoke often of the "cross" before He literally experienced death on the Cross of Calvary. His cross before Calvary, in part, was the crucifixion that He was living out in connection with His divine position. Jesus was very God, and He knew that, but the privileges and prerogatives associated with His divine life were not available to Him as Son of Man. At times, Jesus must have longed to have been able to step out of His humanity and awaken to His experience as God's eternal Son. Yet the mission that He must accomplish, as Messiah and Savior, necessitated that He submit fully to Adam's position and nature. As the Second Adam, His obedience to the Father's will needed to be authentically human. Reliance upon His divine nature would have contradicted the authenticity of His human nature and experience.

The Source of Jesus' Divine Life

Yet Jesus' human life, from conception onwards, was never governed solely by natural human capacities. The presence of divinity was always with Him. Yet that presence of divinity that He depended upon was not His nature as Son of God. Having yielded to His Father's will to undergo the Incarnation, He relinquished any right to draw upon the resources of His divine nature. But another dimension of divine presence was made available by the Father for the Son of Man. As the apostle John asserts, "…for God giveth not the Spirit by measure unto Him. The Father loveth the Son, and hath given all things into his hand." (John 3:34-35, KJV) The Holy Spirit indwelt and filled Jesus' human life, so that divine, supernatural presence and capacity was always with Him. That the presence of divinity within Jesus' humanity was the Holy

Spirit, and not His own divine nature as God's Son, is a matter of immense doctrinal significance.

Real Humanity, Real Obedience

At this juncture, it is critical to note that Jesus in His incarnate life did not have access to the full range of divine capacities that He inherently possessed in the Godhead as the eternal Word and Son of God. He willingly submitted to the conditions and limitations of the Incarnation because our salvation required that He come to earth as the Second Adam. His obedience had to be real, in that it had to be the obedience of one who was fully human. The apostle Paul shows that the Second Adam must reverse Adam's original sin to make redemption possible. "For as through the one man's disobedience the many were made sinners, even so through the obedience of the One the many will be made righteous." (Romans 5:19) Jesus was fully human as we are human, except that He knew no sin. (Hebrews 4:15) Only because Jesus submitted to the humiliation of the Incarnation, accepting the consequences of becoming truly human, can He therefore be legitimately considered an example for those who believe in Him. This means that Jesus refused to take advantage of His inherently divine capacities that had been at His disposal forever in the Godhead. He did not violate the authentic boundaries of the human nature that became His when He emerged from His mother's womb.

Sinless Humanity is Submitted Humanity

Jesus was an authentic human, but not an independent human. He was unwilling to rely upon the resources of His own independent humanity, but only thought and did what His heavenly Father initiated through Him. That meant that the words and works of Jesus were not His own, in the sense of having their origin in His natural human mind apart from the Father's intervention. He only said and did His Father's words and works, thus all that flowed out of Jesus' life was of divine origin. As Jesus stated, "Do you not believe that I am in the Father, and the Father is in Me? The words that I say to you I do not speak on My own initiative, but the Father abiding in Me does His works." (John 14:10) The divinity that He expressed was not His inherent divinity as the Word and Son, but had its source from another member of the Triune Godhead. Jesus' role as a model of desired human behavior has validity because the source of divine agency within Him, prompting and empowering Him to do the Father's works, is the Holy Spirit.

The Holy Spirit: Jesus' Source and Ours

Two issues stand out. First, all humanity needs the presence of divinity in order to realize life's full potential, yet divinity is not inherently present in human nature. Therefore, the divine presence needed by humanity must come from an external source. Second, Jesus modeled human life lived in the fullness of the Holy Spirit. That He qualified as a model of human dependence upon the divine presence meant that His source was not His own divinity, but came from His Father's provision of the Holy Spirit, the same provision the Father makes available to any willing human recipient.

Jesus was divine, but the supernatural reality that He experienced during His earthly pilgrimage did not flow from His divine nature. The dimension of the supernatural Jesus experienced was derived from the Father's provision of the Holy Spirit. When Jesus exemplified an abundance of divine wisdom and power, He did so without violating the nature and conditions of His authentic humanity. His experience, therefore, models for us the very real possibility of being led, equipped and empowered by a source not found in our natural humanity. As we have been given the gift of the Holy Spirit, we have the privilege of tapping into the same source of the supernatural experienced by Jesus Himself.

Authentic Human Living Requires the Supernatural

This means that natural human capacity alone is unfit for the task of emulating the lifestyle of Jesus. Jesus revealed that authentic human living transcends natural capacities. Humanity was created with the capacity not only to relate to God, but to be a living receptacle of divine life. Humanity is regulated by natural conditions corresponding to finitude, yet is also endowed with the capacity to receive and experience the infinite. It could be said that it is not unnatural for humans to participate in the supernatural. Humanity is made with the potential to cross back and forth into both dimensions: the natural and the supernatural. Yet the supernatural must regulate or govern the natural. Paul calls it, walking according to the Spirit (Romans 8:4). When the natural attempts to govern the supernatural, then a fleshly condition appears which grieves the Holy Spirit (Romans 8:6-8).

Jesus set an example for new born Christians in that He never allowed His Adamic nature to dominate His humanity. He made the determination that His human will would respond only to the will of His heavenly Father as revealed to Him by the Holy Spirit. When Jesus completed His redemptive mission by giving Himself up to death on the cross of Calvary, He established for all born again believers coming after Him the possibility of obeying the Spirit's directives rather than yielding to the tendencies of fleshly existence. When one is a believer, the natural realm no longer defines the boundaries of human capacity. Believers have the Spirit's presence to open up the entire realm of the supernatural unavailable to natural humanity.

Spirit Control Opens Up the Supernatural Dimension

More specifically, the believer has died to the natural realm of behavior, having identified with Jesus' cross in baptism, and has turned to the Holy Spirit to provide resources of a supernatural nature befitting the new life now unfolding under the Lordship of Jesus. Whether tasks are clearly extraordinary or are seemingly small and mundane, they take on a radically different character for the believer in that they now are accomplished through a different source. Thoughts and actions are not carried out through self-reliance, but initial submission to the Holy Spirit's control now fuels the believer's behavior. The believer's willing response is now to give way to the Spirit's presence and enablement in the exercise of a given thought or action.

Jesus Unique as Incarnate God and Savior

Only in this context is it possible to consider Jesus' extraordinary human life as a model for emulation. Of course, there are aspects of Jesus' life not meant to be emulated. Most notably, Jesus is God incarnate. He is the eternal Word and Son of God, made flesh for our sakes and our salvation. He is the unique Incarnation of God. No other person is both God and man. It is not possible, nor is it desirable, to emulate Jesus as the absolutely unique God/man. In addition, Jesus is the Jewish Messiah and Savior of the world. This unique mission was meant to be filled by Him and by no one else. He satisfied every requirement in the accomplishment of this unique mission, and His status as Messiah/Savior will never be altered. Jesus is the Jewish Messiah, and the Jews will never need another. Jesus is the world's Savior, and the world will never need another. Jesus' roles as God incarnate, as Jewish Messiah, and as the world's Savior are not open to imitation or emulation. He who would place himself in any such position either is insane or simply a deluded imposter.

We Emulate Jesus in His Total Submission to the Father

Yet other aspects of Jesus' life are meant for our emulation. As a Jew, Jesus not only abided by the standards of the Mosaic Law, but He went beyond mere legal compliance. He set forth the commandment to love God, neighbor and oneself as the summation of all that the Old Testament Law and prophets required of all who desire to do the will of God. He modeled for all who would come after Him what it meant to live in complete adherence to the supreme commandment of love. Jesus calls everyone to do as He did, in emulating His commitment to live out His life in personal relationship with His Father God, never breaking intimate communion and never straying into disobedience in word or deed. He is our model in His refusal to take self-initiative in anything, but was willing to respond to the initiative of His Father in carrying out the words and works that His Father purposed for Him. And in the implementation of His Father's words and works, He never failed to give place to the Holy Spirit's presence and enablement operating through Him as the Father's divine agent of implementation.

Had Jesus done the Father's works through dependence upon His inherent divinity, then He would not have qualified to be our example. We do not, nor will we ever, have a divine nature to be the source of our words and works. But if the same Holy Spirit provided by the Father for Jesus to rely upon is also provided for us, then the possibility now exists for Jesus to be our example.

Chapter 23

JESUS: FIRST GIFT, THEN EXAMPLE
Jesus as Example: Spirit Baptism

Spirit Baptism is Given for Ministry Empowerment

Spirit Baptism May Not Be Chronologically Distinct From Conversion

Clear Logical Distinction

Post Resurrection Appearance

The Disciples' Initial Reception of the Spirit

More to Accomplish After Redemption

Jesus: Baptizer in the Holy Spirit

Spirit Baptism Not Given Until the Day of Pentecost

The Commission Requires Supernatural Power

After Pentecost, Proclamation Without Power

Jesus Is Still the Baptizer

Chapter 23

JESUS: FIRST GIFT, THEN EXAMPLE
Jesus as Example: Spirit Baptism

Spirit Baptism is Given for Ministry Empowerment

The power commensurate with the fullness of Jesus' life, which is the desired norm for carrying out Jesus' commission for His church, comes with the baptism of the Holy Spirit. Spirit baptism, representing the initial filling of the Holy Spirit for the purpose of ministry empowerment, is distinguished from the reception of the Holy Spirit at conversion, when the Holy Spirit originally enters and indwells the individual. These two phases of the Spirit's work may represent different experiences in time, or they may be received simultaneously in such a way that the recipient perceives them virtually as one experience.

Spirit Baptism May Not Be Chronologically Distinct From Conversion

Cornelius and His household seem to have experienced both phases at once, for as they responded with openness to Peter's preaching of the Gospel, the Holy Spirit both converted and empowered them almost simultaneously. (Acts 10:44-48) However, in another Acts passage, the two phases are more sharply differentiated. Paul found in Ephesus a group of twelve men who had received the baptism of John the Baptist. After Paul explained to them the Gospel, they believed in Jesus and were baptized in His name. Immediately following their conversion, Paul then laid His hands upon them to receive the baptism of the Holy Spirit. The Scripture notes, "the Holy Spirit came on them, and they began speaking with tongues and prophesying." (Acts 19:6) In this case, the time differential was brief. In other cases, a much longer period of time can separate an individual's initial reception of the Holy Spirit at conversion from the experience of empowerment that comes with Spirit baptism.

Clear Logical Distinction

The two phases may or may not be set apart in time, which is a chronological distinction. But the primary consideration is not chronological but logical. According to the New Testament, a logical distinction exists between the impartation of the Spirit at conversion and the Spirit's impartation releasing empowerment. The biblical events that establish the logical distinctions of these two impartations are worthy of consideration in this context.

Post Resurrection Appearance

The conversion of humanity awaited the successful completion of Jesus' redemptive work. As Jesus' gave up unto death His human spirit on the cross, thereby completing His part in the prophetic fulfillment of redemption, the Father confirmed the atoning merit of His Son's death by raising Him from the grave to be the firstborn of a new redeemed humanity that eventually will share Jesus' resurrected and immortal humanity. For a designated period of forty days, the resurrected Jesus remained on earth revealing Himself to His disciples. A pivotal moment arrived when Jesus first encountered His disciples as a group. After greeting them, Jesus established His identity by showing them the wounds of His crucifixion.

The Disciples' Initial Reception of the Spirit

After challenging and comforting them with His words, Jesus climaxed the event by initiating a moment of impartation that would alter forever the nature of relationship between God and humanity. Jesus "breathed on them, and said to them, 'Receive the Holy Spirit.'" (John 20:22) As the Lord God first created humanity by breathing "into his (Adam's) nostrils the breath of life," (Genesis 2:7) so the resurrected Jesus recreated sinful humanity by His breath. The new birth, essential to eternal life, now became available to all who would believe. As His disciples believed on Him that day as the resurrected Lord of life, the Holy Spirit came to dwell in them forever.

Over the three year span of time the disciples spent with Jesus during His public ministry, they had enjoyed the accompaniment of the Holy Spirit often. But now, the Holy Spirit came to dwell in them permanently, as freshly born babes of the new creation. (II Corinthians 5:17) Prior to His crucifixion, Jesus had predicted this moment. "And I will ask the Father, and He will give you another Helper, that He may be with you forever; that is the Spirit of truth, whom the world cannot receive, because it does not behold Him or know Him, but you know Him because He abides with you, and **will be in you**." (John 14:16-17)

More to Accomplish After Redemption

The ushering in of the new birth undoubtedly was the single most pivotal event in human history, apart from which no human being would ever see the kingdom of God. (John 3:3) Completing the redemptive phase of His mission, the resurrected Jesus now freely offered His abundant, eternal life to all who would receive Him (John 1:12). Yet Jesus' redemptive triumph propelled Him into other phases of His purpose not possible until the new birth had become available.

Jesus: Baptizer in the Holy Spirit

The most critical function assumed by Jesus after bestowing the new birth was to fulfill His role as baptizer in the Holy Spirit. Every Gospel writer repeated the announcement by John the Baptist that the Messiah would come baptizing in the Holy Spirit. (Matthew 3:11, Mark 1:8, Luke 3:16, John 1:33) The New Testament is clear that the disciples' baptism of the Holy Spirit was a decidedly different experience than their reception of the Holy Spirit for the new birth. (John 20:22) Spirit baptism is identified as a bestowal of empowerment, equipping believers for their mission that requires supernatural enablement. After receiving their commission, the disciples were instructed by Jesus not to go forth immediately, but to go to Jerusalem to wait until they became "clothed with power from on high." (Luke 24:49)

Spirit Baptism Not Given Until the Day of Pentecost

Jesus reiterated His instructions on the day that He ascended to heaven. "And gathering them together, He commanded them not to leave Jerusalem, but to wait for what the Father had promised, 'Which,' He said, 'you heard of from Me; for John baptized with water, but you shall be baptized with the Holy Spirit not many days from now.'" He continued, "…but you shall receive power when the Holy Spirit has come upon you; and you shall be My witnesses … even to the remotest part of the earth." (Acts 1:4-5, 8) It was on the Day of Pentecost, while the disciples were in a Jerusalem room together in prayer, that they received their baptism of power. A noise from heaven like a violent, rushing wind filled the house where the disciples were waiting. Tongues of fire appeared, resting on each of the 120 members of Jesus' church. All were filled with the Holy Spirit, and they "began to speak with other tongues, as the Spirit was giving them utterance." (Acts 2:2-4) They flooded into the Jerusalem streets, continuing to articulate their unintelligible uttering. To their amazement, people from various nations were able to understand what they were saying. "... we hear them in our own tongues speaking of the mighty deeds of God." (Acts 2:11)

The Commission Requires Supernatural Power

A crowd gathered, and Peter rose to preach. He identified the supernatural experience being observed by the people as the baptism of the Holy Spirit coming from the ascended Jesus in heaven. "Therefore having been exalted to the right hand of God, and having received from the Father the promise of the Holy Spirit, He has poured forth this which you both see and hear." (Acts 2:33) Undoubtedly, nothing less than power from on high would suffice to arm the disciples to accomplish the specific task laid out by Jesus prior to His ascension. "And He said to them, 'Go into all the world and preach the gospel to all creation. He who has believed and has been baptized shall be saved; but he who has disbelieved shall be condemned. And these signs will accompany those who have believed: in My name they will cast out demons, they will speak with new tongues; they will pick up serpents, and if they drink any deadly poison, it shall not hurt them; they will lay hands on the sick, and they will recover.'" (Mark 16:15-18) Only the baptism of the Holy Spirit, conveying the Father's promise of power from on high, could open up for the disciples the miraculous dimension required by Jesus' commission.

After Pentecost, Proclamation Without Power

More than twenty centuries later, that same commission still stands as a mandate for the church. Yet most of those centuries have come and gone with generations of Christians attempting to accomplish their commission without the supernatural resources of Spirit baptism. This means that most of the church's history has found the church engaging in the evangelistic enterprise without the attesting supernatural signs of the Holy Spirit. Jesus forbade His earliest disciples to go forth in evangelization without the reception of Spirit baptism. Yet generation after generation of Christians has ventured forth in evangelism without the necessary clothing of "power from on high." They have trusted in proclamation without power, a practice with absolutely no Scriptural foundation. When the ascended Jesus poured forth the baptism in the Spirit upon His original disciples, He established a pattern of ministry intended to be followed by every succeeding generation of believers. "And they went out and preached everywhere, while the Lord worked with them, and confirmed the word by the signs that followed." (Mark 16:20)

Jesus Is Still the Baptizer

Jesus set a precedent for normative church life by assuming His role in heaven as the baptizer in the Holy Spirit. He has never relinquished that role. He is just as desirous today as He was on the Day of Pentecost to pour forth "the Father's promise" of "power from on high" upon any yielded, submitted believer. Because Jesus Himself is baptizer in the Holy Spirit, no believer should refuse to be baptized in the Spirit's power. It simply is a matter of obeying Jesus' plan for the implementation of the Great Commission in the earth.

Chapter 24

JESUS: FIRST GIFT, THEN EXAMPLE
Jesus as Example: Receiver of the Spirit

Source of Miracles
Pattern for the Church
Jesus, Both Giver and Receiver of the Holy Spirit
Modeled Complete Submission to the Spirit
Sanctification By the Spirit
Anointing of Power By the Spirit
The Spirit's Role in Jesus' Conception
Jettisoning of the Spirit
John's Insight
Developing Consciousness of the Spirit's Role
From Indwelling to Spirit Baptism
Supernatural Anointing
Frail Humanity and the Spirit
His Anointing is for the Church
Demonstration of the Spirit and Power

Chapter 24

JESUS: FIRST GIFT, THEN EXAMPLE
Jesus as Example: Receiver of the Spirit

Source of Miracles

Christian opinion for too long has falsely hoisted Jesus onto a pedestal by attributing the miracles that He performed to His divine majesty. Although Jesus deserves all of our praise for His legacy of miraculous works, we are not detracting from the praise that He is due because we recognize that His miracles were accomplished through the Spirit's anointing upon Him. That He ministered so powerfully without relying upon the resources of His own divine nature is an accomplishment of far greater magnitude than had He insisted upon utilizing His divinity.

Pattern for the Church

Furthermore, by doing miraculous works in the weakness of His humanity, while depending upon the Spirit's power, Jesus was demonstrating to His disciples how His supernatural ministry should be continued when He would no longer be physically present. If Jesus depended upon the Spirit to do miraculous works, so can we. If Christians view Jesus' supernatural works as setting a pattern for what the church is to accomplish, then faith is increased within the church to follow through with the challenge of the Great Commission. Incentive is diminished when believers face a daunting assignment with no confidence that supernatural assistance is available. To applaud Jesus for His supernatural ministry, while believing that we are powerless to do similar works, affords Him no glory.

Jesus, Both Giver and Receiver of the Holy Spirit

The same Jesus who stepped into His role as Baptizer of the Holy Spirit on the Day of Pentecost is the One who received and depended upon the Holy Spirit in His incarnate humanity. Giver of the Holy Spirit as God, Jesus also received the Holy Spirit when He became human for the sake of human redemption. Since Jesus' humanity was real, and not augmented by the attributes of His divinity, Jesus' dependence upon the presence and resources of the Holy Spirit were real. We see in the human Jesus, living in the fullness and anointing of the Holy Spirit, a pattern of life as it was meant to be lived in the condition of the Spirit's indwelling and anointing.

Modeled Complete Submission to the Spirit

Jesus lived out His incarnate life with this purpose in mind. He intended for His human existence to be a pattern for His church of what it means to live life in complete submission and compliance with the operations of the Holy Spirit. The apostle John understood the relevance of Jesus' human life for the church. "… as He is, so also are we in this world." (I John 4:17) This is true, both in sanctification and in empowerment.

Sanctification By the Spirit

Jesus kept Himself separated from sin, not by means of inherent holiness, but by yielding completely to the Spirit's control. The Spirit's sanctifying presence is always available to minister to humanity the standards of righteousness. Jesus' personal holiness was maintained on that basis. Jesus stated in John's Gospel, "And for their sakes I sanctify Myself, that they themselves also may be sanctified in truth." (John 17:19)

Anointing of Power By the Spirit

Furthermore, Jesus' anointing of power exemplified in His public ministry was not derived from His inherent divinity, but from His total yieldedness to the Spirit's anointing. On various occasions, Jesus gave authority and power to His disciples to work miracles, even before the Spirit was released to indwell them permanently. (e.g., Luke 9:1-2) He was preparing them for what would come later, after their baptism in the Holy Spirit, when their lives and ministries would be characterized by the supernatural gifts, signs and wonders of the Spirit. Jesus taught His disciples to expect a lifestyle of the Spirit's anointing. "Truly, truly, I say to you, he who believes in Me, the works that I do shall he do also; and greater works than these shall he do; because I go to the Father." (John 14:12) Jesus fully intended that His life of sanctification and power be reproduced by those coming after Him, for the Spirit that filled His humanity would also fill them.

The solid Scriptural foundation for asserting that Jesus' power was derived from the Holy Spirit and not from His inherent divinity deserves further consideration. Traditionally, scholars have skewed the Scriptural perspective of the Spirit's major role in Jesus' life and ministry because of their exaggerated emphasis upon Jesus' divinity. Excessively defensive in response to liberal trends attempting to rob Jesus of His divinity, scholars have failed to embrace the full implications of the doctrine of the Incarnation.

The Spirit's Role in Jesus' Conception

Interestingly, these scholars see no threat in recognizing the Spirit's significant place in Jesus' origins. They view Jesus' unique origin to be the result of His miraculous conception in the womb of Mary by the seed of the Holy Spirit. As recorded by Luke, the angel Gabriel revealed to Mary how Jesus would be conceived. "'And behold, you will conceive in your womb, and bear a son, and you shall name Him Jesus.' ...And Mary said to the angel, 'How can this be, since I am a virgin?' And the angel answered and said to her, 'The Holy Spirit will come upon you, and the power of the Most High will overshadow you; and for that reason the holy offspring shall be called the Son of God.'" (Luke 1:31, 34-35) By placing weight upon the Spirit's role in Jesus' miraculous conception, these scholars are reinforcing Jesus' divine identity. If He was conceived by the Holy Spirit, rather than through natural origins, Jesus' preexistence as God's eternal Son can be defended.

Jettisoning of the Spirit

Once Jesus' supernatural conception is established, these scholars are ready to jettison the Spirit's role in Jesus' sanctification and empowerment, attributing sole responsibility to His inherent divinity. The Scriptural record does not corroborate this interpretation. Wrongly crediting works accomplished through the Spirit's enablement to the inherent power of Jesus' divinity leads to faulty Christological and theological conclusions that have far reaching consequences for Christian living.

John's Insight

Much error may have been avoided had Christian scholarship faithfully interpreted the apostle John's pivotal passage revealing the Father's abundant provision of the Spirit bestowed upon Jesus. Not only had Jesus been born uniquely by the Spirit's conception in His mother Mary, but, as John appropriately indicated, Jesus was endowed with the Spirit's fullness from His conception onwards.[50] (John 3:34-35) Jesus was provided with the full measure of the

Holy Spirit at His conception in His mother's womb, not as a luxury, but of absolute necessity. The reality of His Incarnation required that Jesus' frail, mortal humanity be sustained by the Spirit's sanctifying, empowering presence.

Developing Consciousness of the Spirit's Role

Since the incarnate Jesus did not have the benefit of His omniscient divinity, He was required to develop consciousness of His messianic identity and purpose. His growth and learning was according to patterns of human development. "The Child continued to grow and become strong, increasing in wisdom; and the grace of God was upon Him... And Jesus kept increasing in wisdom and stature, and in favor with God and men." (Luke 2:40, 52) Jesus would have become aware of the prominent place of the Spirit in His life by recognizing that key messianic passages in the Old Testament were meant to be fulfilled by Him. Isaiah prophetically foretold that Jehovah God would put His Spirit upon the Messiah. "Behold, My Servant, whom I uphold; My chosen one in whom My soul delights. I have put My Spirit upon Him; He will bring forth justice to the nations." (Isaiah 42:1) In Matthew's Gospel, this specific prophecy is appropriated personally by Jesus, indicating that He knew that the Spirit was upon Him. "But Jesus, … healed them all, and warned them not to tell who He was. This was to fulfill what was spoken through Isaiah the prophet: 'BEHOLD, MY SERVANT WHOM I HAVE CHOSEN; MY BELOVED IN WHOM MY SOUL is WELL-PLEASED; I WILL PUT MY SPIRIT UPON HIM, AND HE SHALL PROCLAIM JUSTICE TO THE GENTILES.'" (Matthew 12:15-18)

Another prominent prophetic passage from Isaiah figured directly in the formation of Jesus' self-understanding. "The Spirit of the Lord GOD is upon me, because the LORD has anointed me to bring good news to the afflicted; He has sent me to bind up the brokenhearted, to proclaim liberty to captives and freedom to prisoners;" (Isaiah 61:1) Jesus chose the correct moment while reading this passage in the synagogue in His hometown of Nazareth to disclose publicly that He was the anointed One to whom Isaiah was referring. "He entered the synagogue on the Sabbath, and stood up to read. And the book of the prophet Isaiah was handed to Him. And He opened the book and found the place where it was written, 'THE SPIRIT OF THE LORD IS UPON ME, BECAUSE HE ANOINTED ME TO PREACH THE GOSPEL TO THE POOR. HE HAS SENT ME TO PROCLAIM RELEASE TO THE CAPTIVES,' … And He closed the book, gave it back to the attendant and sat down; and the eyes of all in the synagogue were fixed on Him. And He began to say to them, 'Today this Scripture has been fulfilled in your hearing.'" (Luke 4:16-21) Jesus seized this opportunity to declare publicly, not only that He was aware that the Spirit's anointing would rest upon the Messiah, but that He Himself was that very Messiah.

From Indwelling to Spirit Baptism

Timing was extremely important in the providential unfolding of the phases of Jesus' messianic purpose. For instance, Jesus had been filled with the Spirit while in the womb of his mother. Yet He waited until He was thirty years of age, on the occasion of His water baptism by John the Baptist, to appropriate the supernatural power that would accompany His public ministry. Prior to that point, we are not aware of any miracles performed by Jesus. The Spirit's anointing of power that characterized the three years of His public ministry was not manifested until His water baptism. This division of the Spirit's operations in Jesus would have implications for the redeemed company coming after Him. 1) The Spirit's entrance and fullness established in Jesus' life from His conception in the womb is equated with the experience of the new birth in the life of the Christian. The Spirit's sanctifying presence and influence in Jesus' humanity was initiated at His conception. Likewise, the Spirit takes the commanding role in the life of the believer at the moment of conversion. 2) Jesus needed the Spirit's supernatural anointing to confirm His proclamation of the coming of God's kingdom when He began His public ministry. Jesus' anointing corresponds with the occasion of Spirit baptism in the believer's life, releasing supernatural signs and wonders to confirm the preaching of the Gospel to every nation under heaven. Every Christian has some role in the fulfillment of the Great Commission. The Spirit's indwelling occurring at the moment of conversion is not enough to meet the demands of Jesus' mandate. Spirit baptism is the subsequent step after conversion to equip every believer with the supernatural resources needed to fulfill their task.

Supernatural Anointing

Nowhere in the New Testament do we see Jesus asserting His divinity in the carrying out of His mission. Instead, through the years of His public ministry, Jesus yielded fully to His Father's provision of the Holy Spirit. The influence of divinity never left Him, yet the source of supernatural power that He ever relied upon was the Holy Spirit. A statement in Peter's sermon to the Gentiles, recorded by Luke, leaves no question as to the source of Jesus' power. "You know of Jesus of Nazareth, how God anointed Him with the Holy Spirit and with power, and how He went about doing good and healing all who were oppressed by the devil, for God was with Him." (Acts 10:38)

Frail Humanity and the Spirit

Jesus continually required supernatural power in overcoming Satan's strategies, and in releasing people from Satan's bondage. Yet the ultimate release, eternal redemption for Adam's race, could not be won by an exclusively divine being. Only incarnate divinity, the Second Adam, could reverse the curse by sinless obedience and atoning sacrifice. His divinity held in check, Jesus won by

His human reliance upon the Holy Spirit. The Father's power was manifest in His victory, but not through His inherent resources as God's Son. Jesus won in frail, mortal humanity, ever yielding to the control of the Holy Spirit made available to Him. Luke registers the pervasive influence exercised by the Holy Spirit upon the incarnate Jesus. "Jesus, full of the Holy Spirit, returned from the Jordan and was led around by the Spirit in the wilderness ..." "And Jesus returned to Galilee in the power of the Spirit, and news about Him spread through all the surrounding district." (Luke 4:1, 14) In another reference, Matthew reveals the source of His successful assault against Satan's kingdom. "But if I cast out demons by the Spirit of God, then the kingdom of God has come upon you." (Matthew 12:28)

His Anointing is for the Church

The New Testament witness is sufficiently clear to indicate that the source of power operative in Jesus is the same source of power dispensed by Jesus upon His church on the Day of Pentecost. The source of power received by Jesus in His incarnate humanity is the same source of power into which He baptized His church as He equipped His believers with the power to carry out the Great Commission. The source of anointing exemplified in His public ministry is intended to be operative in the lives of all who identify with His name. As Jesus went about the land proclaiming the kingdom of God, He needed the accompaniment and confirmation of the Spirit's gifts, signs and wonders. Those same gifts, signs and wonders also are needed as Jesus' church continues to proclaim the Gospel to a needy world.

In summation, Jesus experienced phases of the Spirit's presence and power in His own humanity in order to prepare the way for the coming operations of the Spirit in the lives of believers. Had Jesus found the source of power for ministry in His own divine nature, His own people would have been powerless in life and ministry, for only Jesus could claim natural divinity as God's only Son. Therefore, Jesus' freely relinquished the privileges of His divinity and humbly submitted to the lowly conditions of Adam's estate for the sake of His church. Jesus relied upon the only source of power made available to Him, the Father's impartation of the Holy Spirit. Allowing His humanity to become a channel for the Spirit's power, Jesus obediently fulfilled His purpose by bringing salvation to Adam's race.

Demonstration of the Spirit and Power

Jesus' ministry of healing, deliverance and reconciliation among the people set a precedent for the church coming after Him. As He had been sent by the Father, He sent forth His church to transmit His Gospel to all nations. As the ascended Lord, the source of His power now could be imparted to them. On the Day of Pentecost, Jesus baptized His church with the same anointing of the Spirit's presence He had known for three years of public ministry. Although weak in His flesh, Jesus had healed the sick, opened the eyes of the blind, loosed the tongues of the dumb, driven demons from the oppressed, and even raised the dead to life. This unparalleled expression of the supernatural was not intended by Jesus to be simply an historical legacy, but a pattern of ministry duplicated by His church where ever His name and Spirit are present. The baptism of the Spirit imparted by Jesus upon the early church was never rescinded, but represents a continuous reservoir of spiritual life and power available to every generation of believers who will partake. Jesus never intended His Gospel to be transmitted in word only, but conveyed to a needy world in demonstration of the Spirit and power. Our role is not to imitate His actions as we remember His deeds, but to participate with Him as He continues to minister to people in the mighty power of the Spirit. Willing vessels free to be used are those submitted to the baptism of the Holy Spirit. No more glorious occupation has ever graced God's children than to be a habitation of the Holy Spirit.

Chapter 25

JESUS: FIRST GIFT, THEN EXAMPLE
Jesus as Example: Empowerment

New Testament Emphasis

Lacking Empowerment

Precise Strategy

Dual Operations of the Spirit

Spirit Baptism is a Logically Distinct Experience

The Spirit's Distinct Workings in Jesus' Incarnate Life

Jesus' Conception is our New Birth; His Anointing is our Spirit Baptism

One Coming, but Two Operations of the Spirit

Spirit Baptism Benefits Church as well as World

Jesus' Strategy: the Gift of Tongues for Every Believer

The Pattern from Paul's Ministry

Tongues Given for Self-edification

Tongues is Not a Spiritual Seizure

Paul Views Tongues as a Form of Prayer

Restraint in the Assembly

Human Volition in the Initial Reception
Worship That Transcends and Humbles the Intellect
Taming the Tongue
Today's Mandate

Chapter 25

JESUS: FIRST GIFT, THEN EXAMPLE
Jesus as Example: Empowerment

New Testament Emphasis

The role of Jesus as Baptizer in the Holy Spirit holds a place of emphasis in the New Testament that is not maintained consistently in Christian history. John the Baptist heralded Jesus as the One who had come to baptize the people in the Holy Spirit and fire, a function implemented only after Jesus had become the risen, ascended Lord. The first official act fulfilled by Jesus after His ascension was to discharge His role as Baptizer in the Holy Spirit. The purpose of Spirit baptism was not to impart the Spirit to the unconverted. Spirit baptism was an additional phase of impartation. His church needed supernatural endowments of power to take the Gospel to the uttermost parts of the earth. Mere human ability and ingenuity would not be sufficient. Jesus never intended for ministry to be attempted without the supernatural provision of the Spirit's baptism.

Lacking Empowerment

Jesus' disciples would seem to have been prepared for ministry prior to His ascension. After all, they had passed through some major experiences since Jesus' death on the cross. First, the disciples had regathered following news of Jesus' resurrection. Then their personal encounter with the risen Christ occurred. In that event, they received the Holy Spirit, becoming new born members of His church.[51] Following their conversion and establishment as His church, they received His commission to take the Gospel to the nations of the world. Yet in spite of the passage of these events, they were not ready to undertake their ministry. Jesus' strategy had not been revealed in full.

While in the company of His church on the day of His ascension, Jesus gave them clear instructions to return to Jerusalem to pray and wait for the Father's promise of Spirit baptism to come upon them. His church obeyed. Within a few days, while the church was gathered in prayer on the Day of Pentecost, the climactic event took place. Every member of the church received the baptism of the Holy Spirit. That very day, the church took to the streets to preach the Gospel to the various people groups assembled in Jerusalem. The power from on high had been sent from Jesus above, equipping believers with supernatural gifts, signs and wonders to accompany their ministry to others.

Precise Strategy

These critical events in the life of Jesus reveal a precise strategy for His ongoing ministry through His church. Certain logical conclusions may be ventured as we examine His strategy. It seems clear that Jesus logically separated the Spirit's work of regeneration from the Spirit's work of empowerment. In the first distinct work of the Spirit in the individual, the Spirit converts the recipient into a new creation inhabited by the Holy Spirit. In the second distinct work, the Spirit overflows the new believer with power, equipping the recipient with supernatural gifts for ministry. Jesus is unequivocal in His strategy to separate logically these distinct operations of the Holy Spirit.

Dual Operations of the Spirit

Because the Spirit's dual operations target different functions, it is more common for these experiences to be separated chronologically. Both experiences usually result in radical change for the individual, but different in kind. The Spirit's work of conversion transforms the individual from a life of self-centeredness and separation from God into an intimate relationship with God that radically alters motives and perceptions. With an entirely new worldview coming into focus, the new believer often is not yet aware of the need to receive the Spirit's power for ministry.

Spirit Baptism is a Logically Distinct Experience

Following the New Testament pattern, as the believer's new identity becomes solidified, the responsibility to minister the Gospel to others should come into focus. Jesus' strategy recognizes the absolute necessity of equipping the believer in the Spirit's supernatural power before venturing into ministry. That additional impartation of the Spirit's power beyond conversion is the baptism of the Holy Spirit. This impartation makes available to the believer a variety of supernatural resources both for personal edification, for ministry to fellow believers, and ministry to persons who have yet to receive Christ. Therefore, because the Spirit's workings in conversion are quite distinct from the Spirit's endowment of power, it is common for believers to experience Spirit baptism as a chronologically separate event from conversion, although a separation in time is not mandatory.[52] Critical to this discussion, however, is the requirement to adhere to Jesus' complete strategy of allowing for two logically distinct operations of the Spirit. To stop at conversion, without extending the mandate of Christ to receive the baptism of the Holy Spirit, results in a deficient Christian experience and church life. Jesus wants the ministry of His church in the earth to be the product of the miraculous power of God. He does not want His church to represent simply the best of human ingenuity and effort, but to reveal the glory and power of God.

The Spirit's Distinct Workings in Jesus' Incarnate Life

When Jesus' pattern of the Spirit's operations is understood, other aspects of the Spirit's work as revealed in the New Testament follow this logical development. Jesus' personal life fits the pattern. We know that at Jesus' conception in the womb of His mother, the Spirit came to inhabit Him and to assist Him to do the will of His heavenly Father. For thirty years, the Spirit's sanctifying presence enabled Jesus to live without sin, even though His humanity was the frail, finite human nature common to Adam's race. Yet when the appointed time arrived for Jesus' to launch out in public ministry, He was visited with a special anointing of the Spirit on the occasion of His baptism at the hands of John the Baptist. We have no record of Jesus preaching or performing miracles until after this special anointing of the Spirit's power.

Jesus' Conception is our New Birth; His Anointing is our Spirit Baptism

Two distinct operations of the Spirit in Jesus' life provide for us a clearer understanding of the pattern of the Spirit's work in the believer. Jesus' conception is analogous to the conversion of the believer, when the Spirit is received to regenerate and sanctify the individual. Yet Jesus gave His church a commission to fulfill, to make disciples of the nations of the world. The Spirit's supernatural power is needed for such a task. The baptism of the Spirit clothes the believer with power from on high, equipping each member with giftings of the Spirit that are miraculous in nature. Spirit baptism for the believer is equated with the descent of the Spirit upon Jesus at His baptism, anointing Him with the Spirit's miraculous power to prepare Him to embark upon His public ministry.

One Coming, but Two Operations of the Spirit

These two distinct workings of the Spirit are not to be understood as receiving the Holy Spirit twice. Jesus was given the Holy Spirit only once, at the moment of conception. From that point forward, Jesus always had the presence of the Holy Spirit within Him. Yet at His baptism, He was visited with an anointing of that same Holy Spirit, enabling Him to utilize supernatural giftings in the exercise of His ministry to people. Believers also receive the Holy Spirit only once, when the Spirit comes to bring conversion. Yet at Spirit baptism, believers are activated by the Spirit's anointing. They are thus equipped to go forth in ministry to people with supernatural giftings of the Spirit.

Spirit Baptism Benefits Church as well as World

Not only an unconverted world benefits from the church's baptism in the Spirit, but the individual members receive ministry from the charismata imparted to the congregation. When the local church is assembled together, individuals are given a variety of gifts to benefit one another. Each member is not given all the gifts, so that individuals can learn to depend upon each other as the Spirit distributes diverse giftings throughout the membership. Special mention, however, should be made in reference to the gift of tongues. Like other spiritual manifestations, tongues is meant to be expressed only through a few individuals when the local assembly is gathered together. Tongues messages are to be spoken sparingly, and only when members are present who exercise the gift of interpretation of tongues that must accompany the gift of tongues in a public gathering.

Jesus' Strategy: the Gift of Tongues for Every Believer

The gift of speaking in tongues is exceptional, however, in that it is a gift given to every Christian who receives the baptism in the Holy Spirit. That is because speaking in tongues functions first in the believer's experience as an initial sign of the reception of the Spirit's baptism. The Acts of the Apostles records that all 120 believers assembled in the Upper Room on the Day of Pentecost spoke in tongues as the sign that the baptism in the Holy Spirit had been released from heaven through Jesus' impartation. On another significant occasion, as Peter was assigned to preach to Cornelius' household, the first expansion of the Gospel to non-Jewish peoples, the Spirit's baptism fell upon every single family member at once while Peter was delivering his sermon. Peter later reported to the Jerusalem church that he had confidence that the Gentiles in Cornelius' house truly had been baptized in the Holy Spirit, because they were given the same gift of tongues that had been visited upon the original disciples on the Day of Pentecost. (Acts 11:15-18) Another event is recorded in the Acts of the Apostles that reveals Spirit baptism being received, with tongues speech being expressed by every recipient. Paul encountered twelve Ephesians, ministered the Gospel to them, baptized them in water, and laid hands upon them to receive Spirit baptism. "… the Holy Spirit came upon them, and they began speaking with tongues and prophesying." (Acts 19:6) In conclusion, since the Great Commission to communicate the Gospel to a lost world is a mandate for every believer, and ministry necessitates the equipping of power from on high through Spirit baptism, it follows that every believer needs the baptism in the Holy Spirit. Since the gift of tongues functions initially in the believer's experience as the sign that Spirit baptism has been received, it is logical to infer that Jesus strategically planned for every believer to receive the gift of tongues.

The Pattern from Paul's Ministry

Further evidence from the New Testament may be garnered from Paul's first letter to the Corinthians. His chief concern in chapter fourteen is to restore order to an unruly congregation, who had fallen into the practice of allowing tongues speech to be voiced too frequently, and without following those utterances with accompanying interpretations of the tongues messages. While providing necessary correction, Paul also reveals important insights concerning tongues as a gift of the Spirit. Paul makes two statements that indicate the high value that he personally places on this gift, while expressing his desire that all believers possess the gift. "I thank God I speak in tongues more than you all;" (verse 18) and "I wish that you all spoke in tongues, ..." (verse 5) Were it not the will of God for all to speak with other tongues, it would not be likely that Paul would state in Scripture his desire for that occurrence.

Tongues Given for Self-edification

Another statement lends further credence to this conclusion. Prior to expressing his desire that all believers speak in tongues, Paul notes, that "one who speaks in a tongue edifies himself." (verse 4) A previous verse augments the significance of that statement. "For one who speaks in a tongue does not speak to men, but to God; for no one understands, but in his spirit he speaks mysteries." (verse 2) It may be inferred from these statements that speaking in tongues is a form of personal prayer that provides spiritual benefit for the speaker. Would it be conceivable that God would play favorites by providing a special prayer language as a means of self-edification only to select members of His church, rather than offering to each member of His church the privilege of utilizing this special language of prayer? After identifying tongues as a form of prayer that builds up the believer, Paul follows by asserting that he desires for every believer to experience this gift.

Tongues is Not a Spiritual Seizure

It is relevant to note in this context that Paul emphasizes the responsibility of the individual believer to exercise self-control in the expression of the gift of tongues. Throughout Christian history, persons have mistakenly believed that tongues was an ecstatic, emotionally-incited experience, seizing the recipient's vocal chords and gushing forth with strange utterances while the speaker remains in a trance-like state. While some historical accounts seem to conform to such a scenario, this description fails to align with the definitive New Testament explanation providing detailed insight as to how this gift is expected to operate in a Scriptural manner.

Paul Views Tongues as a Form of Prayer

Paul makes it unquestionably clear that tongues is simply a form of prayer that is to be uttered in essentially the same manner as one would pray with understanding. He says, "For if I pray in a tongue, my spirit prays, but my mind is unfruitful." (verse 14) Speaking in tongues is praying, but without intellectual comprehension of the content of the prayer. He goes on to say, "What is the outcome then? I shall pray with the spirit and I shall pray with the mind also; I shall sing with the spirit and I shall sing with the mind also." (verse 15) Paul is saying that the same kind of choice is involved for the believer, whether he or she prays with the spirit (speaking in tongues) or prays with the mind (with the understanding). He notes that the same is true also when one sings, whether in the spirit (with tongues) or with the mind (with understanding). Whether praying or singing in tongues, the believer is expected by Paul to exercise the same kind of control as is practiced when one prays or sings with understanding.

Restraint in the Assembly

Furthermore, Paul addresses the case when the believer is in the public assembly of the local church, with no one to interpret his or her tongues speech. He instructs for the believer to remain publicly silent, "and let him speak to himself and to God." (verse 28) It is obvious that if tongues speech is an uncontrollable utterance, a "spiritual seizure" of some sort, then the tongues speaker would be without the power to refrain from exercising the gift when the urge was present, whether in public or in private. Yet Paul instructs that when the tongues speaker knows that one with the gift of interpretation is not present in the assembly, the speaker is to maintain self-control, and pray in tongues only in a private setting.

Human Volition in the Initial Reception

Even when the believer is speaking in tongues for the very first time in the experience of Spirit baptism, the utterance requires the consent of the speaker to vocalize syllables emerging from deep within his/her spirit. When the early church first experienced Spirit baptism on the Day of Pentecost, they "began to speak with other tongues as the Spirit was giving them utterance." (Acts 2:4) It should be noted that the Holy Spirit within them was giving them unintelligible syllables for them to utter, but the act of speaking was their responsibility and under their control. The Spirit gave the utterance, but they did the speaking.

Worship That Transcends and Humbles the Intellect

We have seen that tongues is a form of prayer. More specifically, tongues is an expression of worship so utterly pure and primordial that its meaning transcends conceptual comprehension. As the speaker yields consent to voice this deep form of praise to God, the indwelling Holy Spirit infuses the entire being of the speaker with supernatural power. The utterances are spoken as an act of faith, a total surrender of the voice and tongue to syllables unknown to the intellect. The pride of human intelligence must bow in submission to incomprehensible babblings believed to be the humble articulations of a completely yielded vessel.

Taming the Tongue

James reveals that the person who pleases God perfectly is able to control the tongue. The one who can control the tongue can control all of his actions. (James 3:2) Yet he laments that "no one can tame the tongue; it is a restless evil and full of deadly poison." (verse 8) When the pride of godless humanity in early civilization overstepped permitted boundaries, and the people designed a city with a tower that they intended to reach to heaven (Tower of Babel), God stepped in to put a stop to their prideful ambition. They had been one people with the same language. God said, "Come, let Us go down and there confuse their language, that they may not understand one another's speech." (Genesis 11:7) After their language was confused, they were scattered abroad over the face of the earth, and they stopped building the city. (verses 8-9) How fitting that when God finished His redemptive work in Jesus Christ, He gave His redeemed community a "new tongue," (Mark 16:17) a universal language in the Holy Spirit to unite His people in the presence and power of Jesus Christ!

Today's Mandate

Jesus and Paul have revealed a comprehensive pattern for individual and corporate experience that must be heeded if normative Christian living is to occur. Jesus' role as Spirit baptizer must be heeded, entreating every believer with the mandate to receive the supernatural impartation of Spirit baptism as a necessary preparation for effective Christian life and ministry. Every believer is responsible for receiving the resources Jesus imparts in Spirit baptism self-edification, corporate participation and ministry penetration. Speaking in tongues is not an optional gift accompanying Spirit baptism, but is both an initial sign of the baptism's reception, as well as a new language of prayer bringing personal edification that ignites participation in the supernatural dimension on a continuous basis. Like praying in the language of one's understanding, praying in the language of the Spirit is a controlled action free to occur whenever the speaker is willing. When contemporary Christianity rediscovers and implements the biblical pattern concerning Jesus as Baptizer in the Holy Spirit and the Pauline revelation concerning speaking in tongues, revival will ignite the church with lasting reformation looming on the horizon.

Chapter 26

JESUS: FIRST GIFT, THEN EXAMPLE
Jesus as Example: Speaking in Tongues

Jesus' Master Plan
New Testament Pattern
After the Apostolic Era
Significance of Tongues Lost
Monastic Preservation
The Church Fathers and Beyond
Protestestantism and Cessationism
George Fox and the Quakers
The Camisards
Jesuits and Jansenists
Wesley and Subsequence
Mother Ann Lee and the Shakers
Edward Irving and the British Revival
The Catholic Apostolic Church
The New Apostolic Church
Irving's Contributions Not Perpetuated

Irving's Christological Foundations
Phoebe Palmer and American Methodism
The Holiness Movement
Benjamin Irwin and the Fire-Baptized Holiness Church
Charles Parham and Spirit Baptism
The Emergence of William Seymour
Los Angeles Stirrings
The Azusa Street Revival
Forgotten Azusa Street Factors
Factors Carried into the Pentecostal Movement
Pentecostal Denominations
"Volitional tongues" Not Yet Recovered
The Charismatic Movement
Charismatics Receptive to "Volitional Tongues"
Value of "Volitional Tongues"
A Truth for All Christians
The Pauline Context
I Corinthians 14
"Third Wave" Neo-charismatics
Contemporary Independents
Final Test

Chapter 26

JESUS: FIRST GIFT, THEN EXAMPLE
Jesus as Example: Speaking in Tongues

Jesus' Master Plan

Jesus was no stranger to the experience of speaking in tongues. He announced to His followers as He was preparing them for their future mission that one of the signs to be expected among new converts would be that "they will speak with new tongues." (Mark 16:17) After completing His redemptive work and ascending to heaven, Jesus as Baptizer in the Holy Spirit poured forth upon His church the anointing of the Spirit to empower them for their mission. As this baptism descended upon the faithful, the first noticeable sign of their reception was the experience of speaking in tongues.[53] It is highly improbable that the reigning Lord responsible for this infilling would have been surprised at the manifestation of tongues visited upon the upper room disciples on that momentous day. Especially, in view of the fact that the tongues visitation on the Day of Pentecost was not just a one time event, but became a usual occurrence whenever believers were baptized in the Spirit,[54] adds to the probability that tongues speech from the start had been a part of Jesus' master plan to equip His people with power for life and ministry.

New Testament Pattern

Tongues speech functioned in the New Testament era both as an initial sign of the Spirit's empowerment and as a gift of worshipful utterance both for personal and corporate edification. We believe that Jesus established this pattern for His people following His resurrection, and intended for these multiple functions of tongues to constitute the normative behavior for His church after His ascension to heaven. Paul's first letter to the Corinthian church reveals that the earliest Christians adhered to Jesus' pattern. Paul reveals further insight on the nature of the gift of tongues as prayerful utterance transcending the intellect and subject to the speaker's control.[55] After the biblical era, however, little evidence exists that the pattern established by Jesus and recorded in Paul's writings continued in the church's doctrine and practice. Not only was tongues as the initial evidence of Spirit baptism lost to the body of Christ in early development, but tongues as a gift of the Spirit suffered misunderstanding and disintegration.

After the Apostolic Era

Soon after the apostolic era, the church no longer viewed Spirit baptism as a necessary stage of empowerment to prepare the believer for ministry, but merely co-opted the terminology as another way of speaking about the Spirit's coming at conversion. Spirit baptism was relegated to the convert's experience of receiving the Holy Spirit following the rite of water baptism.[56] The majority of initiates coming into the church in this early period were adult converts, although infants of church members were also baptized.

Water baptism was the central event of Christian initiation. Following this rite, hands were laid upon the recipient, whether adult or infant, with the expectation of the Spirit's coming. Adults at times would receive manifestations of the Spirit during these occasions. With infants, the church recognized the possibility that spiritual manifestations could occur during a future stage in life. The delay between water baptism and later manifestations, however, did not imply that the manifestation stage was to be viewed as a separate phase of the Spirit's work. The time of manifestation was seen to be an extension of the initial coming of the Spirit. Later manifestations were understood theologically as two parts of one event, i.e., the event of Christian initiation. The notion of a separate, subsequent experience of Spirit baptism for the purpose of ministry empowerment was no longer recognized.

Significance of Tongues Lost

With Spirit baptism no longer viewed as a separate, subsequent experience from conversion, tongues lost its significant function as a sign of initial reception. Tongues became only one of several spiritual manifestations that could occur during the rite of water baptism. For three centuries, spiritual manifestations continued to occur sporadically in local congregations, but tongues was not expected to be integral to the experience of every Christian. Furthermore, as the bishops of the churches took on added responsibilities and roles formerly shared by the laity, the ministry of the gifts of the Spirit easily became the exclusive function of church leadership. By the fourth century, in most sectors, even the initiation rite of laying hands upon the newly baptized for Spiritual impartation became purely ritualistic. The vast majority of believers no longer experienced or even expected to be endowed with supernatural power or gifted with supernatural manifestations.

Monastic Preservation

Manifestations of the Spirit never disappeared from Christendom, but shifted mostly to the monastic context. Through the Middle Ages and into the Scholastic Era, the Spirit's signs and gifts came to be seen as rewards for extraordinary ascetic discipline, reserved for masters of mystical achievement. Manifestations appeared only in connection with exceptional individuals as "evidence of extreme piety."[57]

The Church Fathers and Beyond

The doctrine and experience of tongues speech gained only limited mention throughout the era of the Church Fathers. Tertullian (160-220) lauded the vitality of the churches under his influence by noting an abundance of Spiritual manifestations, including the gift of tongues and interpretation of tongues. Novatian (d. 250) spoke of the presence of tongues and other charismata among contemporary churches in his time. Hilary of Poitiers (315-367) defended the orthodoxy of the gifts of tongues and interpretation of tongues in the fourth century. Pachomius (290-346), instrumental in the founding of communal monasticism, on a particular occasion after he had prayed for three hours, is said to have been able to converse with a visitor in Latin, although he never learned the language.

After a lengthy absence in which the practice of speaking in tongues virtually disappeared from the literature of the church, evidence of the gift reappeared among certain notable monastic figures after the dawning of the next millennium. Hildegard of Bingen (1098-1179), Dominic (1170- 1221), Anthony of Padua (1195-1231) and Clare of Montefalco (1268-1308) are among those who evidenced this gift, although other manifestations of the Spirit such as healing often attracted more attention.

Protestestantism and Cessationism

With the advent of Protestantism in the sixteenth century, miraculous manifestations were not emphasized. The chief Reformers, Luther, Zwingli and Calvin rejected the legacy of Catholic miracles, particularly as they were used to substantiate Roman dogma. Consequently, Protestantism became identified with the cessationist theory of miracles. In reaction to Catholic miracles that seemed to be outside Biblical perimeters, most Protestants reasoned that miracles were confined to the New Testament era, when the fledgling Gospel needed supernatural confirmation in order to gain initial acceptance. Protestants placed miracles on the periphery of Christianity, so that they were viewed to be expendable as the Gospel gained a measure of permanence in the world. How ironic it is that the personal experience of Protestantism's founder, Martin Luther, represented an obvious contradiction to the cessationist theory. He sought and received a number of notable healing miracles in the course of his life and ministry. The Protestant movement, however, failed to follow Luther's lead.

George Fox and the Quakers

A significant exception to Protestant cessationism was George Fox (1624-1691), British founder of the Society of Friends. A reactionary movement to the rigid religious uniformity of seventeenth century Anglicanism, the "Quakers" as they were called, viewed miracles to be integral to the intensely personal version of Christianity that they espoused. Fox viewed the wellspring of supernatural manifestations visited upon his ministry as a recovery of the original Pentecost. "...we received often the pouring down of the spirit upon us, and the gift of God's holy eternal spirit as in the days of old, and our hearts were made glad, and our tongues loosed, and our mouths opened, and we spake with new tongues, as the Lord gave us utterance, and as his spirit led us, which was poured down upon us, on sons and daughters."[58] Fox acknowledged the necessity of the Spirit's empowerment upon his church, and viewed tongues as a sign of this anointing. Other aspects of the doctrine and practice of the Society of Friends lacked Biblical foundations, however, and did not sustain widespread influence. Also, Fox's early emphasis upon supernatural manifestations was not maintained within the Quaker tradition.

The Camisards

Another fringe group kept miracles alive within Protestantism in the eighteenth century. As the persecution of the Protestants in Catholic France resurfaced in the early 1700's, the Huguenots split into two factions. One of those groups, the Camisards (known also as the Prophets of the Cevennes Mountains) claimed to be inspired directly by the Holy Spirit. Ecstatic utterances characterized the movement, and children as well as adults were among the "gifted." Utterances included tongues and interpretation of tongues, although prophetic utterances predominated. Camisards who fled to England were known as French Prophets. Extremist practices surfaced among the French Prophets, as children were organized into strict training programs and instructed in the ways of prophecy. In some instances, children three years of age and younger were said to have been used for such purposes.

Jesuits and Jansenists

Within Catholicism after the Reformation, evidence of the miraculous continued to be found, mostly in monastic and missionary settings. Jesuit founder Ignatius Loyola (1491-1556) was reported to have received visions that altered the course of his life. His disciple Francis Xavier (1506-1552) was known to have experienced significant miracles as he labored in distant Japan and the West Indies spreading the Jesuit message. Francis depended upon the gift of tongues on several occasions to preach the Gospel to people groups whose language he had never learned. Jansenism, a radical Augustinian movement, sprang up in the mid-seventeenth century Catholicism. The papacy dealt severely with this group, whose doctrinal sympathies were judged by Rome to be too Calvinistic. The Jansenists were known for their signs and wonders, spiritual dancing, healings, and prophetic utterances. Some reportedly spoke in tongues.

Wesley and Subsequence

A doctrinal development in eighteenth century English Protestantism contributed by John Wesley (1703-1791) set a precedent for later Pentecostals to advocate that Spirit baptism is a distinct, subsequent experience from conversion. Wesley established the Methodist movement within Anglicanism, an organization that became an independent Protestant denomination after his death. He taught that each Christian should experience a second work of grace beyond conversion, which he identified to be sanctification. Although Wesley emphasized sanctification as a process, spanning the lifetime of the believer, he ventured that this second phase of the Spirit's work often was inaugurated instantaneously.

Successors of the Wesleyan tradition built upon this foundation to introduce a doctrine of subsequence, leading ultimately to the development of Pentecostalism in the American context. Wesley also rejected the cessationist theory typical of Protestantism. He saw no Scriptural basis for the cessation of supernatural gifts of the Spirit, and personally reported an experience of miraculous healing when beset by a serious illness. Yet without question the emphasis of Wesley's doctrine and practice rested on the side of the fruit of the Spirit and the virtues of holiness rather than upon the gifts of the Spirit and supernatural power.

Mother Ann Lee and the Shakers

Mother Ann Lee (1736-1784) and a group of followers relocated from her native England to New York in the American colonies in 1774. The organization that she founded, the Shakers, based their credibility upon direct revelations of the Spirit. Prophetic visions were frequent. Speaking in tongues was integral to the early experience of the movement. Mother Ann not only spoke in tongues, but would write lengthy messages "in the Spirit." A Presbyterian minister who visited revival services in New York in 1779 became convinced that the manifestations that he witnessed were signs of "the baptism of the Spirit." However, questionable doctrines and practices of this fringe movement severely limited its widespread influence in American Christianity.

Edward Irving and the British Revival

Scotsman Edward Irving (1792-1834), a noted London pastor with the Church of Scotland, became convinced that miraculous gifts, signs and wonders of the Holy Spirit had been restored to the church after reports reached him from reliable sources of outbreaks of charismata from the west of Scotland in the summer of 1830. A visitation of similar manifestations within his own congregation led to his dismissal, paving the way for the creation of an independent church pastored by Irving where gifts of the Spirit were welcomed and encouraged. This new congregation founded in 1832, the Newman Street church, became a center for charismatic activity in the London area. Eventually, a London Council of seven churches was formed with Irving as President.

The Catholic Apostolic Church

Irving's untimely death due to illness in 1834 led to significant changes. An apostolic team of leaders raised up at Newman Street assumed control, relocating the headquarters of the movement to rural Albury, south of London. An international organization was formed under apostolic authority, the Catholic Apostolic Church (CAC). Soon, the new organization evolved into a formalistic, ritualistic entity, vastly different from the spontaneous, charismatic fellowship that once thrived under Irving's leadership at Newman Street.

The New Apostolic Church

Another organization, the New Apostolic Church (NAC), was formed in Germany in the 1860's, as German members of the CAC were excommunicated for appointing their own apostles. The CAC had locked themselves into an apostolic college of only twelve, so that after the last apostle died in 1901, the organization was unable to perpetuate itself. The NAC, with unlimited apostles, expanded internationally during the twentieth century, and continues to be a thriving organization. Although the NAC is less ritualistic than was the CAC, gifts of the Spirit have been relegated to the apostles only. Relevant to our study is the presence of a contemporary organization (the NAC), affirming the authenticity of continuing charismata of the Spirit, tracing its roots back to Edward Irving and the Newman Street church.

Irving's Contributions Not Perpetuated

More important than the groups that were produced by the original movement are the theological formulations contributed by Irving in response to the early outbreak of the charismata. Irving's writings became eclipsed after his death by the preponderance of literary minutia generated by adherents of the CAC. The apostles dramatically altered the character of the CAC from her Newman Street beginnings, and resented being labeled "Irvingite" by outside observers.

The CAC's self-conscious break from Irving's foundational legacy led to the rapid loss of historical memory of Irving's writings related to the charismata. There is a sense in which Christianity has been robbed of invaluable prophetic vision and theological wisdom contributed by a Pentecostal pioneer who forged his way ahead more than seventy years before the appearance of the Pentecostal movement with no guide but the Spirit's illumination and the truths of Scripture. Irving's insights offer biblical, Christological and ecclesiological structure for the proper understanding and expression of the charismata.[59]

Irving's Christological Foundations

Irving formulated biblical, Christological foundations for the manifestations of the Spirit. He articulated a doctrine of subsequence, recognizing the Spirit's indwelling of the newly converted believer as being distinct from the event of Spirit baptism, releasing the first fruits of the Spirit's power upon the believer to equip for ministry. First fruits are less than the full harvest of power to be manifested at the time of Jesus' Second Coming, but are nonetheless minimally equivalent to the anointing that was upon the incarnate Christ as He ministered the works of the Father in His earthly ministry.

The gift of tongues figured significantly in Irving's scheme, serving as the "standing sign"[60] of Spirit baptism, as well as being "a great instrument for personal edification."[61] The deficiency in Irving's perspective comes in his explanation of the believer's appropriation of the gift of tongues. For Irving, the role of the believer is subsidiary to the Spirit's sovereign choice to bestow the gift. The believer is admonished to desire earnestly the gift, to petition the Father with confidence, and to tarry until the gift is received. Even with the monumental breakthroughs contributed by Edward Irving, his failure to incorporate into his system this Pauline revelation of "volitional tongues" resulted in the restriction of the experience of tongues and Spirit baptism to a limited circle of "gifted" beneficiaries who were privileged to gain the coveted prize.[62] In spite of this major limitation, Irving's Newman Street church came close to recovering for Christendom the Pauline perspective, through the influence of experienced leaders such as Emily Cardale and Mary Caird. Had Irving himself been able to recognize that the reception of Spirit baptism is essentially nothing more than utterances in tongues as a devotional prayer language, to be exercised as simply and freely as the practice of praying regularly in one's understanding, his movement possibly could have catapulted itself out of obscurity into a place of precipitating a major Pentecostal revival ahead of the Azusa Street phenomenon.

Phoebe Palmer and American Methodism

Turning to the American context in the nineteenth century, a Methodist woman named Phoebe Palmer devoted more than forty years of her life to an influential teaching ministry aimed at encouraging Methodists to receive sanctification through an instantaneous experience that she identified to be the baptism of the Holy Spirit. She utilized Pentecostal language to characterize this crisis experience of perfect holiness possible for the believer. The gift of tongues and other charismata, however, were not integrated into her agenda.

The Holiness Movement

By the 1860's, a Holiness movement materialized within Methodism, advocating sanctification as a distinct experience for believers, and promoting revivals within the churches. "Higher life" conferences in Keswick, England in the late nineteenth century paralleled the American emphasis upon holiness as a distinct work of grace in Christian experience. As Holiness advocates within Methodism became disillusioned with denominational resistance to their emphasis upon sanctification as an experiential priority, a "come-outer" movement during the 1890's swept through Methodism as hundreds of Holiness devotees abandoned their institutional affiliation to form various independent holiness organizations around the country. Out of this milieu, sympathetic to multiple works of grace, crisis experiences and revivalism, Pentecostalism would be born.

Benjamin Irwin and the Fire-Baptized Holiness Church

A former Baptist minister, B. H. Irwin, successfully organized Holiness groups into a denomination that swept through the Midwest, becoming known as the Fire-baptized Holiness Church (1895). Irwin concluded that a third experience beyond sanctification was possible for believers. Challenging Palmer's theory, Irwin contended that the third and not the second experience was "the baptism with the Holy Ghost and fire" or just "the fire." No specific sign indicated to the recipient that "the fire" had been obtained. As Spirit baptism was received, any number of manifestations could occur: screaming, shouting, falling into trances, speaking in tongues, or experiencing "the jerks." By 1900, Irwin was not content with three works of grace. He concluded that additional baptisms are necessary for the perfection of the Christian. He employed chemical jargon in the naming of these successive baptisms: dynamite, lyddite and oxidite. A seventh baptism was added (celenite). Most members of the group, however, never accepted these progressive stages of perfection. A moral failure brought to light in 1900 led to the departure of Irwin as overseer of the denomination, and the organization never regained its original influence.

Charles Parham and Spirit Baptism

Charles Parham was a former Methodist minister who became

independent after 1895 as the "come-outer" movement impacted Methodism. From his Methodist background, Parham accepted the teaching that sanctification was a second work of grace beyond conversion, and was influenced additionally by Irwin that a third work of grace was desirable. Located in Topeka, Kansas, Parham began the Bethel Healing Home (1898) and the Bethel Bible School (1900). Late in 1900, Parham and his students reached the conclusion that the Scriptural evidence for determining that one had received the baptism in the Spirit is speaking in tongues. As the school conducted a watchnight service on December 31, 1900, a service extending into the new year, student Agnes Ozman requested prayer from Parham to receive Spirit baptism. Her experience of speaking in tongues was so captivating that she continued at length in prayer, unable to communicate in her own language for three days. Parham and other students also received the evidence of speaking in tongues. Convinced that his teaching represented the recovery of the upper room experience on the Day of Pentecost, Parham closed the school and took his ministry on the road.

The Emergence of William Seymour

Twentieth century Pentecostals recognize Parham as being the father of the "classical Pentecostal doctrine" helping to ignite the modern Pentecostal movement. Yet his message failed to gain acceptance initially. For four years, he and his group labored in obscurity. In 1905, he found enough support in Houston, Texas to locate his headquarters there. He founded another school in Houston, "The Bible Training School." Parham's decision to teach was significant, for one of the enrollees in his school was William J. Seymour. Seymour was a black evangelist from Louisiana, desirous of receiving biblical training from Parham. Seymour eagerly adopted Parham's Pentecostal teaching. Already convinced that sanctification was a second work of grace, Seymour now embraced Spirit baptism as a third blessing for the believer's empowerment, evidenced by the experience of speaking in tongues.

Los Angeles Stirrings

In the winter of 1906, Seymour was contacted by members of a storefront Holiness congregation in Los Angeles, California, recruiting him to be their pastor. Seymour accepted, and journeyed by train to assume his new position. Seymour preached only a few sermons, but found himself locked out of the building of his new pastorate. Members were not prepared to accept Seymour's doctrine of Spirit baptism. Even though Seymour had not yet received the experience, his preaching emphasis upon speaking in tongues alienated his hearers.

The Azusa Street Revival

Without a job or a home of his own, Seymour was given temporary shelter and dedicated himself to a season of intense prayer. Eventually, a family took him in and persuaded him to offer services in their home. The tide turned in favor of Seymour and his message, and crowds flocked to the home meetings. Interest was so high that a former church building was secured at 312 Azusa Street. Calling themselves the Apostolic Faith Mission, the group began services in April under Seymour's pastoral leadership. The opening of the mission coincided with a stirring revival among the core members of the new church. Seymour and others received the baptism in the Holy Spirit. The Los Angeles media publicized the Azusa Street events. Attendance mushroomed, and revival broke out in the services. Seymour printed a newsletter highlighting the Pentecostal outpouring, and news spread to Holiness denominations throughout America. Revival flourished to the extent that services at times at Azusa Street became consecutive, continuing without interruption, night and day. Pentecostal missionaries from Azusa

Street spread the message of Spirit baptism around the world. Revival was unbroken for three years (1906-1909). The Azusa Street revival spawned a worldwide Pentecostal movement whose influence has continued into the twenty-first century.

Forgotten Azusa Street Factors

Several factors that contributed to revival at Azusa Street were not perpetuated within the Pentecostal movement that followed the initial revival. The humble circumstances of the mission encouraged people of all races, classes and cultural backgrounds to feel on equal footing at Azusa Street. Seymour recognized that the true foundation for the revival was the presence of interracial, intercultural unity, providing an atmosphere of humility and brokenness among the people that invited the Spirit's presence and Pentecostal power. In addition, Seymour was an exceptionally humble leader, willing to be a background figure courageous enough to allow the Holy Spirit to move freely without hindrance. Issues of character, giving room for the sovereign move of the Spirit, were easily swept aside by the sensationalism of the recovery of Pentecostal manifestations.

Factors Carried into the Pentecostal Movement

On the other hand, the manifestation and magnification of the doctrine of Spirit baptism, with the accompanying reaffirmation of the New Testament practice of speaking in tongues as the initial sign of this subsequent blessing of Christian empowerment, was a positive factor from Azusa Street that was disseminated and institutionalized within the Pentecostal movement. The fact that some Pentecostal denominations accepted sanctification as a second work of grace, as in the cases of Parham and Seymour, while others viewed sanctification as a part of the conversion experience, thus rendering Spirit baptism as a second rather than a third distinct Christian experience, proved to be only a minor difference among the throng of Pentecostals that were establishing their permanent place within the worldwide community of Christians.

Pentecostal Denominations

As Pentecostal denominationalism passed the baton to the next generation, dynamic features of Pentecostalism experienced a measure of ossification. Denominations maintained the concept of subsequence for Spirit baptism, and insisted upon tongues as the initial sign, but spontaneity of experience gave way to structured worship and formality. Pentecostals yielded to pressures to conform to mainstream Christian practices, which brought increased acceptability within society, but resulted in a de-emphasis of Pentecostal distinctives. We must note, however, that the positive consequence of Pentecostal acceptability meant that this new movement had earned a place within the landscape of Christendom that could not be ignored.

"Volitional tongues" Not Yet Recovered

Both the Azusa Street revival and the Pentecostal denominations brought prominence to Spirit baptism and tongues as the initial sign of reception, while failing to recover the Pauline emphasis upon "volitional tongues."[63] We remember that Irving's Newman Street church had established the value of tongues as a language of prayer, available to every believer, but had not provided a viable means for implementing tongues for everyone. Consequently, only a select group actually received tongues, forming an elite group of the "gifted," who had attained preferential status within the church because of their positive results. Even Irving, whose teaching on tongues as a gift has yet to be exceeded, did not find himself among the "gifted" few.

Seymour and Azusa Street proved to be more successful in the ministry of implementation, in their focus upon the empirical verifiability of Spirit baptism by means of the tongues experience. This focus was transmitted into the Pentecostal movement. Yet with the gains of Pentecostalism, the outcome fell short of restoring Paul's "volitional tongues." Pentecostalism maintained the "tarrying" facet of receiving tongues,[64] meaning that the desire for tongues must be matched by the appropriate timing and subjective feeling for satisfactory appropriation to take place. While many would conclude the process having attained a successful outcome, others mystifyingly would fail to gain the coveted prize.

The Charismatic Movement

New dynamics dominated the scene as the Charismatic movement came into prominence in the 1960's. The Charismatic movement flooded both Protestantism and Catholicism, and to a lesser extent, Eastern Orthodoxy, with a fresh wave of Pentecostal awareness and experience. Renewal groups sprang up within mainline Christian denominations, providing validation and encouragement for the experience of Spirit baptism as a distinctive work of the Holy Spirit. Innovation marked the Charismatic movement, in that tongues was no longer seen by some to be the necessary sign of Spirit baptism, but only one among other possible manifestations that could characterize the reception of this distinctive blessing. Most groups preferred tongues as the initial sign, but the door was opened for believers to claim possession of the experience without having spoken in tongues.

Charismatics Receptive to "Volitional Tongues"

Despite this innovation, the Charismatic movement contributed a breakthrough on a major scale that other previous groups sympathetic to Pentecostalism had failed to provide. "Volitional tongues" became a prominent teaching within various Charismatic circles, recovering a basic practice common to New Testament

Christianity in the days of the apostle Paul but soon abandoned by the churches. Research has not yet uncovered the source or sources within the pre-Charismatic milieu responsible for reintroducing "volitional tongues" as a Pentecostal truth. The teaching surfaced probably in the 1940's, possibly through the ministry of Smith Wigglesworth and possibly in the Latter Rain revival that began in Canada in 1948. Pentecostal leaders who successfully transitioned into the Charismatic movement, and who were prominent advocates of the "volitional tongues" perspective, were Oral Roberts (**see Appendix 2 for Oral Roberts' personal comments concerning "volitional tongues, prepared especially for this book**), David du Plessis, Demos Shakarian and Kenneth Hagin, among others. Yet regardless of the initiating agent or agents fostering widespread acceptance of this teaching, it is undeniable that the Charismatic movement was responsible for preparing the way for an unprecedented number of initiates to receive the manifestation of speaking in tongues throughout the world, spanning every Christian denomination.

Value of "Volitional Tongues"

Among the practical consequences of the widespread acceptance of "volitional tongues" promoted by the Charismatic movement are the demystification and desubjectification of the experience. Armed with the knowledge that speaking in tongues may be commenced at will, the believer will tend to experience Spirit baptism more quickly without waiting for a special timing or feeling. Once baptized in the Spirit, believers will more frequently practice tongues as a regular language of prayer, realizing that the original experience was simply one of numerous experiences of personal empowerment meant to continually build up the believer for Christian living. The Holy Spirit is always ready to stir the human spirit to pray in the heavenly language of tongues. The responsibility rests with the believer to vocalize those utterances that flow from deep within the human spirit through the urging of the Holy Spirit.

A Truth for All Christians

The Charismatic movement became a vehicle for awakening the church to a truth of New Testament experience that for centuries has been forgotten by Christendom. The teaching of "volitional tongues," while being a Charismatic distinctive, is, more importantly, a biblical, New Testament distinctive. A truth revealed to the church through Paul, this teaching was meant to be believed and implemented by all Christians. The human spirit was created to engage in continuous communion with the indwelling Holy Spirit, and the expression of tongues is a primary means of maintaining intimacy with Jesus and experiencing His ministry in continuous relationship.

The Pauline Context

Perhaps the radical implications of this teaching can be highlighted more clearly if the primary Scriptural text from Paul's writing is accentuated. Paul articulates the nature and proper expression of the gift of tongues in I Corinthians 14. More is said in this chapter about speaking in tongues than anywhere else in the New Testament. In this context, a paraphrase of key verses in this chapter specifically focusing upon tongues is ventured, in expectation that readers will grasp Paul's mindset in a fresh way, bringing enhanced insight and vision of this invaluable truth.

I Corinthians 14

"When the believer is speaking in tongues, he is not speaking to men but to God. He is speaking mysteries to God flowing out of his human spirit. (2) When one is speaking in tongues, he is being edified and built up in his faith. (4) Therefore, I wish that all of you would enter into the practice of speaking in tongues. (5) Speaking in tongues is a form of prayer, yet not a conceptual expression of the intellect, but a prayer originating from the human spirit. (14) Just as the believer chooses to pray or sing to God with intellectual comprehension, so should the believer choose to pray and sing to God in tongues. Yet when believers are gathered together in worship, consideration must be made for the good of the assembly. Even though I am thankful that I speak in tongues privately more than all of you, I control myself when I am worshipping with others. In the assembly, five words that can be understood are better than ten thousand words spoken in tongues. (18-19) During worship, it is best for only two or three of you to bring a message in tongues, and only when one is present to interpret each message through the gift of interpretation. Otherwise, it is better to refrain from speaking in tongues in the assembly, but to continue to pray in tongues in your private devotions to God." (27-28)

"Third Wave" Neo-charismatics

An extension of the Charismatic movement has been the emergence of what has been labeled the "Third Wave" of Pentecostalism (Neo-charismatics). The Charismatics sought to bring renewal in the Holy Spirit to denominational Christianity. Neo-charismatics established their identity outside structures of the denominational church. Within Protestantism, Third Wave groups proliferated by the thousands. While most of these groups remained small and limited in influence, others developed highly organized entities similar to major corporations, with branches extending in some cases even beyond national borders. Neo-charismatics have been responsible for spawning "mega-churches" and "mini-denominations" significantly impacting worldwide Christianity. Many of the largest churches in the world today have been produced by the Third Wave movement originating out of the Charismatic movement. In addition, thousands of parachurch ministries that are Charismatic in orientation, but not denominationally related, have found their place in Christendom as a result of the Third Wave movement.

Contemporary Independents

These independent Neo-charismatics in the modern world are a force to be reckoned with. Some operate with a "corporate" infrastructure, supporting hundreds of affiliate churches and ministries. Some are loosely assembled, while others are maintained by authoritarian government under singular or group leadership. An "apostolic" movement is thriving within this milieu, as churches have ordered themselves under the leadership of apostles in an effort to recover this New Testament pattern. In line with the focus of this chapter, we have observed general continuity in belief and practice with the Charismatic movement. The independents view Spirit baptism as a distinct experience, subsequent to conversion, for the basic purpose of equipping the believer with the supernatural power of the Spirit. When compared with the original Charismatics, attempting to influence mainline denominations with the Spirit's gifts, signs and wonders, the independents are more insistent in their belief that speaking in tongues is the initial sign of the baptism in the Holy Spirit. They are less likely to compromise this tenet of "classical Pentecostalism." In addition, they have perpetuated the Charismatic recovery of "volitional tongues," thereby fostering the concept that tongues should be a frequent, normal practice in the devotional life of every Christian.

Final Test

We have reached a pivotal point, where the focus should now be turned to the central, underlying issue, which is Christological foundations. All aspects of our belief and practice, in order to be authentically Christian, must conform to the biblical revelation concerning the person and work of Jesus Christ. We must have the courage to submit ourselves regularly to the process of reform. Every aspect of what we believe and how we practice our beliefs should be scrutinized rigorously according to theological reflection centered upon Christology. Put simply, if what we believe and practice is not in accordance with the life and ministry of Jesus Christ, and the New Testament witness of His ministry, then our experience must be reformed accordingly. Christology is our standard as we conclude our process of reflection and reform.

Chapter 27

CHRISTOLOGICAL RECOVERY
The Theory of the "Push Button" Divinity of Jesus

Modern Christologies Fall Short

Christology Must Be At the Heart of Expansion

Traditional Standards Blended With the Pneumatological Dimension

Implicit Christology of the Current Church

Jesus' "Divinity Button"

Distances Jesus From Us

Resembles Eutycheanism

Challenges the Integrity of Jesus' Humanity

Incarnation Not Understood or Honored

Theory Transgresses the Incarnation

False Protection of Divinity

Deactivation of Divine Attributes Essential

Deactivation of Divinity Allows Jesus' Obedience to be Genuine

Jesus' Supernatural Dimension From the Holy Spirit
Jesus a Real Person of Faith
His Father's Works Through the Spirit
From Baptism to Baptizer
No More Excuses For Sinning!
No More Excuses For Powerlessness!
No Apologies For Being Human
Jesus Needed No Unfair Advantage
A Tsunami of Praise

Chapter 27

CHRISTOLOGICAL RECOVERY
The Theory of the "Push Button" Divinity of Jesus

Modern Christologies Fall Short

Our intention is not to advance novelty, but to stimulate recovery. For centuries, Christology has deviated from the biblical norm of the nature of Jesus' person and purpose. Previous chapters addressing how Jesus' incarnate life was lived in dependence upon the sanctifying and empowering presence of the Holy Spirit, thus making possible the church's ability to carry out Jesus' Great Commission and to take seriously His purpose as Baptizer in the Holy Spirit, show plainly the glaring deficiencies in traditional and modern Christological orientations.

Christology Must Be At the Heart of Expansion

While Neo-charismatic expansion of the present day church has tapped into the experiential roots of biblical Christianity, doctrinal and Christological models have not followed suit to authenticate, unify, and envision fresh horizons for present consolidation and future exploration. Just as the New Testament church advanced into uncharted territory, supported by the secure bedrock of the apostle's doctrine, the current expansion and diversification of the Gospel needs doctrinal moorings. The contemporary Independent constituency must have a Christological foundation at the heart of its expansion, for the Holy Spirit's activity, no matter how dynamic, must always center upon the foundation of the Jesus of Scripture, and accentuate the Gospel proclamation.

Traditional Standards Blended With the Pneumatological Dimension

Spirit-filled Christology meets the standard, by blending the traditional model culminating with the refutation of semi-Pelagianism at the Council of Orange, with the pneumatological dimension that has been omitted from otherwise orthodox presentations of Jesus' person and work. The "cessationist theory" has dominated the arena of academic education for too long, and must be replaced with a Christological model that is faithful to Jesus' mission and His ecclesiological mandate. For more than a hundred years, since Pentecostalism burst upon the map of world Christianity, the most dynamic sector of the church has revisited the Book of Acts experiential scenarios, without a Christological foundation to establish and guide its rapid advancement.

Implicit Christology of the Current Church

No official debate has ever been engaged to address the issues of this false Christology, which I have labeled as the theory of the "push button" divinity of Jesus. As an unnamed and implicit presupposition, passing from generation to generation without question, this opinion concerning Jesus Christ has loomed in the background for centuries, ensnaring devotees who would never have dreamt of straying from the proven paths of orthodoxy. I believe that this "push button" theory, while appearing to avoid the glaring errors of the ancient Christological heresies, has made its bed with the modern church in such a way that changes necessary for the health and vitality of contemporary Christianity are being thwarted.

Jesus' "Divinity Button"

Most adherents of this view have at least some knowledge of Jesus as having two natures, both divine and human. But the underlying erroneous assumption ensnaring every victim of this view is the notion that Jesus, while experiencing His life as a human, kept in continuous reserve the full range of His divine attributes. When needed, He did not hesitate to activate them for His purposes (to push His divinity button). While maintaining His human consciousness, Jesus at times activated His divine consciousness, providing Him with access to the totality of Divine attributes that were available to Him as the eternal Son of God. Holders of this view assume the constancy of Jesus' human life, but view Him as having a continuous reserve of divine resources at His disposal, which He was able to activate at will according to the needs of the moment. For instance, divine omnipotence was activated when Jesus gave sight to the blind, healed the lame, raised the dead, calmed the storm and walked on water. When He revealed personal details from the past history of the woman at the well, Jesus pushed His "divinity button" in order to tap into His eternal omniscience for such information.

Distances Jesus From Us

The danger with such a view is that it appears on the surface to do justice both to divine and human attributes in Christ, and provides a convenient explanation for His supernatural capabilities. On a psychological level, this view allows devotees conveniently to "pedastalize" Jesus by interpreting accounts of His extraordinary achievements as being the result of activating His divine nature, thus eliminating believers from any connection between Jesus' works and their own. The "push button" divinity theory safely distances Jesus and His experiences from the daily life of believers, insulating them within a "comfort zone" of mediocrity. For instance, if we believe that Jesus achieved sinlessness because of His inherent divinity, having resources at His disposal that are unavailable to us, then we have both minimized the human accomplishment of Christ's obedience and eliminated any connection between His holiness and our challenge to participate in His sanctification. Likewise, if we view His many miracles as being expressions of His divine nature, meant only to confirm His identity as Son of God, then we have removed ourselves as believers from any possibility of serving as vehicles for supernatural works as we engage in ministry in His name.

Resembles Eutycheanism

The "push button" divinity of Jesus view appears to give place to Christ's full and complete divinity, thus it easily attracts the devotion of believers who wish to protect and preserve orthodox and conservative Christianity. Unwarily, however, it resembles Eutychean types of Christologies which tend to overemphasize the role of Christ's divinity in His incarnate experience. For instance, Eutychean artistic representations of Christ abound throughout history. Christ is often depicted with a glow of light surrounding His body, something like a divine aura. Some images of Christ find Him with a halo, or portray Him with an angelic or mystical presence. At the root of such images is Eutycheanism, the view that Christ's divine nature so dominated His incarnate personality that His human traits were blended or absorbed into the majesty of His divinity. Christ's humanity effectively was "divinized" at conception, leaving little room for any point of identification with our true humanity.

Challenges the Integrity of Jesus' Humanity

The "push button" theory shares with Eutycheanism the common error of docetism,[65] but varies in its details. The "push button" theory attempts to be true to Christ's continuous and real humanity, but allows Him the option of accessing the full range of divine attributes at will, without seeing this as a threat to Jesus' human integrity. What appears to be a faithful recognition and appreciation of Christ's uniquely divine capabilities in reality represents a serious doctrinal error equally as dangerous as Eutycheanism. Whereas Eutycheanism presents a Jesus whose human attributes are compromised by the overpowering dominance of His continually active divinity, the "push button" theory portrays a Jesus who activates His divinity at will when challenges to His humanity prove to be too challenging. With Eutycheanism, true human attributes are swallowed up by the dominance of Jesus' divinity, whereas with the "push button" theory, genuine humanity is only a temporary reprieve from frequent excursions into the supernatural realm of His divinity. Both theories undermine and invalidate the authenticity of Jesus' true humanity. Invariably, Christologies which compromise Jesus' humanity are victimized by an improper, unbiblical doctrine of the Incarnation.

Incarnation Not Understood or Honored

This brings us to the most serious problem facing today's church. The prevalence of the "push button" theory, especially among those who are committed deeply to the defense of conservative orthodoxy within Christendom, brings to light a fundamental flaw at the heart of modern conservatism. The Christian doctrine of the Incarnation is neither understood nor honored in the belief and practice of the church. If Christians of all denominations and backgrounds simply adhered to the apostle John's supreme Scriptural affirmation concerning the Incarnation: "the Word was made flesh," (John 1:14) then our view of Jesus Christ would undergo a purification process with the potential of revolutionizing every phase of the Christian church. Following the New Testament meaning of "flesh," i.e., the Greek word "sarx," the humanity assumed by the Son of God in the Incarnation event is the sphere of earthly, human life in its totality. Our understanding of Christ must not stray on any level from the true integrity of His humanity.

Theory Transgresses the Incarnation

The "push button" theory attempts to play tricks with the doctrine of a real Incarnation. The implication of this view is that Jesus was able to trespass His incarnational conditions and boundaries at will, transforming instantaneously from finitude to infinity and from creatureliness to Creator, and then reversing this operation to return to conformity with His human nature. Yet how preposterous it is that advocates of this theory seem to think that such maneuverings represent no contradiction to the reality of Jesus' Incarnation. Some logical reflection upon the biblical doctrine of the Incarnation will reveal that the "push button" theory and other Christologies attempting to mix active divine attributes with the human life of Jesus have no biblical foundation. Being incompatible with the church's doctrine of the Incarnation, these views also end up threatening the credibility of Christ's atonement and nullifying the link between Christology and responsible Christian living.

False Protection of Divinity

A longstanding false presupposition continues to block most Christians from correctly understanding the workings of the Incarnation. People suppose that the truth of Jesus' divinity somehow is threatened if His divine attributes are held to have been inactive during His incarnate life. The paradox is that the only viable defense of Jesus true divinity is upheld when His divine attributes are understood to have been inactive. This means that in the eternal councils of the Trinity, the Son of God chose to become the object of Incarnation for the sake of human salvation. The eternal Son of God agreed to become the incarnate Son of Man. While condescending to the limitations of human nature,

He temporarily ceased to be active in His divine nature and consciousness. For His Incarnation to be authentic, He was fully active as a human, while being deactivated of divine attributes. Any activity of His divinity during the brief period of His incarnate mission would have violated the authenticity of His humanity. Having successfully accomplished His mission, Jesus returned to His Father's throne, regaining access to the divine attributes that always have belonged to Him as the eternal Son of God.

Deactivation of Divine Attributes Essential

This description of the workings of the Incarnation both does justice to the authenticity of Jesus' real humanity while it maintains the necessity of Jesus' essential divinity. For Jesus voluntarily to have deactivated His divinity because of His desire to bring reconciliation between God and humanity hardly represents a threat to the doctrine of His true deity. It is the prerogative of deity to assume the nature of humanity and to live within those limitations, if so determined by the members of the Trinity. Because Jesus chose not to activate His divine attributes throughout His redemptive mission on earth in no wise poses a contradiction to His essential nature as the divine Son of God. In contrast, however, it is not consistent with the nature of humanity to manifest divine attributes. Attributes of finitude and infinity, of creatureliness and of Creator God, are not logically interchangeable. By definition, the meanings of divinity and humanity are incompatible. To admit belief in the Incarnation, while contending that Jesus manifested attributes of His divine nature, represents logical contradiction. The Incarnation of the Son of God is an essential biblical reality. Therefore, the inactivity of Jesus' divine attributes during His redemptive mission is a necessary consequence of His Incarnation, and represents the only logical conclusion that preserves Jesus' essential divinity and His authentic humanity. Jesus was no less God for undertaking the ordeal of the Incarnation and remaining faithful to the limitations of His assumed humanity. In fact, it gives

His people cause for offering unto Him the greatest glory and the highest praise!

Deactivation of Divinity Allows Jesus' Obedience to be Genuine

Without Jesus' complete Incarnation, allowing Himself no recourse to the resources of His divine nature, Adam's race would yet be in sin, and Jesus' redemptive work would stand for nothing. The Old Testament required that the final sacrifice for human sin must come from the "Lamb without blemish." For Jesus' shed blood to be efficacious to atone for the sins of all humanity, He Himself must be sinless. The author of Hebrews tells us that Jesus was "tempted in all things as we are, yet without sin." (Hebrews 4:15) It is obvious that Jesus' humanity must be authentic in order for His obedience to be genuine. Had He relied upon His divine nature in any manner in His resistance against sin, His obedience would have been something other than human, and would not have been applicable to Adam's race. For Jesus to have maintained obedience based upon the resources of His divinity would have made a mockery of the meaning of obedience. Divinity cannot be tempted by sin. (James 1:13) Temptation simply does not apply to God. God is Holy, and cannot contradict Himself. In contrast, for one who is completely and inviolably human to never commit a single sinful act, was of supreme significance for the human race. The shed blood of Jesus at Calvary was efficacious to wash away all human sin because Jesus' obedience qualified Him to be the prophetic "Lamb without blemish." The victory was won because Jesus met every redemptive requirement without ever contradicting His incarnate nature and experience. The "push button" theory represents a false Christological opinion that nullifies the biblical doctrine of human redemption.

Jesus' Supernatural Dimension From the Holy Spirit

It should be clear at this point that the contemporary church must not fail to take seriously the doctrine of Jesus' Incarnation. The health and vitality of our faith is dependant upon viewing Jesus with complete consistency, in that His incarnational limitations were never violated by excursions into the realm of His divine nature and consciousness. Everything done by Jesus was within the parameters of His human nature and consciousness. Yet a consistent incarnational Christology must give an accounting for the obvious inbreaking of the supernatural in Jesus' life, particularly during the three years of His public ministry. This leads us to the critical juncture in this attempt to lead the church into a recovery of the incarnational Christology of the Scriptures. Divine resources were available to Jesus. Jesus operated freely in the realm of the supernatural. An incarnational Christology recognizes that supernatural, divine resources were active in Jesus. Yet the source of divine activity in Jesus is key to the discussion. Jesus did not rely upon His own divine nature to tap into the supernatural, for He had willingly rendered dormant His own divine attributes. Rather, Jesus relied upon the divine resources of the Holy Spirit, whose presence had been indwelling Him since His conception in His mother's womb.

Jesus a Real Person of Faith

A true doctrine of the Incarnation brings to the forefront the role of the Holy Spirit in the life of Jesus. Once the option has been eliminated of Jesus depending upon the resources of His divine nature, we are liberated to see the biblical portrayal of the human Jesus operating as a person of faith. Weak in His humanity, Jesus was strong in faith. He lived His life in complete dependence upon His relationship with His heavenly Father, and His Father's provision of the Holy Spirit. Since conception, Jesus had been filled with the Holy Spirit "without measure." (John 3:34) In the weakness of His humanity, Jesus always had accessibility to the Holy Spirit. Yet the Spirit did not function without Jesus' yieldedness and cooperation. When facing real human temptations, or Satan's fiery darts of oppression, Jesus did not push his divinity button to activate His divine nature or consciousness. Rather, He leaned upon His Father's presence, and drew from the Spirit's comfort and strength. Jesus kept His humanity pure, and gave no place for the devil, as He allowed the Holy Spirit continuously to fill Him and impart divine resources for His every task.

His Father's Works Through the Spirit

The Holy Spirit had indwelt Jesus' from conception onwards, but when Jesus' embarked upon His public ministry at the time of His water baptism, He received a special anointing of the Spirit's power, allowing the supernatural works of the Father to be manifest in His life from that time forward. Isaiah had prophesied that the coming Messiah would receive the Spirit's anointing, releasing upon Him the power "to bring good news to the afflicted; …to bind up the brokenhearted, to proclaim liberty to captives, and freedom to prisoners; …" (Isaiah 61:1) Not by pushing His divinity button, but by yielding to the Spirit's anointing, Jesus was enabled to fulfill completely Isaiah's prophecy. Luke notes of "how God anointed Him with the Holy Spirit and with power, and how He went about doing good, and healing all who were oppressed by the devil; for God was with Him." (Acts 10:38) Jesus did not claim to have performed the mighty works of the Father by means of His own inherent divinity, but gave rightful credit to the Spirit operating within Him. Lecturing the Pharisees, Jesus revealed the source of His delivering power. "But if I cast out demons by the Spirit of God, then the kingdom of God has come upon you." (Matthew 12:28) Jesus never attempted to step outside the boundaries of His weak and frail humanity in the accomplishment of mighty miracles. Yet supernatural power flowed from His humanity, because He remained dependent upon the Holy Spirit, the source of His power. Though by nature He was God, Jesus condescended to our weak nature. Yet His incarnate humanity did not limit the supernatural power that flowed through Him because He exercised faith in His Father and the provision of the Holy Spirit freely given to Him.

From Baptism to Baptizer

This leads us to the revolutionary dimension of a consistent incarnational Christology, for it contains immense application for healthy and vital church life capable of precipitating revival to the highest degree. Jesus' walked in the Spirit's sanctification and anointing of power on earth. He then, after paying the price on Calvary's cross for our sins, rose from the dead to breathe regenerative life upon His disciples. He ascended as the risen Lord to become the Baptizer of the Holy Spirit upon His church. When He imparted the Holy Spirit unto every believer, He endowed them with the same sanctifying presence that enabled Him to resist sin and live with a pure conscience before the Father. When He poured out from heaven the Pentecostal baptism of the Holy Spirit, He equipped His church with the same supernatural anointing that characterized His public ministry.

No More Excuses For Sinning!

If Jesus turned to the resources of His divine nature in the accomplishment of His sinless life, then we are off the hook. We have no divine nature to activate when sin's temptations beckon. We can yield to sin, then rely upon the familiar excuse, "but I'm only human." We continue in sin because that is what humans do. Such a scenario has a major problem. It is not biblical. Jesus Himself taught us, "you are to be perfect, as your heavenly Father is perfect." (Matthew 5:48) Drawing from the model of Jesus' sanctification, believers need not despair in striving against sin, for the example of His incarnate life continually calls us to turn to our heavenly Father in complete dependence, knowing that the Spirit is ever present to give us strength that is beyond our own ability to obey the will of God. Not only is Jesus our comforting presence to provide us with courage and motivation to resist sin and its destructive influence, but He also is our source of grace, providing forgiveness and restoration when we fail in our struggle with sin. By adopting a right understanding of Jesus' Incarnation, familiar excuses to sin based upon our humanity can be discarded for good. The Spirit empowers us in our humanity to walk in obedience to our Father's will. We are free to live by the faith of Jesus, who shared our common humanity, yet overcame sin's temptations by the same Spirit that sanctifies us.

No More Excuses For Powerlessness!

Furthermore, if Jesus activated His divinity button in order to perform the miraculous works dotting the landscape of His public ministry, then we are justified in lacking faith to pray for others with the expectancy that signs, wonders and miracles will follow. Our excuse for not acting is as follows. "Sure, Jesus worked miracles. After all, He was God. I'm only human." However, our faithlessness is not justifiable. The Bible presents Jesus as the incarnate Christ. Although eternally God, Jesus became fully human. He refused to activate His divinity during His earthly sojourn. He lived by faith, as we are called upon to live, in dependence upon the Holy Spirit. Yet His Father appointed Him to minister miraculous works in confirmation of the coming kingdom of God and as an expression of the Father's love for hurting humanity. Jesus performed those mighty works, in obedience to His Father's will, without ever violating the confines of His weak and frail humanity. He stepped out in faith, and gave place to the Spirit's power, and mighty works were the result. Jesus imparted to His people the same Holy Spirit, and sent upon His church the Spirit's baptism of power.

He commissioned us to "preach the gospel to all creation," while promising that attesting miracles will accompany our proclamation. "And these signs will accompany those who have believed: in My name they will cast out demons, they will speak with new tongues; they will pick up serpents, and if they drink any deadly poison, it shall not hurt them; they will lay hands on the sick, and they will recover." (Mark 16:15, 17 18) This commission has never been rescinded, and remains the church's obligation as long as Jesus tarries in His Second Coming.

No Apologies For Being Human

The Christian church will move to a new level of maturity and faith when we allow ourselves to be delivered from an unhealthy, negative complex about humanity. It is a serious, unscriptural mistake to equate our humanity, which was created good, with evil and sin. The problem with the human race is not that we are humans, but that we are sinners. Jesus came to deliver us from sin and its power, so that we can be reconciled to God, others and ourselves. He came that we may enjoy abundant life, which includes the full, creative potential of our humanity. Jesus epitomized that abundant, human life. He assumed the same human nature that we possess, and lived His life within the same environment and conditions that we face. And His life was full of joy. He showed us that we can live free from sin and its power, through the indwelling, sanctifying life of the Holy Spirit. The believer who knows his standing in Christ does not have to apologize for being human. We know that we are the temple of the Holy Spirit.

Jesus Needed No Unfair Advantage

Docetic Christologies rob us of our hope of being free from the domination of sin. They make Jesus' humanity different than ours. They give Jesus unfair advantage against sin by attributing His sinlessness to divine capacities not available to us. The standard line is, "Sure Jesus didn't commit sin. He was God. We sin because we are just humans." Yet Jesus needed no unfair advantage. The writer of Hebrews restores our hope. He reveals the authentic Jesus, who "had to be made like His brethren in all things." (Hebrews 2:17) Jesus had all the power of divinity at His disposal, yet He refused to compromise that integrity of His humanity. He needed to win the victory as man, that His brother men might reap the rewards of His conquest. The only advantages that Jesus had are advantages available to every believer: our intimate relationship with Father God, and the indwelling presence of Jesus through the Holy Spirit.

A Tsunami of Praise

This concludes the synopsis of *Spirit-filled Christology*. This doctrinal treatment regarding the person and purpose of Jesus Christ holds the potential for reform. Reflecting upon these truths compels action. The Holy Spirit will be released to glorify Jesus among His people. A tsunami of praise will be set in motion that will envelop the earth. Praise will not be independent, but we will enter as one body into the high praises of Jesus as they crescendo to the Father. "And the earth will be full of the knowledge of the Lord as the waters cover the sea." (Isaiah 11:9)

APPENDIX 1

60 Affirmations of SPIRIT-FILLED CHRISTOLOGY

Introduction

In 529, the bishops of the Council of Orange submitted their 25 Articles in opposition to semi-Pelagian doctrine and to affirm the initiative of God's grace both in conversion and sanctification.

In 1517, Martin Luther submitted his 95 Theses in opposition to abuses related to indulgences and the sacrament of penance and to affirm the Biblical meaning of true repentance.

In 2006, I am submitting the 60 Affirmations of Spirit-filled Christology in opposition to docetic Christologies and to affirm Jesus' Incarnation and anointing by the Holy Spirit as the standard for Spirit-filled living in today's church.

These standards are in the form of affirmations in order to facilitate their use as confessional statements of faith. I recommend that Christians affirm these faith declarations on a daily basis to renew consciousness and encourage active response to the dynamic operations of the Spirit in this time of expanding worldwide revival!

THE 60 AFFIRMATIONS

1

Jesus Christ is fully God, eternally pre-existent, and sharing the same divinity with the Father and the Holy Spirit *"In the beginning was the Word, and the Word was with God, and the Word was God."* (John 1:1)

2

In the eternal counsels of the Trinity, the Son of God consented to become human for the sake of the salvation of the human race (Psalms 40:7-8, Hebrews 10:9-10, John 17:24).

3

At the appointed time, the eternal Son of God became incarnate in the person of Jesus Christ (Galatians 4:4; Hebrews 2:14-17). Maintaining His divine identity, He was conceived in the womb of His mother Mary through the agency of the Holy Spirit (Luke 1:35).

4

Jesus' human nature was of the substance of His mother's humanity, i.e., the mortal and corruptible flesh (sarx) of the human race that He came to redeem. *"And the Word became flesh, and dwelt among us, ..."* (John 1:14)

5

Christians naively dismiss the significance of Jesus' humanity, thinking that overemphasis upon Jesus' deity at the expense of His humanity is a virtuous exchange. Few realize that our redemption is null and void if Jesus is not fully human as well as fully divine.

6

If the Son did not become what we are as the Second Adam, then that which He did not assume in His Incarnation remains under the curse of sin. Jesus took all that we are so that reconciliation, redemption and relationship with the Father could apply to our whole humanity. *"For since by a man came death, by a man also came the resurrection of the dead. For as in Adam all die, so also in Christ all shall be made alive."* (I Corinthians 15:21-22, Romans 5:18-19)

7

Jesus' divine attributes and consciousness were deactivated when He became human, so that the authenticity of His humanity would not be compromised. *"...although He existed in the form of God, did not regard equality with God a thing to be grasped, but emptied Himself, taking the form of a bondservant, and being made in the likeness of men."* (Philippians 2:6-7)

8

Jesus was very God, and He knew that, but the privileges and prerogatives associated with His divine life were not available to Him as Son of Man.

9

The status of Jesus' divinity was not threatened by the deactivation of His divine attributes and consciousness in the Incarnation event, in that His identity as the Son of God is eternal in scope, and is not jeopardized by the temporal restraints that were self-imposed for a brief time for the sake of human redemption. (John 17:5)

10

Since the incarnate Jesus did not have the benefit of His omniscient divinity, He was required to develop consciousness of His messianic identity and purpose. His growth and learning was according to patterns of human development. *"The Child continued to grow and become strong, increasing in wisdom; and the grace of God was upon Him… And Jesus kept increasing in wisdom and stature, and in favor with God and men."* (Luke 2:40, 52)

11

Consciously, Jesus knew that He was Son of God, but He had no memory of His life and experience as a member of the Godhead. He knew that He had an identity beyond His human life and experience, but He gave up His natural access to His divine identity from conception to the grave.

12

Jesus was no less God for undertaking the ordeal of the Incarnation and remaining faithful to the limitations of His assumed humanity. In fact, it gives His people cause for offering unto Him the greatest glory and the highest praise!

13

Jesus assumed humanity for the purpose of redemption. He became the Second Adam in order to reverse the curse upon humanity due to the disobedience of the first Adam. In Adam's place, Jesus countered the first Adam's disobedience by offering the Father true human obedience all His life long, culminating in His death on the cross. *"For as through the one man's disobedience the many were made sinners, even so through the obedience of the One the many will be made righteous."* (Romans 5:19)

14

Jesus, God's Son, came into the very place where sin abounded, taking into His own person the human nature entrapped by sin, bringing reconciliation and righteousness into the arena formerly under sin's control.

15

While living within the limitations and boundaries of His human nature, Jesus was subject to the common temptations of the human race. *"For we do not have a high priest who cannot sympathize with our weaknesses, but one who has been tempted in all things as we are, yet without sin."* (Hebrews 4:15)

16

Jesus resisted all temptations to sin all His life long. The status of Jesus' holiness was moral, in that He maintained His human life in unwavering obedience to His Father's will.

17

His moral obedience was not a sham, done only in the guise of humanity, and really accomplished by His divine prowess. Far from it. Jesus' flesh was identical to the flesh of Adam's race when He lived out His life in complete obedience to the will of His Father. Glory be to Jesus!

18

Jesus' sinlessness was attained through continuous reliance upon the sanctifying presence of the Holy Spirit, and not through His inherent divinity. *"And for their sakes I sanctify Myself, ... "* (John 17:19) *"...although He was a Son, He learned obedience from the things which He suffered; and having been made perfect, He became to all those who obey Him the source of eternal salvation; ... "* (Hebrews 5:8-9)

19

Jesus calls everyone to do as He did, in emulating His commitment to live out His life in personal relationship with His Father God, never breaking intimate communion and never straying into disobedience in word or deed. He is our model in His refusal to take self-initiative in anything, but was willing to respond to the initiative of His Father in carrying out the words and works that His Father purposed for Him. *"I do nothing on My own initiative, but I speak these things as the Father taught Me."* (John 8:28)

20

When the time arrived for Jesus to lay down His life for the sins of the world on Calvary's cross, He was fully qualified to be the spotless Lamb of God (Leviticus 14:10, John 1:29, Hebrews 10:10-12). The Father's acceptance of Jesus' sacrifice on the cross was based upon the lifelong offering of moral obedience, and not upon holiness as an inherent quality of His divinity. We have cause to praise Jesus not only for His sacrifice upon the cross, but for His daily sacrifices of authentic human obedience!

21

We must learn not to shy away from Jesus' sinlessness in mortal, corruptible humanity, but glory in it. Humanity achieved eternal victory in Jesus' moral triumph against sin. Because of it, our fallen nature is now restored before the Father. We are accepted and justified with our holy God because Jesus took our nature and made it sinless (Romans 8:3, II Corinthians 5:17).

22

When Jesus entered into His public ministry following His baptism, He worked miracles to glorify His Father, to show that His character was fully compassionate to meet human need, and to confirm His Messianic purpose. *"And Jesus was going about all the cities and the villages, teaching in their synagogues, and proclaiming the gospel of the kingdom, and healing every kind of disease and every kind of sickness. And seeing the multitudes, He felt compassion for them, ..."* (Matthew 9:35-36) *"...He went about doing good, and healing all who were oppressed by the devil; for God was with Him."* (Acts 10:38) *"The Son of God appeared for this purpose, that He might destroy the works of the devil."* (I John 3:8)

23

The Holy Spirit indwelt and filled Jesus' human life, so that divine, supernatural presence and capacity was always with Him. Jesus never attempted to step outside the boundaries of His weak and frail humanity in the accomplishment of mighty miracles. Yet supernatural power flowed from His humanity, because He remained dependent upon the Holy Spirit, the source of His power.

24

That the presence of divinity within Jesus' humanity was the Holy Spirit, and not His own divine nature as God's Son, is a matter of immense doctrinal significance. (John 3:34-35, Isaiah 42:1, Matthew 12:15-18, Isaiah 61:1, Luke 4:16-21)

25

The divinity that He expressed was not His inherent divinity as the Word and Son, but had its source from another member of the Triune Godhead. Jesus' role as a model of desired human behavior has validity because the source of divine agency within Him, prompting and empowering Him to do the Father's works, is the Holy Spirit. *"You know of Jesus of Nazareth, how God anointed Him with the Holy Spirit and with power, ..."* (Acts 10:38) *"And Jesus, full of the Holy Spirit, ...was led about by the Spirit ...And Jesus returned to Galilee in the power of the Spirit; ... "* (Luke 4:1, 14) *"But if I cast out demons by the Spirit of God, then the kingdom of God has come upon you."* (Matthew 12:28)

26

Christian opinion for too long has falsely hoisted Jesus onto a pedestal by attributing the miracles that He performed to His divine majesty. Although Jesus deserves all of our praise for His legacy of miraculous works, we are not detracting from the praise for which He is due because we recognize that His miracles were accomplished through the Spirit's anointing upon Him. That He ministered so powerfully without relying upon the resources of His own divine nature is an accomplishment of far greater magnitude than had He insisted upon utilizing His divinity.

27

By doing miraculous works in the weakness of His humanity, while depending upon the Spirit's power, Jesus was demonstrating to His disciples how His supernatural ministry should be continued when He would no longer be physically present. If Jesus depended upon the Spirit to do miraculous works, so can we. *"And He has said to me, 'My grace is sufficient for you, for power is perfected in weakness.' Most gladly, therefore, I will rather boast about my weaknesses, that the power of Christ may dwell in me. ...for when I am weak, then I am strong."* (II Corinthians 12:9-10)

28

Had Jesus activated the attributes of His divine nature during His incarnate mission, whether in resisting temptation or in working miracles, He would have violated the standards of redemption set by His Father. (Matthew 27:42, Luke 22:42)

29

It is not consistent with the nature of humanity to manifest divine attributes. To admit belief in the Incarnation, while contending that Jesus manifested attributes of His divine nature, represents logical contradiction. The Incarnation of the Son of God is an essential biblical reality. Therefore, the inactivity of Jesus' divine attributes during His redemptive mission is a necessary consequence of His Incarnation, and represents the only logical conclusion that preserves Jesus' essential divinity and His authentic humanity.

30

After His resurrection from the dead, Jesus rose as the Redeemer for all humanity. His act of breathing upon His disciples to receive the Holy Spirit represented the inauguration of the new birth within human history. Collectively, His new born disciples were constituted as the first members of the Christian church. *"...Jesus came and stood in their midst, and said to them, 'Peace be with you.' And when He had said this, He showed them both His hands and His side. The disciples therefore rejoiced when they saw the Lord. Jesus therefore said to them again, 'Peace be with you; as the Father has sent Me, I also send you.' And when He had said this, He breathed on them, and said to them, 'Receive the Holy Spirit.'"* (John 20:19-22)

31

Jesus' breath of regenerative life upon those disciples signifies the birthday of the church. From this point forward, all members of the human race willing to receive Jesus as the resurrected Redeemer may become sons and daughters of God, and members of the church. *"But as many as received Him, to them He gave the right to become children of God, even to those who believe in His name, ..."* (John 1:12)

32

The faith to receive Jesus and His salvation must never be considered a work on our part, something done to earn our salvation. That would leave room on our part for boasting that we had contributed to our own salvation. Paul approves of boasting only in God, whose graciousness solely is responsible for our salvation. *"And what do you have that you did not receive? But if you did receive it, why do you boast as if you had not received it?"* (I Corinthians 4:7)

33

Human works can neither add nor take away from the finished work of Jesus Christ on the cross. Justification is based solely upon the victory that was finished on the cross, and it is actualized in the individual simply by believing in the accomplishment of Jesus. *"For by grace you have been saved through faith; and that not of yourselves, it is the gift of God; not as a result of works, so that no one may boast."* (Ephesians 2:8-9)

34

Jesus' presence, blessings and power are not external goals to be acquired by superior spiritual performance, but are freely bestowed giftings that accompany Christ's presence. The Spirit does not respond to the believer's works, but leads the believer to respond to the works of Christ in His continuing mission in the earth. *"But when He, the Spirit of truth, comes, He will guide you into all the truth; for He will not speak on His own initiative, but whatever He hears, He will speak; and He will disclose to you what is to come. He will glorify Me, for He will take of Mine and will disclose it to you. All things that the Father has are Mine; therefore I said that He takes of Mine and will disclose it to you."* (John 16:13-15)

35

When Christians are found to be trying to impress God, to measure up, to do something for God, or to obtain the blessings of the abundant life by spiritual performances, they are displaying symptoms of immature, fleshly behavior.

36

Christians do not live **for** Jesus, but rather, have died to self life and have become **vessels of the indwelling Christ** through the Spirit's presence. *"I have been crucified with Christ; and it is no longer I who live, but Christ lives in me; and the life which I now live in the flesh I live by faith in the Son of God, who loved me, and delivered Himself up for me."* (Galatians 2:20)

37

We have trouble really believing that our Gospel is a Gospel of grace. Rather than gratefully receiving Jesus Christ and the full endowment of giftings and benefits associated with His baptism in the Spirit, we are tempted to fall back into carnality by attempting to do something for God to reciprocate for our good fortune. *"But if it is by grace, it is no longer on the basis of works, otherwise grace is no longer grace."* (Romans 11:6)

38

Becoming new born believers carries with it the responsibility of abiding in Jesus (John 15:4) and contributing to the task of the Great Commission He assigned to the church prior to His ascension. The church has been commissioned by Jesus to make new disciples, and to transmit His Gospel to the uttermost parts of the world. (Matthew 28:19-20, Mark 16:15-16)

39

Jesus required that His church receive the Holy Spirit's baptism of empowerment before venturing out to begin the implementation of His Commission. *"And behold, I am sending forth the promise of My Father upon you; but you are to stay in the city until you are clothed with power from on high."* (Luke 24:49) *"…He commanded them not to leave Jerusalem, but to wait for what the Father had promised, … for John baptized with water, but you shall be baptized with the Holy Spirit not many days from now."* (Acts 1:4-5)

40

Following His ascension, Jesus assumed His role as Baptizer in the Holy Spirit. *"He will baptize you with the Holy Spirit and fire."* (Matthew 3:11) On the Day of Pentecost, He baptized His church with power from on high, enabling them to confirm the proclamation of the Gospel with signs, wonders and miracles following. *"Therefore, having been exalted to the right hand of God and having received from the Father the promise of the Holy Spirit, He has poured forth this which you both see and hear."* (Acts 2:33)

41

The same Jesus who stepped into His role as Baptizer of the Holy Spirit on the Day of Pentecost is the One who received and depended upon the Holy Spirit in His incarnate humanity. Giver of the Holy Spirit as God, Jesus also received the Holy Spirit when He became human for the sake of human redemption.

42

Since the Day of Pentecost, the baptism of the Holy Spirit has been available for all new born believers, representing a subsequent experience of power following conversion. (Acts 2:38-39)

43

Although Spirit baptism may be received in chronological simultaneity with the new birth, nonetheless logically it should always remain a distinct experience from conversion. The Holy Spirit comes to indwell the believer at conversion, bringing forgiveness and regeneration. In Spirit baptism, the Holy Spirit equips supernaturally the regenerated believer with gifts, signs and wonders for the expressed purpose of carrying out Jesus' Commission. *"…but you shall receive power when the Holy Spirit has come upon you; and you shall be My witnesses both in Jerusalem, and in all Judea and Samaria, and even to the remotest part of the earth."* (Acts 1:8)

44

Reception of Spirit baptism is evidenced by speaking in unknown tongues, as was typical in the Book of Acts. *"And they were all filled with the Holy Spirit and began to speak with other tongues, as the Spirit was giving them utterance."* (Acts 2:4)

45

Speaking in tongues is foremost a language of prayer, and may be spoken at will as a prayerful and empowering form of communication with God the Father. *"For one who speaks in a tongue does not speak to men, but to God; ..."* (I Corinthians 14:2) The human spirit was created to engage in continuous communion with the indwelling Holy Spirit, and the expression of tongues is a primary means of maintaining intimacy with Jesus and experiencing His ministry in continuous relationship. *"...in his spirit he speaks mysteries."* (I Corinthians 14:2) Secondarily, it is a gift to be expressed in an orderly fashion among believers when an interpreter of tongues is present. (I Corinthians 14:27-28)

46

Like praying in the language of one's understanding, praying in the language of the Spirit is a controlled action free to occur whenever the speaker is willing. *"What is the outcome then? I shall pray with the spirit and I shall pray with the mind also; I shall sing with the spirit and I shall sing with the mind also."* (I Corinthians 14:15) When contemporary Christianity rediscovers and implements the biblical pattern concerning Jesus as Baptizer in the Holy Spirit and the Pauline revelation concerning speaking in tongues, revival will ignite the church with lasting reformation looming on the horizon.

47

We have seen that tongues is a form of prayer. More specifically, tongues is an expression of worship so utterly pure and primordial that its meaning transcends conceptual comprehension. *"For if I pray in a tongue, my spirit prays, but my mind is unfruitful."* (I Corinthians 14:14) As the speaker yields consent to voice this deep form of praise to God, the indwelling Holy Spirit infuses the entire being of the speaker with supernatural power. *"One who speaks in a tongue edifies himself; ..."* (I Corinthians 14:4) The utterances are spoken as an act of faith, a total surrender of the voice and tongue to syllables unknown to the intellect. The pride of human intelligence must bow in submission to incomprehensible babblings believed to be the humble articulations of a completely yielded vessel.

48

Jesus' lived an authentically human life in complete dependence upon the Holy Spirit. He exemplified a life of consistent faith in His Father's provision through the Spirit. Weak in His humanity, He was strong in faith. *"In the days of His flesh, when He offered up both prayers and supplications with loud crying and tears to Him who was able to save Him from death, and who was heard because of His piety, ..."* (Hebrews 5:7) This life of complete dependence not only enabled Him to meet the requirements for redemption, but also served to demonstrate in His own life the pattern of Spirit-filled living He intends for believers to follow.

49

Jesus' holiness was through moral obedience in dependence upon the sanctifying presence of the Holy Spirit, not through the inherent holiness of His divine nature. By intention, He set a pattern for sanctified living for all believers, in that the Holy Spirit is present in all believers to produce sanctification in union with His holy humanity. *"For since He Himself was tempted in that which He has suffered, He is able to come to the aid of those who are tempted."* (Hebrews 2:18)

50

The personal mission and destiny of the life of the individual believer can be achieved only as the Holy Spirit is given freedom to enforce the Lordship of Jesus in every facet of thought and action.

51

Jesus purposefully did not activate the supernatural attributes of His divine nature, and depended upon the Spirit's power in the living out of His miraculous ministry. He desires for His church, through the experience of Spirit baptism, to work the same and even greater works than did He in the exercise of His public ministry. *"Truly, truly, I say to you, he who believes in Me, the works that I do shall he do also; and greater works than these shall he do; because I go to the Father."* (John 14:12) The same Holy Spirit that empowered Jesus is available to empower His church in the world today.

52

Jesus lived out His incarnate life with this purpose in mind. He intended for His human existence to be a pattern for His church of what it means to live life in complete submission and compliance with the operations of the Holy Spirit. This is true, both in sanctification and in empowerment.

53

Had Jesus' done the Father's works through dependence upon His inherent divinity, then He would not have qualified to be our example. We do not, nor will we ever, have a divine nature to be the source of our words and works. But if the same Holy Spirit provided by the Father for Jesus to rely upon is also provided for us, then the possibility now exists for Jesus to be our example. *"... as He is, so also are we in this world."* (I John 4:17) *"...the one who says he abides in Him ought himself to walk in the same manner as He walked."* (I John 2:6) *"For you have been called for this purpose, since Christ also suffered for you, leaving you an example for you to follow in His steps."* (I Peter 2:21)

54

It is futile to attempt to follow the example of Jesus' lifestyle without having first received Him as gift. Humanity devoid of the Holy Spirit is powerless to emulate the lifestyle Jesus modeled.

55

The baptism of the Spirit imparted by Jesus upon the early church was never rescinded, but represents a continuous reservoir of spiritual life and power available to every generation of believers who will partake. Jesus never intended His Gospel to be transmitted in word only, but conveyed to a needy world in demonstration of the Spirit and power. *"And my message and my preaching were not in persuasive words of wisdom, but in demonstration of the Spirit and of power, so that your faith would not rest on the wisdom of men, but on the power of God."* (I Corinthians 2:4-5) *"For the kingdom of God does not consist in words, but in power."* (I Corinthians 4:20)

56

When He imparted the Holy Spirit unto every believer, He endowed them with the same sanctifying presence that enabled Him to resist sin and live with a pure conscience before the Father. When He poured out from heaven the Pentecostal baptism of the Holy Spirit, He equipped His church with the same supernatural anointing that characterized His public ministry. *"And as for you, the anointing which you received from Him abides in you, …"* (I John 2:27)

57

If Christians view Jesus' supernatural works as setting a pattern for what the church is to accomplish, then faith is increased within the church to follow through with the challenge of the Great Commission. *"These signs will accompany those who have believed: in My name they will cast out demons, they will speak with new tongues; they will pick up serpents, and if they drink any deadly poison, it will not hurt them; they will lay hands on the sick, and they will recover."* (Mark 16:17-18)

58

Incentive is diminished when believers face a daunting assignment with no confidence that supernatural assistance is available. To applaud Jesus for His supernatural ministry, while believing that we are powerless to do similar works, affords Him no glory.

59

Jesus' taught His disciples to expect a lifestyle of the Spirit's anointing. Jesus fully intended that His life of sanctification and power be reproduced by those coming after Him, for the Spirit that filled His humanity would also fill them. *"But you have an anointing from the Holy One, and you all know."* (I John 2:20)

60

Our role is not to imitate Jesus' actions as we remember His deeds, but to participate with Him as He continues to minister to people in the mighty power of the Spirit. *"And they went out and preached everywhere, while the Lord worked with them, and confirmed the word by the signs that followed.*" (Mark 16:20) Willing vessels free to be used are those submitted to the baptism of the Holy Spirit. No more glorious occupation has ever graced God's children than to be habitations of the Holy Spirit.

APPENDIX 2

ORAL ROBERTS' LETTER

**ORAL ROBERTS
UNIVERSITY**

Oral Roberts
Founder/Chancellor

December 12, 2005

Dr David Dorries
c/o ORU
Tulsa, OK

Dear Dr. Dorries:

The term, "volitional tongues," is one I've never heard of. It was at the seminars I led at the pre-opening of ORU in the first 3 buildings that the Lord gave me the term, "The prayer language of the Holy Spirit," and the extended teaching of praying in tongues at will, and, of praying back to our minds the interpretation.

To help me expound this revelation of the Apostle Paul were special spiritual charismatic leaders such as Dr. Jim Brown, Dr. William Reed, Tommy Tyson, Jean Stone, Howard Ervin, Dr. John Peters, Harald Bredesen — and others, mostly historic ministers; also, Dennis Bennett of the Episcopal church in Van Nuys, California.

The Pentecostal was David du Plessis from South Africa, who was prominent in the "open door" of Pope John between the Pentecostals and Catholics in the early 60's. There were others I had teaching with me who also had fresh revelations of tongues which was new at the time.

I think the best thing God enabled me to do was (1)

introducing the prayer language and interpretation to the mind, which came out of my own experience as I walked the bare grounds trying to know how to build ORU from "nothing," and that along with seed-faith became the answer; (2) bringing these leaders mostly from historic churches to share with the 300-600 groups who came at my invitation where we boarded them free as our seed for 10 days at a time.

There were other "break-outs" of this revelation in Catholic groups and others that we later heard about.

God bless you in your most important work.

Sincerely,

Oral Roberts

Oral Roberts

The text below represents the question that I sent to Oral Roberts and other scholars in December of 2005. The letter from Oral Roberts (Appendix 2) is in response to this question. I am deeply grateful to Chancellor Roberts for the time and effort that he expended in reply to my question, as well as for his permission to publish his letter.

"I am in the process of completing a chapter on the history of speaking in tongues for a book that I am writing. I have not been able to identify what person or group recovered the teaching that I call "volitional tongues," that is, the realization that speaking in tongues can be spoken at will by any believer. I believe that speaking in tongues is the prayer language of the human spirit, as moved upon by the indwelling Holy Spirit. This seems to be the teaching of Paul in I Corinthians 14, but was lost to the church for centuries. It seems to have been recognized by many when the Charismatic Movement came into prominence in the 1960's, yet the perspective of "volitional tongues" must have come in earlier, possibly in the 1940's or 1950's. People that I have spoken with have suggested several possibilities for the recovery: Smith Wigglesworth, John G. Lake, Latter Rain Movement (Canada - 1948), Oral Roberts, Demos Shakarian and Harold Bredesen. I believe that "volitional tongues" was an important breakthrough, in that believers began recognizing that they can pray in tongues at will, ushering in the Spirit's anointing and supernatural communication. This allows other gifts to be quickened to the believer, and, as Oral Roberts has taught us, to pray back the interpretation to oneself. Prior to this insight, people felt that they had to be in a special emotional state to speak in tongues, which made the experience too subjective and sporadic. Many struggled to "work up" the right feeling or spiritual state. The apostle Paul wanted believers to pray in tongues at will, thus frequently and regularly. Please help me discover who helped recover to the church this important Pauline teaching."

David W. Dorries, Ph.D.

Oral Roberts University

ddorries@oru.edu

APPENDIX 3

HOW TO RECEIVE JESUS AS YOUR PERSONAL SAVIOR

"But as many as received Him, to them He gave the right to become the children of God, even to those who believe in His name, …" (John 1:12)

The Gospel is not about what we must do to acquire Jesus and His salvation. The Gospel is about what Jesus did to provide salvation for the human race, freely and without condition.

Change in our lives comes only after we receive Jesus, not before. Only when He has been invited to come in does the process of change begin. The Holy Spirit accompanies Jesus, and makes change possible. Receiving Jesus only requires that we come empty handed, as sinners. We come, willing to receive Jesus as a gift. We know that we have not earned, nor do we deserve, the salvation Jesus provides. We come, as needy people, willing to receive.

"For by grace you have been saved through faith; and that not of yourselves, it is the gift of God; not as a result of works, so that no one may boast." (Ephesians 2:8-9)

No one is excluded from the offer of salvation through Jesus Christ. Jesus was not ashamed to become human. He lived a life of complete human obedience and gave Himself up to death on the cross for our sakes. What He did for humanity applies for every member of the human race.

"He Himself is the propitiation (appeasement, satisfaction) for our sins; and not for ours only, but also for those of the whole world." (I John 2:2)

Pray this prayer to God now, with sincerity, and Jesus gladly will come to dwell in you permanently as your Savior and Lord.

"Dear Father God, thank you for Jesus, and for His life, death and resurrection for my sake. I come to You as a sinner, not worthy of Your salvation. I ask for Jesus to come into my life at this very moment through the Holy Spirit. I receive forgiveness for all my sins, and I accept a new beginning in life with Jesus as my Lord. Father, now I know that I am a new born believer. I know that I now have life, abundant and eternal. Guide and control my life, from this day forward. Amen!

Dear Reader, if you have received Jesus Christ as your personal Savior as a result of this book, I would be thrilled for you to share the good news with me!

Either email, write or call me at the following locations:

David Dorries
ddorries@oru.edu

Kairos Ministries International
P. O. Box 575
Coweta, OK 74429

918.495.6894

Visit my website at:
www.kairostime.com

APPENDIX 4

HOW TO RECEIVE THE BAPTISM OF THE HOLY SPIRIT

When Jesus baptized His disciples in the Holy Spirit on the Day of Pentecost, He was making Spirit baptism available for all Christians for all times. In fact, He requires that all Christians receive this *"power from on high"* (Luke 24:49) before trying to carry out His work. The best of human strength is woefully inadequate to fulfill the purposes of Jesus Christ in the earth. We need the supernatural resources of Spirit baptism in order to implement the will of God.

Our confidence that we have received the baptism of the Holy Spirit is the experience of speaking in tongues. Since it is a form of prayer, it is an utterance that the believer is able to control. When Spirit baptism was first released by Jesus upon His disciples, **they "began to speak** *with other tongues, as the Spirit was giving them utterance."* (Acts 2:4) Notice that the believers did the speaking, not the Holy Spirit. Some people have the idea that speaking in tongues is like a spiritual trance beyond the control of the speaker. That idea is not biblical. Paul taught that speaking in tongues is a voluntary practice. *"…I will pray with the spirit…and I will sing with the spirit…"* (I Corinthians 14:15 NKJV) He instructed believers not to speak in tongues in the assembly when an interpreter is not present. In that instance, it is better to "keep silent in the church; and let him speak to himself and to God." (I Corinthians 14:28) This implies that tongues speech is able to be controlled. Viewing speaking in tongues as a frenzied activity performed in a trance-like state is the stuff of pagan religions, not the biblical practice of tongues speech in Christian experience.

Like prayer, speaking in tongues is meant for every Christian, because it is a means for the believer to experience inner communion with the Holy Spirit. This practice ushers the believer into the supernatural realm of the Spirit's power. The believer is built up in the Spirit's strength, and becomes available to operate in all the gifts of the Holy Spirit. God does not show partiality. He would not allow these privileges to a few of His children, while depriving others. Paul made the appeal to all Christians when he said, *"I wish that you all spoke in tongues, ..."* (I Corinthians 14:5) Spirit baptism has been released upon the church, and continues to be available to all.

For anyone desiring to receive the baptism of the Spirit, keep in mind that praying in tongues soon will become as simple for you as praying to God in your own understanding. Your first step is to ask Father God to baptize you in the Holy Spirit. Begin thanking and praising Him, but do not allow yourself to speak in your own language or any known language. Speak only in "syllables of faith."[66] Begin exercising your vocal chords. Allow sounds to be vocalized, without expecting to understand what you are saying. While speaking these unknown utterances, force yourself to stop. Then start up again. This will assure you that you have chosen to speak in tongues, and can do so at will, anytime.

Focus upon Jesus as you allow your new tongues to flow. You are now baptized in the Holy Spirit! Speak in tongues freely and frequently. You will find yourself more receptive to the things of God. Be open to receiving other gifts of the Spirit (I Corinthians 12:8-10) You will never be the same!

Dear Reader, if you have received the baptism of the Holy Spirit as a result of this book, I would be thrilled for you to share the good news with me!

Either email, write or call me at the following locations:

David Dorries
ddorries@oru.edu

Kairos Ministries International
P. O. Box 575
Coweta, OK 74429

918.495.6894

Visit my website at:
www.kairostime.com

END NOTES

[1] I wish to thank two persons who played roles in the title that I have chosen for this book. My friend and colleague, **Dr. Daniel Thimell**, suggested the term *Spirit-filled Christology* as the name for the Christological perspective presented therein. **Chancellor Oral Roberts** helped me indirectly with my subtitle. He founded a seminary as part of his university for the express purpose of **merging theology and the power of the Holy Spirit**. See Chancellor Roberts' articulation of his vision for the seminary in his autobiography, *Expect a Miracle*, Nashville, TN: Thomas Nelson Publishers, 1995, p. 321.

[2] Oral Roberts, *Expect a Miracle*, Nashville, TN: Thomas Nelson Publishers, 1995, p. 321.

[3] My source for these statistics is *World Christian Trends AD 30-AD 2200*. David B. Barrett and Todd M. Johnson, Pasedena, CA: William Carey Library, 2001, p. 4.

[4] As defined in *The New International Dictionary of Pentecostal Charismatic Movements* (ed., Stanley M. Burgess, Grand Rapids, MI: Zondervan, 2002, p. xvii-xviii), "'neocharismatic' is a catch-all category that comprises 18,810 independent, indigenous, postdenominational denominations and groups that cannot be classified as either Pentecostal or charismatic but share a common emphasis on the Holy Spirit, spiritual gifts, Pentecostal-like experiences (*not* pentecostal terminology), signs and wonders, and power encounters."

[5] Another leader who resisted the anti-intellectual bias of Pentecostal/Charismatic expansion to found an accredited graduate school, Regent University, also offering first-rate theological education, is Pat Robertson. In addition, Pentecostal denominations have pursued excellence in theological education, e.g., Assemblies of God Theological Seminary and the Church of God Theological Seminary. Fuller Theological Seminary, although not Pentecostal/Charismatic in orientation, for decades has provided solid academic theological training for P/C students.

[6] Dr. Flip Buys, *Manila T.O.P.I.C. Report*, online at www.puk.ac.za/theology/manil.htm.

[7] The original Definition of Faith was the confessional statement produced at the Council of Chalcedon (451). The Definition of Faith gained significance

through the centuries of Christian history as recognized by all major branches of Christendom because it captured the church's orthodox beliefs concerning the person and work of Jesus Christ by beautifully summarizing the conclusions of the four major ecumenical councils in the suppression of Christological heresies.

[8] The Bible confirms Jesus' historical existence. Yet beyond the Scriptures, other religious and secular writers confirm His historical existence.

[9] Although Joseph was Jesus' earthly father, he was not so biologically. Jesus' supernatural conception will be considered later.

[10] The names of Jesus' four brothers were James, Judas (Jude), Joseph and Simon. The number of sisters is not known precisely, but legend suggests two (Mary and Salome) or possibly three. Scholars differ as to whether they were the younger brothers and sisters of Jesus, born to Mary and Joseph, or Joseph's children from a previous marriage.

[11] Jesus did not shun family connections as he formed His ministry team. Even His own family was well represented. Two of Jesus cousins were among the twelve disciples, James and John, who were brothers. Two of Jesus' brothers (James and Jude) and another cousin (Simeon) would become leaders in the early church, but did not follow him before His death. Two other brother combinations made up the original twelve (Andrew and Peter, James and Matthew). Jesus' positive attitude about family members participating in the leadership of His team indicates that he did not attempt to separate family life from ministry.

[12] See biblical examples of Jesus' sensitivity to individuals; Zaccheus (Luke 19:1-10), Bartimaeus (Mark 10:46-52), and the unnamed woman with a hemorrhage (Luke 8:43-48).

[13] T. W. Manson confirms that the Jewish notion of Messiah was tied closely to the nationalistic hopes of Israel. "For that history shows that the Jews of Palestine were only too ready to welcome any promising champion of the cause of Israel and to take up arms in a holy war for the kingdom of God." *Servant Messiah*, Cambridge: Cambridge University Press, 1961.

[14] No scholar exegetes more accurately and convincingly on the topic at stake, i.e., that the Day of Pentecost was not the birthday of the church, than does Howard Ervin. Several of his publications establish this position, including *Conversion-Initiation and the Baptism in the Holy Spirit*, Peabody, MA: Hendrickson Publishers, 1984, p. 133ff.

[15] An enemy of Jesus during His lifetime, James became one of Jesus' ardent disciples after his dramatic conversion. The resurrection persuaded James that his brother was the Messiah. Another brother, Jude, was also a post-resurrection convert. Jude authored one of the books of the New Testament, bearing his name.

[16] *The Apology*, Chapter 50. Tertullian (160-220) was from Carthage, Africa, and was an eloquent writer and defender of early Christian doctrine.

[17] As biblical scholar F.F. Bruce has stated, "When at last a Church Council – the Synod of Carthage in A.D. 397 – listed the twenty-seven books of the New Testament, it did not confer upon them any authority which they did not already possess, but simply recorded their previously established canonicity." *The Books and the Parchments*, London: Pickerikng and Inglis, 1950, p. 111.

[18] Traditionally, such writings are called apologetics. Apologetical writings have served to defend the church against false charges levied against her doctrines and practices. Writers of apologetics are known as apologists.

[19] Donald G. Bloesch, *Essentials of Evangelical Theology*, Vol. 1, San Francisco, CA: Harper and Row, 1982.

[20] The apocryphal writings represent a collection of early church literature not ultimately included in the New Testament scripture, yet considered valuable enough to have been read among the assemblies as Christians congregated for worship.

[21] Relevant verses are located in *The Epistle of Barnabas* 5:10-13.

[22] A limited number of early Jewish converts to Christianity called the Ebionites adopted a perverted view of Jesus, but their teachings never mounted a serious challenge to the church at large.

[23] Arius published a popularly written book of his teachings entitled, *The Banquet*. Although lacking theological acumen, Arius' attractive presentation of his ideas managed to entice many followers.

[24] Heresy generally means an opinion contrary to the accepted standards of a group; in this case, the Christian church.

[25] Polytheism is belief in the existence of more than one God. Prior to endorsing Christianity as the state religion, the Roman Empire permitted polytheism. The Roman Pantheon, a temple of public worship, housed the images of a multitude of gods.

[26] Orthodoxy is a term used to represent the essential, normative doctrines held by the Christian church at large. They constitute the foundation of doctrinal truth, without which the church would fail to retain her identity as the church of the Holy Scriptures.

[27] Perhaps the most thorough and influential of Athanasius' anti-Arian works is *Orations Against the Arians*.

[28] The Nicene Creed as we know it today contains some changes that were added to the original creed at the Council of Constantinople in 381. The substance of the creed remains the same. Further doctrinal conflicts resulted in the need to explicitly affirm the eternal divinity of the Holy Spirit, as well as the Son. The original creed focused upon the Father-Son relationship, and the divinity of the Spirit was added at Constantiople. The revised creed, nonetheless, retained the original name.

[29] Cyril's masterful refutation of Nestorianism is best represented in three letters, two of which were addressed to Nestorius, and the third to John, bishop of Antioch. These letters are reproduced in J. Stevenson's book, *Creeds, Councils and Controversies,* London: SPCK, 1966.

[30] I do not consider the emergence of Socinianism in the late 1500's to have been a major threat to orthodoxy. This reformulation of ancient Nestorianism, encouraged by Michael Servetus' radicalism, produced a minor Reformation undercurrent that surfaced much later in the form of rationalistic expressions of anti-Trinitarianism. Unitarianism was spawned from this milieu.

[31] Since Jesus was born of a virgin, he did not share the natural seed of David. But since Hebrew genealogy traces ancestry through the father's lineage, Jesus' lineage rightfully follows that of Joseph, His earthly father. In two Gospels, Matthew and Luke, Jesus' genealogy through Joseph is traced back to His father, David.

[32] References to the sacrificial animals being required to be without defect are numerous: Leviticus 1:3, 10; 3:1, 6; 4:3, 23, 28, 32; 5:15, 18; 6:6; 9:2-3; 14:10; 22:19; 23:12, 18; Numbers 6:14; 28:3, 9, 11, 19, 31; 29:2, 8, 13, 17, 20, 23, 26, 29, 32, 36.

[33] Eduard Schweizer, *Theological Dictionary of the New Testament,* VII, ed. Gerhard Kittel and Gerhard Friedrich, Grand Rapids, MI: Eerdmans Publishing Company, 1971, p. 135.

[34] Ibid, p. 139.

[35] Ibid.

[36] This quote is from article 31 of the Creed. The Athanasian Creed actually was not written by Athanasius, but first appeared in the sixth century, and has unknown authorship. It is highly regarded in the West, but is not recognized by Eastern Orthodox churches.

[37] "St. Irenaeus," in *A Dictionary of Christian Theology*, ed. Alan Richardson. London: SCM Press LTD, 1969, p. 175.

[38] Thanks to the scholarly work of George Dragas, Athansian authorship of *Against Apollinaris I and II* has been proven. See Dragas' study, *St. Athanasius Contra Apollinarem*, Athens. Church and Theology VI, 1985.

[39] The eight ecumenical councils of the early church, whose findings are recognized by all major branches of Christendom, are as follows: Nicaea I (325); Constantinople I (381); Ephesus (431); Chalcedon (451); Constantinople II (553); Constantinople III (680-681); Nicaea II (787); and Constantinople IV (869-870).

[40] The Definition proceeds with the assumption that Mary's humanity is the common humanity of all persons.

[41] For a careful study, defending the orthodoxy of Irving's Christology, see my book *Edward Irving's Incarnational Christology*, Fairfax, VA: Xulon Press, 2002.

[42] Henry Cole, *The True Signification of the English Adjective Mortal, and the Awfully Erroneous Consequences of the Application of That Term to the Ever Immortal Body of Jesus Christ, Briefly Considered,* London: j. Eedes, 1827, p. 5.

[43] Weimar Edition, W, 10/I/2, 247, quoted I.D.K. Siggins, *Martin Luther's Doctrine of Christ*, New Haven: Yale University Press, 1970, p. 159.

[44] The term, semi-Pelagianism, was not coined until the Scholastic era.

[45] *On the Predestination of the Saints* and *On the Gift of Perseverance,* included in *A Select Library of the Nicene and Post-Nicene Fathers of the Christian Church*, ed. Philip Schaff, vol. V (Saint Augustin: Anti-Pelagian Writings), Grand Rapids: Eerdmans Publishing Company, 1956.

[46] Various degrees of adherence to the Augustinian system of doctrine were evident in the movement to resist semi-Pelagianism. The dominant party standing against semi-Pelagianism did not come from sympathizers of Augustine's absolute predestination theory, but rather from moderate Augustinians.

[47] Philip Schaff, *History of the Christian Church, A.D. 311-600*, Vol. II, Edinburgh: T. and T. Clark, 1891, p. 858.

[48] Thomas Aquinas, *The Summa Theologica*, II-I, q. 109, art. 6, obj. 1 and 2. Ed. Anton C. Pegis, *Basic Writings of Saint Thomas Aquinas*, Vol. II, New York: Random House, 1945, p. 987.

[49] *Institutes of the Christian Religion*, ed. John T. McNeill, trans. Ford Lewis Battles, Volume I, Philadelphia: The Westminster Press, 1960, p. 593 (III.3.1).

[50] This Scriptural phrase conveys a double meaning; "… for He gives the Spirit without measure." (vs. 34) 1) This refers to the Father's bountiful provision of the Holy Spirit to His people in a general sense. 2) More specifically, this phrase refers to the Father's provision of the Holy Spirit given without measure to Jesus. Verse 35 confirms the reference to Jesus in this context, when it is said, "The Father loves the Son, and has given all things into His hand."

[51] Jesus' resurrection signaled the completion of His redemptive work. He appeared to His disciples immediately following His resurrection to substantiate His identity and to breathe upon them the regenerative life of the Holy Spirit (John 20:22).

[52] An exceptional case is the experience of Cornelius and his household, recorded in chapter ten of the Acts of the Apostles. God sent Peter to preach to them, their first exposure to the Gospel of Jesus Christ. Before Peter could complete his message, the Holy Spirit came upon the entire group. Not only did they believe in the Gospel, bringing the Spirit's regeneration into their lives, but simultaneously they received the Spirit's power. Here, no chronological separation occurred between the reception of the Spirit imparting regeneration and the reception of the Spirit's power, evidenced by the utterances of tongues speech coming from the newly converted. Generally, such cases are the exception rather than the rule. For most people, a chronological as well as a logical separation occurs in the Spirit's dual operations.

[53] Tongues speech was the obvious initial manifestation exhibited by the early believers on the Day of Pentecost when Jesus first exercised His role as Baptizer in the Holy Spirit. "And there appeared to them tongues as of fire distributing themselves, and they rested on each one of them. And they were all filled with the Holy Spirit and began to speak with other tongues, as the Spirit was giving them utterance." (Acts 2:3-4)

[54] Among other prominent Biblical accounts of tongues speech being the initial manifestation when believers received their baptism in the Holy Spirit, two are worthy of mention. 1) Pentecostal baptism was extended to the non-Jewish

world for the first time when Peter was sent to Caesarea to preach the Gospel of Jesus to the household of Cornelius. "While Peter was still speaking these words, the Holy Spirit fell upon all those who were listening to the message. All the circumcised believers who came with Peter were amazed, because the gift of the Holy Spirit had been poured out on the Gentiles also. For they were hearing them speaking with tongues and exalting God." (Acts 10:44-46) 2) Paul found in Ephesus twelve men who had been disciples of John the Baptist, but who had not heard of the Gospel of Jesus. After Paul's instruction, they believed in Jesus and submitted to baptism as new converts. Paul then led them into the baptism of the Holy Spirit. "And when Paul had laid his hands upon them, the Holy Spirit came on them, and they began speaking with tongues and prophesying." (Acts 19:6)

[55] Paul's concept, that the speaker in tongues is under voluntary self-control, is identified throughout this chapter as "volitional tongues."

[56] An excellent source for understanding the early church context for charismatic manifestations is *Christian Initiation and Baptism in the Holy Spirit*, by Killian McDonnell and George T. Montague, Collegeville, Minnesota: The Liturgical Press, 1991.

[57] From the article, "A History of Speaking in Tongues and Related Gifts," by George H. Williams and Edith Waldvogel, *The Charismatic Movement*, ed. Michael P. Hamilton, Grand Rapids, MI: Eerdmans Publishing Company, 1975, p. 71.

[58] George Fox, *The Works of George Fox*, Vol. III, New York: AMS Press, 1975 (reprinted from the edition of 1831), p. 13.

[59] Several of my publications provide insight regarding Irving's Christological and Pneumatological contributions. David W. Dorries, *Edward Irving's Incarnational Christology*, Fairfax, VA: Xulon Press, 2002; David W. Dorries, "Edward Irving and the 'Standing Sign' of Spirit Baptism," in *Initial Evidence*, ed. Gary B. McGee, Peabody, MA: Hendrickson Publishers, 1991; D. W. Dorries, "West of Scotland Revival (1830)," in *The New International Dictionary of Pentecostal Charismatic Movements*, ed. Stanley M. Burgess, Grand Rapids, MI: Zondervan, 2002. Look for reprints of various Irving writings, such as *The Day of Pentecost or The Baptism with the Holy Ghost*; *On the Gift of the Holy Ghost, Commonly Called Supernatural*; and *The Church, With Her Endowment of Holiness and Power*. These works are edited by David W. Dorries.

[60] Edward Irving, *The Day of Pentecost or The Baptism with the Holy Ghost*, Edinburgh: John Lindsay, 1831, p. 28.

[61] Edward Irving, "On the Gifts of the Holy Ghost, Commonly Called Supernatural," in *The Collected Writings of Edward Irving in Five Volumes*, vol. 5, ed. Rev. G Carlyle, London: Alexander Strahan, 1864, p. 548.

[62] I stand in strong disagreement with Dallimore's basic conclusions regarding the life and ministry of Edward Irving, yet I find his explanation plausible as to the success some of Irving's followers experienced in receiving manifestations, while Irving himself most probably never received tongues, interpretation of tongues, or prophecy. States Dallimore, "It is evident Irving did not want any gift which needed some form of human inducement. The gift of tongues did not come as a direct action from heaven, but means were employed to bring it about. Miss Cardale was considered especially proficient in this regard and made it her practice to say to a seeker, 'Yield your tongue, yield your tongue, yield your tongue to the Holy Ghost!' Likewise, Mary Caird, with her mystical but forceful personality, did much instructing as to how to speak in tongues and was exceptionally successful in the task. Irving condoned these practices, but he wanted something better for himself. He dare not accept any form of the gifts which might leave him with the least doubt as to the supernaturalism of the phenomena… He anticipated the coming on him of 'the power' in what he spoke of as 'a mighty seizure of the Holy Ghost, …'" Arnold Dallimore, *Forerunner of the Charismatic Movement: The Life of Edward Irving*, Chicago: Moody Press, 1983, pages 134-135. Irving's use of the term "seizure" in reference to the Spirit's coming in Spirit baptism is revealing, for it implies a sovereign imposition of the Spirit upon the recipient leaving no question as to the supernatural origin of the event. He uses the term on another occasion as he describes Mary Campbell's (she became Mary Caird in 1831) initial reception of the gift of tongues. Irving states, "She has told me that this first seizure of the Spirit was the strongest she ever had; …" Edward Irving, "Facts Connected with recent manifestations of the Spirit," *Fraser's Magazine*, January, 1832, page 761.

[63] The author encountered new information just prior to the publication of this book that could not be integrated into the text. What we have described as the Pauline concept of "volitional tongues" appears to have been implemented to a degree by William Seymour and the Azusa Street workers. Refer to these sources: Cecil M. Robeck, Jr., *The Azusa Street Mission and Revival*, Nashville, TN: Thomas Nelson, 2006, p. 140; and Mrs. Charles Fox Parham, *The Life of Charles F. Parham*, Joplin, MO: The Tri-State Printing Company, 1930, p. 169. Apparently, the Pentecostal movement dropped the baton by failing to carry this elusive truth into succeeding generations.

[64] This was a carryover from the "camp meeting" format common to the American Methodist background familiar to early Pentecostals. Responding to an "altar call," potential recipients of various experiences knelt at the altar to tarry for an expected spiritual outcome.

[65] As noted previously, docetism is the basic Christological error of minimalizing Christ's true humanity. Various Christologies are docetic when they devalue or even deny the real humanity and/or true human body of Jesus Christ. Classic examples of heresies whose Christologies are docetic: Gnosticism, Apollinarianism and Eutycheanism.

[66] I first heard the phrase, "syllables of faith," from Pastor David Ingles of Walnut Grove Church in Broken Arrow, Oklahoma. His ministry in leading persons to receive Spirit baptism is one of the most effective I have had the privilege of witnessing.